T0007244

"A generation of radicals comes to life in their own words and feelings as compassionate, complicated, frequently attractive and certainly compelling human beings."
    –*This Magazine*

"The result is a beautifully written, evocative and often moving account of the betrayal of a generation's hopes."
    –*Maclean's*

"The tone is at the same time detached and passionate; idealistic and skeptical; innocent and cynical; gentle and harsh. But what better tone to capture the nuances of that crazy doomed dream know as the Canadian Communist Party."–*Calgary Herald*

"Often moving ... the true story of a human drama."
    –*Toronto Star*

"Weisbord pieces together an amazing story of power, corruption and repressive politics."
    –*Kitchener-Waterloo Record*

"With a skillful blend of personal recollections and historical data, Weisbord paints a gripping picture of the conditions that fired the early communists."
    –*Kingston Whig-Standard*

"The book is a gripping collage of highly personal accounts from key players and bit players, man of whom had kept silent for more than twenty years about their roles in that tumultuous period."
    –*Ottawa Citizen*

THE STRANGEST DREAM

Canadian Communists,
The Spy Trials, and
the Cold War

MERRILY WEISBORD

REVISED THIRD EDITION

Véhicule Press

Published with the generous assistance of the Canada Council for the Arts, the Canada Book Fund of the Department of Canadian Heritage, and the Société de développement des entreprises culturelles du Québec (SODEC).

Cover design: David Drummond
Typeset in Minion by Simon Rodchenko
Printed by Livres Rapido Books

Published originally by Lester & Orpen Dennys Ltd., 1983
First Véhicule Press edition with new preface, 1994

LIBRARY AND ARCHIVES CANADA CATALOGUING IN PUBLICATION
Title: The strangest dream : Canadian communists,
the spy trials, and the cold war / Merrily Weisbord.
Names: Weisbord, Merrily. author.
Description: Third edition. | Includes bibliographical references and index.
Identifiers: Canadiana (print) 20220183031 | Canadiana (ebook)
20220183090 | ISBN 9781550655995
(softcover) | ISBN 9781550656053 (HTML)
Subjects: LCSH: Communists—Canada—Biography. | LCSH:
Communism—Canada—History—20th century. | LCSH:
Subversive activities—Canada—History—20th century. | LCSH:
Trials (Espionage)—Canada—History—
20th century. | LCSH: World politics—1945-1989.
Classification: LCC HX103 .W44 2022 | DDC 335.430971—dc23

Published by Véhicule Press, Montréal, Québec, Canada
www.vehiculepress.com

In Canada distributed by LitDistCo
www.litdistco.ca

In USA distributed by Indepdendent Publishers Group
www.ipgbook.com

Printed in Canada on FSC certified paper

Contents

PREFACE TO THE THIRD EDITION 13

PREFACE TO THE SECOND EDITION 21

INTRODUCTION 31

Chapter One
The First Contingent 41

Chapter Two
The Third International 59

Chapter Three
Seditious Utterances, Unlawful Associations 69

Chapter Four
Inroads 77

Chapter Five
Vortex 86

Chapter Six
The Second Contingent 97

Chapter Seven
Party Life 119

Chapter Eight
The Phoney War 140

Chapter Nine
Underground 146

Chapter Ten
Total War 156

Chapter Eleven
A Communist Member of Parliament 170

Chapter Twelve
The Bomb 190

Chapter Thirteen
The Spy Show 198

Chapter Fourteen
The Fred Rose Case 211

Chapter Fifteen
Evidence 227

Chapter Sixteen
The Denouement 233

Chapter Seventeen
The Post-War Labour Putsch 249

Chapter Eighteen
The Final Years 268

Chapter Nineteen
The Revelations 279

AFTERWORD 290
UPDATE ON PSEUDONYMS USED IN THE BOOK 297
RESPONSE FROMR READERS TO THE FIRST EDITION 303
THREE LETTERS 311

NOTES 319
BIBLIOGRAPHY 324
INDEX 333

For my mother and my father

ACKNOWLEDGEMENTS

To all those who spoke to me about their belief in communism.

To the Canada Council for its support.

To Josh Freed whose encouragement and clarity were vital,
to Phyllis Amber for her constant support, to Tom Fairley and
Janet Hamilton who guided me editorially.

To Arnie Gelbert, my true and valorous comrade.

The Strangest Dream

Last night I had the strangest dream
I never dreamed before,
I dreamed the world had all agreed
To put an end to war.

I dreamed I saw a mighty room
The room was full of men,
And the paper they were signing said
They'd never fight again.

And when the paper was all signed
And a million copies made,
They all joined hands and bowed their heads
And grateful prayers were prayed.

And the people in the streets below
Were dancing round and round,
And swords and guns and uniforms
Were scattered on the ground. *

* "Strangest Dream," music and lyrics by Ed McCurdy, sung by Pete Seeger.
Copyright © 1956 by Folkways Records & Service Corp.

Preface to the Third Edition

"Whatever the outcome, a cover imposes an intimate
relationship between author and image... The jacket touches
my words, it's wearing me."

–Jhumpa Lahiri, *The Clothing of Books*

The Strangest Dream has been in print since 1983, and this edition
is clothed in its fourth cover. The first edition was written in my
mid-thirties. I was a single parent with three children, finally all at
school. I had a Canada Council grant and I was free, blessed, inter-
viewing, researching, writing. I held my first published book and
marvelled. Just the fact of it was enough. It's only now that there
is to be the choice of a fourth cover, that I study it, and realize that
this first cover pleases me.

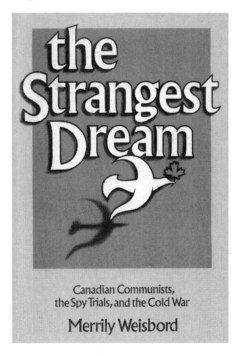

The design, white type against a red background, reflects Canadian communists' hopes for peace, shadowed, but not overwhelmed, by the hammer and sickle, the symbol of Soviet communism.

As the 2022 edition is being prepared, I receive an email and a picture of the new cover from Véhicule Press's co-publisher, Simon Dardick.

> Designer David Drummond, who has done many award-winning covers for us and other publications, likes to think outside the box. See his note below.
> Simon

FROM: DAVID DRUMMOND

> Very different look for this one. Sometimes I approach non-fiction covers as if they were illustrations for Op ed columns in the *New York Times*. Here the inverted hammer and sickle reveal a "C"—for Canada. The inverted symbol also works well with title—*Strangest Dream*.

I see the graphic strength of the cover with its red background, but this is not my book. I write to Simon:

> I REALLY don't like the reductionist cover. It ties the book stereotypically (which the book does not) to the Russian Revolution and the Soviet Union.

If the cover were aesthetically problematic, which it decidedly isn't, I wouldn't react so vehemently. But this cover undermines the reason I wrote the book. It is particularly upsetting at a time when the words, "communist, socialist, Marxist, left-wing radicals," associated with Russian communism and the hammer and sickle, remain viable Cold War smears to discredit legitimate dissent.

Unsure of my reaction, I ask writers and friends whom I respect, for their gut reaction to the cover. I email excerpts of prevailing themes to Simon, saying, "It seems the hammer and sickle icon has knee-jerk, Russian, Cold War associations."

FROM L:
This cover does not represent the book I read. It feels like the raising of a frightening flag, the symbol of a threat that overshadowed decades of misguided North American politics.

FROM R:
It's a bit too "God that Failed" kind of Koestlerish.

FROM S & E:
Where is the 'dream'??

FROM E:
It doesn't evoke the idealism, passion, and humanity of the characters you portray.

FROM C:
The intimacy is nonexistent.

Looks like a book about Russia.

I send a poster to Simon with a more amenable message.

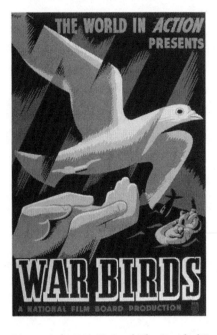

Harry Mayerovitch, 1943, National Film Board of Canada

Simon responds:

Hi Merrily,
The process continues.
David thought he would try something simpler that projected
optimism. This is a very rough draft—he would sharpen it up
if this is the right direction.

Simon sends a new cover whose colours remind me of the Chinese
communist flag. Then, ten days later, this:

CANADIAN COMMUNISTS,
THE SPY TRIALS, AND
THE COLD WAR   MERRILY WEISBORD

Jhumpa Lahiri says a cover imposes an intimate relationship between author and image, which is why it can lead to a sense of complete alienation. She would like to back away from covers she dislikes, and I would like to bury this one. But I can't, it's touching my words. Not only my words but the history of my parents and their friends. This is a book about Canada's radical roots, and it is also, personal.

I contact Simon, trying to be understood:

> The dream was not frayed. It was perhaps, the strangest dream, but it was a great ideal, and still is.
>
> The disillusionment came for party members, not with the dream, but with what it was associated with. This is a book about people who had the strangest, but laudable, dream.

Simon, too, reacts to the problematic fraying flag, but he likes its movement. He sends an email and new rendition of the flag-cover.

THE
STRANGEST
DREAM

CANADIAN COMMUNISTS,
THE SPY TRIALS, AND
THE COLD WAR   MERRILY WEISBORD

> The cover must not have elements that are counter to the theme of the book. No question. But the cover also does not have to contain all the elements. This cover is vibrant, positive, and somewhat enigmatic, simply because of the title, which is great. It has a good vibe. Let the title and subtitle carry the day. With this cover, you want to open the book.

I tell Simon I am concerned about the flag drooping, its crumpled look, and the difficulty reading the 'D" and the "T." And I worry that Simon's patience must be running out.

Soon after, Simon sends a "warmer version" with blue skies in the background.

> I think David addressed our issues. He rearranged the sky behind the subtitle so it stands out more. In terms of the drooping flag, etc., there is only so much he can do re the flag. But the direction of the flag indicates movement in the wind. Merrily, this is a perfect cover. It's an optimistic cover

18

and we should not fiddle with it. We all love it at this end and can't wait to show our sales reps. Our sales meeting with them is next week.

The upcoming sales exigency, and my appreciation of the rare, consultative process among publisher, designer and author, produces the final cover, the cover you hold in your hands.

I wrote *The Strangest Dream* out of love for my parents, to better understand their history, and the context of the choices they made. I tried to evoke not only the struggle "to make a better world," but the warmth, generosity, songs, theatre, art, and exhilaration of party members for whom comradeship meant a way of life. These comrades may no longer be alive, but their age-old dream of a just and equal society resonates, and lives on.

Merrily Weisbord
May, 2022

Preface to the Second Edition

Time has passed. Many of the people I spoke to for this book are dead. Fred Rose is dead. Bob Haddow, Fred Taylor, Harry Binder, Irving Myers, Henri Gagnon, Allan Harrison.

Lea, amazing Lea Roback, is ninety years old.

The discrepancy between what I knew of my parents and the distorted cold war perception prompted me to write *The Strangest Dream*. "If we forget our history," said Carlos Fuentes, "We forget ourselves." And if we forget ourselves, we have no vantage point from which to assess the many manufactured images of who we are and what we value.

I am currently making a film about Canadian writer, Ted Allan, who worked with Dr. Norman Bethune's mobile blood unit during the Spanish Civil War. Most Canadians don't know who Ted Allan is, or the names of any other prominent left-wing figures. Or even that Canada had a rich tradition of left-wing political action and thought. Raymond Boyer's trial made front page Cold War news but the day after he died, I found only one small obit. I had begun to think of *The Strangest Dream* as a link to a disappearing history and imagination.

Now, seen against the dissolution of Soviet communism, it underscores the ideological anguish of our time.

What now?

What do we believe now after the death of what was at once a most noble dream and a soul-destroying nightmare?

Is global capitalism all there is?

What remains of the impulse for social justice?

What, if anything, is the legacy of the strangest dream?

Increasingly, children of communists have been trying to answer these questions by reclaiming their past. Two American women who read this book wrote me about their work-in-progress. The first was plucked, age eight, from a warm bed in Queens, bundled onto a train to Mexico, hidden with campesinos in a walled courtyard, and then flown to Czechoslovakia where she was raised from age eight to twenty-one. Her father was a known communist, Party leaders were in jail, the Rosenbergs on trial—her parents chose exile. Prague is the city of her adolescence, Czech her language of poetry and love. Her experience of communism is different from mine but by our third meeting we were singing, "If I had a hammer, I'd hammer in the morning, I'd hammer out love between my brothers and my sisters all, all over this land."

Students at the Lenin School in Moscow in the twenties, Spanish Civil War volunteers in the thirties, and striking seamen in the forties, felt the heady joy of belonging to an international communist community. I, and children of communists around the world, have the songs.

The second woman's family also fled the congressional committees, arrests, imprisonments of the Smith Act (1948) which made it illegal to be a communist in the United States. She is writing a history of the American left-wing expatriate community in Mexico, in which she was raised.

Canadian Len Scher, whose father was blacklisted in the fifties, recently published *The UnCanadians*, the first book to expose the extent and effect of our home-grown witch-hunts.

Another communist kid wrote and performed an off-Broadway show called *Confessions of a Red Diaper Baby*. He said he grew up thinking the Knicks were a communist organization, "They passed the ball a lot, they were into sharing." His father's vision of utopia was "everyone should have plenty of money, plenty to eat and plenty of sex."

The Strangest Dream resurrects the radical, activist, socialist, communist, alternative part of our proper Canadian selves. The left-wing belief in economic justice is as much our heritage as bottom-line economics. Union battles are as relevant to how this country works as Confederation. And iconoclastic thinking is just as necessary and still as suspect. After much lobbying, the ideological grounds which banned many of the people in this book from entering the United States (McCarran Walter Act, 1952), were finally revised (Immigration Act of 1990) and now ex-Party members can, theoretically, visit the US without humiliation.

But the spirit of the witch-hunts lives on.

In 1989, I was banned from South Africa. I had a visa, but it was revoked by the Home Minister in Pretoria. How did the Home Minister know me? And why, despite my sorry record as an activist (I never joined anything), was I banned? I called the South African consulate and an indiscreet employee told me, "They have some sort of file on you. Some recommendation."

"What sort of recommendation?" I asked.

"Police."

"But I don't have a police record."

Besides, I thought, our secret police, the Canadian Security Intelligence Service (CSIS), a.k.a. the RCMP, are not supposed to have commerce with your apartheid police.

A large, blond South African vice-consul stamped "Canceled" on my visa and refused to tell me why I was banned. Once an investigation was started, it went into the intelligence pool, she said. Telling why would jeopardize security sources. "After they looked at your boo...uh, application..."

Book? But this book has the distinction of being equally well received by *This Magazine* and *Legion*, and it was never published outside Canada. Are the politics of the fathers and mothers visited on the children? Or is it really because I chose to write about it? Come on. This is a free country, isn't it?

With the help of a lawyer friend, I applied for my files from CSIS data banks SIS/P-PU-005, 010, 015. Months later, our intelligence service answered. They couldn't help me because they didn't know my birthday. I wrote back in sympathy. Finally, they informed me I did not have a file in PU-005 or PU-015. As for SIS/P-PU-O10, the data bank on people of ongoing interest to CSIS, they wouldn't tell me if I had a file or didn't have a file because to do so would be a threat to national security.

As one friend said, if you didn't have a file before, you sure have one now.

To this day, I don't know how and why I was banned from South Africa. It is hard to believe it is solely because of my parents or this book. But when I search the nooks and crannies of my secret history, the only serious political involvement I find that might, perhaps, be held against me, are the days and months I hid Fred Rose.

Fred Rose was not a relative of FLQ Paul Rose and we didn't study him in school although he was the only Communist Party candidate ever elected to Parliament in Canada. He served three years as MP for Montreal-Cartier and in 1946 was named by Soviet defector Igor Gouzenko as a leader of a network that gave official secrets to the Soviet Union. He was sentenced to six years in penitentiary, served five and then went to Poland to work. The Canadian government amended the Citizenship Act and took away his citizenship. He had been stateless in Poland for over thirty years when I started this book, and I was the only journalist he ever accepted to see.

Fred Rose died in 1983, age seventy-six, in Warsaw. I was in Montreal with his daughter Laura as she discussed funeral plans long distance with her mother in Poland. Laura had been petitioning the Canadian government to allow her father to end his days in Canada and it had seemed possible until another spy affair slammed all doors shut. Now, despite the state funeral offered by the Polish government, Laura wanted her father home.

We phoned the Canadian Department of External Affairs to make sure they would allow the corpse of Fred Rose into Canada. Then we contacted the Polish Consulate who recommended the body-shipping branch of the Polish Ministry of External Affairs, acronym BONGO. The cost of shipping a body was prohibitive. The only way to get Fred Rose out of Poland and into Canada was to cremate him. He was not a religious Jew so it was not imperative that he be buried whole. Laura and her mother noted that he had escaped the Holocaust but not the ovens. For $1800 US., BONGO arranged the whole thing.

Laura Rose was too busy repatriating her mother to handle the urn or the funeral, so Fred Rose was delivered to my house in a plain, brown box. Inside, swaddled in newspapers, was an unadorned, metal urn.

I had a marble mantle but it wasn't my place to expose Fred. I put him in the closet to await burial. He stayed in the closet for months while the family and the few remaining apparatchiks decided what was appropriate. Every day he was with me, I knew he was there. And CSIS must have known it too. Perhaps they had an informer in the closet. They had one reporting from the national women's group, NAC, so they must be very diligent. If I'm not on their bad list because of my parents, or this book, it must be because I provided a safe house for Fred Rose's remains.

Not long ago, I was in Plattsburgh, speaking to students at the State University of New York and I recounted this story. My theme, far-fetched for most North Americans, was censorship in a free society, something I learned about at my mother's knee. I told the students my parents had been communists. And even though Marxism was one of the most important political philosophies of the last centuries, communists in Canada were arrested, jailed, deported, and spied on, for their beliefs. In Quebec, houses were padlocked because they contained communist literature.

I described the moldy pamphlets and magazines in my library that my parents had buried in the earth—a 1938 *Labour Monthly* with articles by John Strachey and Ivor Montagu, a 1949 *Masses and Mainstream* with writing by Gwyn Thomas, Louis Aragon, Langston Hughes. I told them there used to be an illegal printing press in my friend's basement and another in the country, close to where I now live. That we were very careful about how we spoke on the telephone because we knew phones were tapped. That I was ten when Ethel and Julius Rosenberg, the mother and father of Michael, ten, and Bobby, six, were executed.

Some children I played with didn't know their parents were communists because they belonged to "closed sections." Most kids who knew, knew not to tell—even much later.

I was drawing a line from past to present, trying to show the students why my experience makes me see the world differently from them. Describing an alternative perspective, so they could see it too. I told them I'd recently co-written a book based on the television series, *The Valour and the Horror*, the only unofficial series about Canadians in the Second World War. I outlined the fallout from the TV broadcast and the companion book, an object lesson in the workings of censorship in a free society.

It began with a stacked Conservative Party Senate Subcommittee investigation of the film series. Parliament buildings. East Block. The women's toilet smelled. Pipes exposed. Fake paneling in the hearing room, buckling rug, fluorescent lights. Film director Brian McKenna was called to testify. When he said our airmen killed "women and children," the Bomber Command veterans sitting opposite me visibly recoiled. A sound, like someone hit in the stomach, came from them—a chorus of "No's," heckling, jeers. The man on my left muttered that the series was an attack on military historian Charles Stacey as well as the High Command. The man on my right, the brother of a dead hero who had led all his men, marching and piping into a lethal ambush, said so quietly that I asked him to repeat it, "I've been bombed by our own planes, waves and waves of them." The lone Liberal senator said, "If you guys were not aiming for civilian areas, you were awfully bad shots because you certainly bombed the place all to pieces." Then a senator asked McKenna if he believed the Holocaust occurred.

The accusation of Holocaust denial made public the censorship issue and brought our secret, almost dirty little problem, out into the open. The public wanted to decide whether they watched the series, or not. The Senate Committee, on the other hand, wanted the CBC not to rebroadcast the films in their original form. Based on accusations of inaccuracies offered by Defense Department historians, they wanted Canada to "evaluate the degree to which government-financed agencies dominate news and public information broadcasting, the implications of this dominance, and whether it is in the public interest." In other words, they wanted an end to arms length public broadcasting.

CBC board member John Crispo, a known advocate of selling the CBC to private investors, wrote Arnie Gelbart, the producer of the series, to express his "utter contempt" for Gelbart and everyone involved in the production. He concluded, "you and your ilk" are a disgrace to what the valiant veterans fought and gave their lives for.

What ilk was that we wondered?

Next, CBC President Gerard Veilleux, appointed by the Conservative government, ordered a "Special Review." The CBC's Ombudsman chose three consulting historians—one of the co-authors of *The Official History of the Canadian Army* criticized by the series, another who had already attacked the series in print, the last designated by the family of Bomber Harris to write the introduction to his memoirs.

For us, this was a year of *tsouris* (a good Yiddish word for heartache and trouble) and a tremendous waste of energy. My co-writer, Merilyn Simonds Mohr, bombarded by late-night phone calls from irate veterans, felt like a leper in Kingston, her military-dominated city. Arnie Gelbart, almost bankrupted by the briefs, interviews, press campaign, time without money, remembered the 1950's witch-hunts. There was stress, crisis, and little time for private life. I understood the strain on marriages during the Cold War show trials. And why several of us were becoming ill. Finally, things calmed down emotionally. Then, at bedtime in my house in the country, three miles from the closest village, the doorbell I had installed so my daughter wouldn't scare me when she came to visit, rang. And the bailiff delivered a 500 million dollar law suit.

The 221-page document said it was in the Public Interest at all times "to have the capacity to recruit volunteers for the armed forces." Therefore, it was necessary to promote public confidence in "the integrity, competence, and morality of the leadership of

Her Majesty's Armed Forces and Her Majesty's governments." (All of them?) We had to adhere to a minimum standard of historical writing "as enunciated by Louis L'Amour, the very popular writer of romantic 'Wild West' fiction." (The Louis L'Amour standard?) And we were under a "positive duty" not to utter false (?) innuendo.

My co-defendants were surprised by the tactics and exercise of power in the censorship campaign against *The Valour and the Horror*, but I wasn't. What surprised me was how incredibly confining are the bonds of self-censorship that powerful lobbies would have us impose. How constrained independent creative people are by market forces, broadcast illusions of objectivity, the onus to prove ourselves innocent of libel, the litigious power of monied men. How very easy it is to be a heretic. How little it takes.

In 1983, when I first said publicly that my parents had been communists, I felt brave. Standing in front of the Plattsburgh students in these *glasnost* times, I feel freer of the cold war stigma, more open to investigating the extent to which upbringing is part of one's destiny. I tell the students about Fred Rose, South Africa, *The Valour and the Horror*, my parents, to shake up their complacent view of freedom, censorship, the North American experience. So they will be alert, aware, prepared to act.

Is this my destiny?

I have a persistent nostalgia for The Brotherhood of Man. I prefer the 1937 concept of global, collective security, to paranoid national security. When contemporary political leaders say "new world order," I remember Mussolini, Hirohito and Hitler in Arthur Szyk's 1941 cartoon collection, *The New Order*. I know the contents of Khrushchev's secret speech to the 20th Congress of the Soviet Union. I am wary of "isms" and principles that crush people. I sing Paul Robeson's lullaby "Oh, My Curly-Headed Baby" to straight-haired kids. I understand ex-communist Ted Allan, lolling on the beach, a drink clinking in his hand, protesting, out of nowhere, to no one, "No, I don't. I don't feel guilty at all."

John Kenneth Galbraith worries about naïve countries that embrace laissez-faire capitalism without realizing the extent to which capitalism was forced to change itself—forced, I'd say—by the existence of an alternative and by the courage of people with an alternative belief. Now that there is no longer a significant socialist model, we, more than ever, need people with socially-responsible philosophies and visions of human organization that counterbalance capitalism's inhumane imperatives and protect our hard-won rights. We need to remember the conflicts and ideals of the labour and left-wing radicals who went before, to realize the endangered status of their passion. Our young people need to know how we got welfare, minimum wage, unemployment insurance, Medicare, so they understand how to keep them. Because "the past is never dead," as William Faulkner said, "it's not even past." By what methods do people's movements affect government? What are unions for? Who are our unsung heroines and heroes? Where are the books, films, TV series, CD-ROMs on the protest movements of Canada? What, besides money, can we aspire to?

After eight decades of organizing, Lea Roback says we have to keep fighting. Social programs, VIA Rail, generic drugs, Indigenous peoples' rights, public broadcasting, no onus libel laws, racial, religious, gender, creed equality, employment security, NAC. Because of Lea and the grassroots activists around her, I don't believe in the simplistic finality of the "collapse of communism"— i.e. dead Bolshevik experiment = dead socialist causes. Those inspired by left-wing courage and its generous vision of human potential, believe that people can work together to make a better world. They have hope—a basic element in human survival.

That is why I welcome the 1994 edition of *The Strangest Dream*. Canada's left-wing history is a vital link to contemporary survival. It seems to me worth remembering.

Merrily Weisbord,
May 1994

Introduction

I BEGIN TO WRITE a book about communists so I can understand my parents and the ethos in which I was raised. I expect to find the warm, communal, and hopeful spirit that I remember as a child. I remember, "All people are equal, all people are capable of good, there is tremendous potential in the human spirit."

I will write an ode to my father and my mother. I will sing them to the rest of the world.

"Go see Lea," people tell me. Lea, at seventy-nine, is still "the fireball." Thin, wiry, she welcomes me into her apartment, telling, asking, cursing in English, French, German, and now that she is older, an increasing amount of Yiddish. Independent and intensely social, Lea has never married. Yet, she shares her life generously. As she talks, her face is a blur—glasses, a nose—in constant motion. In amazing detail, she describes a world in which elections were rigged, workers were "frightened stiff," and communists landed "in the clink." Thirty years after she quit the Party, she has as much contempt for "bastard bosses," corrupt lawyers, and Liberal party hacks as she has love for her comrades. She relives for me her experience in Nazi Germany and her union battles of the thirties. Between tapes she walks me around the block for fresh air. In everything Lea says, I recognize the values of my childhood: human dignity, social and economic equality, justice for all. Her earthy philosophizing has the familiar ring of "the voice of humanity singing a hymn to a new world in birth."[1] I savour the sureness.

I speak to other children of communists. Jerry, a Marxist philosopher at the University of London, sings communist youth songs for me and says, "I used to believe very strongly that most people are nice and all communists are nice and all nice people are communists. The two were practically coincident." Laura Rose describes "a togetherness, a common goal, a common bond, such warmth and goodness between the people themselves." When her father, Fred Rose, was away—in prison, underground, or, later, in the House of Commons—Laura was cared for by her mother and a close group of friends who, Laura says, were "like parents to me." Irene Kon, daughter of Norman Bethune's mentor Louis Kon, remembers discussions in her home about politics and art, beginning in the morning when all four family members would go into the bathroom. "My mother would be in the bathtub," she says, "my father shaving, my brother on the john, and me brushing my teeth, all in the all-together, arguing, discussing." Irene learned to think, to make decisions, to have a sense of social responsibility very early in life. Her father treated her as an equal, her opinion was asked, and when she spoke, the group around her listened. She developed a social and political context in which to see herself and, she explains, "a sense of my own worth and value that nothing can take away." Harry, the child of communists who came to Canada after the 1917 Russian Revolution, recognizes that his communist education destined him from age seven to seek as his empire "a better world. There was no other objective and no other life that was worthwhile, and my mother encouraged me in this."

Harry's conviction, Irene's ease with thought and discussion, and Laura's and Jerry's feeling of being among friends are gifts of my youth. I was fourteen when Khrushchev's denunciation of Stalin ended my parents' commitment to the Communist Party, when my family's image of "a better world" disintegrated. It was a while before my mother and father would relax from the responsibility of saving the world, before their fear of late-night knocks on the door would fade. I live now in a world where not all people are nice, where very few people in North America are still communists. The story rests, until now.

Yet, as others look for touchstones in Israel or the Hebrides, and still others search out the graves of their ancestors, I try to reclaim my past. Through discussion and reading, I attempt to understand "the richness of expectation"[2] I had as a child and, later, its context: international communism, Russian style. I tape-record

32

my meetings with people who formed part of the communist community, if they will permit, or take notes, if they are frightened. Like a melody, communist ideals and enduring friendships weave through their testimonies. Often, the counterpoint is the controlling effect of Party policy and Soviet power on their lives. Few leave me with an idealized vision.

My research begins to centre on the post-war spy trials and, especially, on Communist Party of Canada (CPC) leader Fred Rose, first elected to the House of Commons in 1943, and arrested and convicted in 1946 for "communicating official secrets to a foreign power." Fred Rose is the only member of Parliament ever elected as a communist in Canada, and he is the man for whom I was named, Rose, Merrily. I read diaries and biographies of Mackenzie King, Royal Commission transcripts, court documents, and I keep copious files. The trials are a recurrent theme in my interviews. I know nothing about them, but I think I am going to prove that Fred Rose was framed. It is hard to get people to talk about this sensitive, fear-ridden subject. Because of a liking and respect for my parents, people meet with me when they will talk to no one else. But most of those who know are still scared. They remember the "bad times" of the spy trail witch hunts, and they know that the smear is extant. Even today association with the trials could ruin their lives. I collect clues, track down each lead, and conclude that Fred Rose and other communists did communicate classified information to the Soviet Union during the Second World War. It is a fact. One ex-communist says, "There was no choice for a communist." Another says, "We would have done anything to help the Soviet Union." It is a jolt of reality, sharp as a cold shower.

I go to see Fred Rose in Poland, where he has lived since serving his six-year prison term in St. Vincent de Paul Penitentiary for conspiracy. He and Fanny, his wife of over fifty years, live in a two-room apartment overlooking Warsaw's Old Square. On Victory Day, from their third-floor window, we see actors unfurl Red flags in the square, now crowded with people and orchestras from the surrounding villages. Inside, on a stereo cassette, Rose listens to his music—Beethoven, Paul Robeson, Dinah Shore. Fanny has learned to warm the beds with hot-water bottles and be in line early enough to buy food. He chain smokes, directs me to references in books on French Canada and labour history, to his copies of *Hansard*—1943, 1944, 1945—where his House of Commons speeches are recorded. Friends in Montreal remember him as "132 pounds of contained velocity." The blond, trim moustache of the forties is gone, but traces of the natty style remain in his 1920 Jewish-immigrant jive: "Listen, sweetheart," he says when I am slow to understand him, "Sure, kid," when I finally get the point. There is, as a Canadian reporter remembered, "a certain kind of dignity to him." He is physically ailing, but mentally and emotionally undaunted. We cover the early history of the Communist Party in Quebec. He will not discuss: Euro-communism, the Soviet government or the Canadian Communist Party after 1946. "I don't know, kid. I was already in the coop at this point." I ask questions of him and his wife. Why don't they talk? Why haven't they come back to Canada? They smile at my enthusiasm. Fred has twice been refused permission to visit Canada. They are not physically strong enough to "join the battle." It is a young person talking to an old, old world.[3]

The more I research, the more I see the international importance of the Canadian spy trials. They are the first big show trials in the West. Communists are denounced as traitors, and tarred and feathered publicly. Red-baiting destroys the popular-front groups and the lobby for the international control of atomic weapons. It destroys the militant unions and is used to discredit the Canadian attempt to keep its unions independent of the American Internationals. The trials are the basis for a tidal wave of anti-Russian propaganda. They prepare the way for the North Atlantic Treaty Organization (NATO) and the era of atomic diplomacy. They justify the growth of secret security services.

I find out exactly what official secrets were given by whom to whom. It is important to take the measure of the beast. I want to know every detail of the crime that was, at the time, considered worse than murder. I learn that the Soviet government, with the help of Canadian communist leaders, secretly collected information, some classified, such as the results of advanced research on optics, radar, and explosives. I learn that the Canadians who gave information did so because they believed it was right. My research seems to implicate unnamed Canadian public figures. I wonder why they were not publicly investigated. As I ask more questions, it becomes obvious that politically the Second World War was another world—one in which not only communists embraced the Soviet ally. But it has become official policy to repress the realities of the anti-fascist alliance. I worry that my documents contravene the Official Secrets Act. I begin to fear the Royal Canadian Mounted Police. I hide papers, talk elliptically on the phone. I read books on other communist trials and books on treason. I dissect the documents from the Fred Rose appeal with a lawyer friend, who repeats incredulously, "This betrays all the tenets of natural justice." I am not sure what is right and what is wrong.

I drive tens of blocks east of St. Lawrence Boulevard— "The Main"—past Papineau, to the French-Canadian east end of Montreal, to speak to Henri Gagnon, head of the Young Communist League (YCL) in Quebec before the war and the Communist Party's provincial organizer after the war. He clears the galley-proofs of his current book off the kitchen table, where he then serves me Christmas ham. Henri is in his late sixties. His hair, slicked down and brushed back, gleams. He pads comfortably around the kitchen, telling me that he joined the Third International in the thirties "because of the class struggle." Then, I hear the theme that will play at varying volumes throughout my talks with French-Canadian militants: I hear for the first time about the 1947 split within the Party between the French-Canadian communists and the Toronto-based Central Committee.

Henri arranges for me to see Emery Samuel, who has come from Vancouver to speak to journalists and university students about the revolutionary history of Quebec. Emery logged in the north woods of Quebec, then studied at the International Lenin

School in Moscow. He is an old-time story-teller and a trained polemicist. He talks to me about "the best days" of his life "in the Party," then, like an echo of what others have said, about his expulsion and ostracism in 1947.

I phone "David," an ex-member of the Central Committee's Political Bureau, now a successful businessman living in Toronto. David's politics changed in 1956 with Khrushchev's revelations about Stalin, but his bulldog tenacity and dogmatism have not. He makes it abundantly clear that he doesn't want to talk. "Everything written about the Party is crap." I tell him I want to understand my parents' experience. I am interested in the Cold War trials begun in 1945 in which Fred Rose was convicted. Without hesitation he says, "He was guilty. And Ethel and Julius Rosenberg were guilty. We were controlled by the Soviet Union."

I go back to see Lea and ask how she felt in 1956 when Khrushchev's speech to the Twentieth Congress of the Soviet Communist Party finally revealed to her the horrors of the Stalinist purges. After years of animating Marxist study groups, smuggling banned literature in Montreal, managing Quebec's only left-wing bookstore, organizing workers in sweat-shops and on factory assembly lines, Lea quit the Party. There was no one in the Central Committee who would help her make sense of the shocking perversion of everything she believed. Instead, the Canadian party leaders attempted to ignore and whitewash what she felt desperately needed mass discussion. "There was no one to talk to." Yet, she has no regrets. "I learned a lot. We had the challenge of fascism, the beginning of women's work, the beginning of the trade-union movement, our young people learned initiative and motivation. No years were wasted. Our lives were enriched." She quit the Party with the Yiddish curse, "*Fardrait zich ayereh kepp*"— "Screw up your own heads."

This book is not a song but the complex story of an idealistic, hard-working group of Canadians who believed that they could make a better world. They joined the Communist Party at a time when it was fighting for unions, for the unemployed, and against fascism. They thought of themselves as revolutionaries—in the heroic mould of the Russian worker pitted against the armies of the tsar, in the valiant tradition of the Chinese guerillas battling the Japanese Empire. They saw themselves in the image of Rosa Luxemburg and the Spartakusbund fighting the shadow armies of the German militarists. Party members braved police clubs on picket lines, at May Day parades, in demonstrations. They printed and handed out Marxist, union, and civil-rights literature when to do so was "subversive," an act of courage. External persecution served to strengthen the Party's hold on their lives. In their devotion to the cause, they accepted the Party discipline deemed necessary to build an organization that could withstand severe repression. In time, the subordination of individual responsibility to the greater good became submission. Members, to stay members, submerged the iconoclastic impulse that had led them to the Party. The hierarchical Party structure allowed the Soviet Communist Party to treat the Canadian party with the cynicism it still shows to all national communist movements other than its own, and the Central Committee of the Canadian party did the same to the French-Canadian communists in Quebec.

This is not the book I thought I would write. Only the chapter on the effect of the Khrushchev revelations about Stalin allows me to write with clear emotion, with respect for the vision of a just world and sadness for the loss of that belief. It was Marx who suggested that men make history but not in the circumstances of their own choosing. This book is meant, then, to depict the circumstances in which men and women from varied backgrounds chose to be communists. It is their story, culled from their words.

For many, the decision to speak to me was not a simple matter. Even now, there is prejudice and discrimination against former communists. Under the Internal Security Act, or McCarran-Walter Act, of 1952, absorbed into the Immigration and Nationality Act of the United States Section 212(D)(3), a high percentage of ex-communists can still not enter the United States. The now-computerized "Black Book" includes a file of out-dated lists given decades ago to the American immigration authorities by the municipal and provincial Red Squads and the RCMP: lists of known communists, lists of subscribers to left-wing newspapers, lists of union leaders, study-group members, Spanish Civil War veterans, and lists from over thirty-five Popular Front groups of the thirties and forties. Many who joined the Communist party in the thirties but left it on or before 1956 have been pulled off trains, buses, planes, escorted by armed guard, and turned back at the border. To be granted temporary visiting privileges requires time, money, fingerprinting, repudiation of subversive allegiances, and pro-American vows. The complicated procedure of having one's name removed from the list takes a minimum of two years and at least $5,000. It requires an affidavit which, according to an immigration lawyer, "many find demeaning" and letters of reference from five individuals who are then themselves subject to investigation. Each applicant must file his fingerprints with both the FBI and the RCMP. Proof has to be supplied that the applicant has been actively engaged in opposing communism. Depending on the person's age, the date he left the Party, whether his adhesion had been voluntary or involuntary, and the tenor of the police reports, the United States Immigration Department will or will not allow the applicant to enter the United States. If an ex-communist succeeds in having his name removed from the blacklist, he is reclassified and given Defector Status.

A painter responsible for Spanish Civil War posters, Russian relief posters, and, most damning, Fred Rose election posters asked that I use a pseudonym for him so he can continue seeing art shows in New York, as did a professional who lost clients because his name was once mentioned in connection with the 1946 spy trials. A grandmother asked that I use her first name only so she can visit her grandchildren in the United States. A respected artist won't let me publish the impressive graphics he did in the thirties and forties because it would mean forfeiting a consulting contract. Yet, whenever people allowed it, I used their full names. Failing that possibility, I asked that, "for history, for the grandchildren," I use, at least, their given or Christian names. In circumstances in which adverse repercussions were an overriding concern, I created fictional names or pseudonyms which are introduced in quotation marks.

So pervasive is North American's obsession with communism that the past is often rewritten, seen through the distorting lens of a justified paranoia. Communists have given valuable material on popular-front groups to libraries, censoring or burning all references to the Communist Party. Others have published evocative pieces on the thirties, talking only in generalities, however, about "the left wing." Biographies of union leaders have been published omitting the fact of the subject's alliance with the Communist Party. Social Democrats and Liberals pretend that they never met and conferred with communists. And it is either difficult or impossible to get access to official or public documents on controversial periods and subjects. The crucial November, December 1945 entries in the Mackenzie King diaries, when the decision was made to proceed publicly against the communists, are inexplicably lost, as are the official transcripts of the Fred Rose trial. Exhibits and other materials relating to the government's position in the spy trials are kept sealed. In fact, the name Fred Rose still rings alarm bells in the Justice Department. To see files concerning him one needs permission from government officials in charge of state information. In my library research in Ottawa, I constantly met government employees who, fascinated, nervous, and at the mercy of government directives concerning "sensitive" material, whispered with me in corridors about Fred Rose. "The RCMP has all the information you need," said an archivist, "but you'll never see it."

That the state's concern with secrecy is out of all proportion to the threat of the man himself or of the Party is an indication of the excesses and distortions that have skewed our historical vision. Only die-hard activists such as Lea and Henri can keep their equilibrium. Committed to social change, each in his own way is beyond the reach of conventional sanctions, and can therefore embrace and acknowledge the past. They would do the same thing again, they say, only better. Henri's last word is "*Un bon monde là-dedans*"— "Good people in there." I hear the same theme repeated by Gérard Fortin, a tough seaman and bush-worker organizer who was almost killed by goons in a northern logging camp: "When I see my past, giving everything for the Party, being ready to give my life if necessary, I think it was like a new religion. But at least it was for the working class."

I return to my tapes, to the many people with whom I spoke, to the source.

CHAPTER ONE

The First Contingent

Montreal. 1932

THE BITING MARCH WIND cut through Fred Rose's heavy overcoat, through his tailored vest, into his bones. The only warmth was the crowd around him—his comrades and the thousands of workers who had followed them into the streets. Finns, Ukrainians, Jews, Slavs, French Canadians, from labour unions and associations for the unemployed, had surged onto The Main, a brass band leading with songs of the Russian Revolution. They were ten thousand strong, and as they marched angrily up the street, Fred Rose thought he could hear the crisp, clear notes of revolution.

It hadn't taken much for the one hundred or so Montreal communists to mount this protest. In 1932 the majority of the city's workers were poor or unemployed, destitute. Their hope was dry as tinder and their anger ready for the spark. This time they had been pushed too far. Only twenty-four hours before, police had thrown another jobless worker, Nick Zynchuk, out of his home. Then, as Zynchuk had walked back up the stairs to his flat to retrieve his few possessions—trousers, a hat, an old suitcase—a police officer had coolly drawn his service revolver and shot him in the back. It was murder. Within hours of the shooting, outrage at the utter contempt of the act had spread among thousands of workers. Now, despite a provincial ban on demonstrations, they had dared to come together to express their rage: in each person's heart was the conviction that the dead man could just as easily have been him.

As the crowd strode towards Mount Royal cemetery, where Zynchuk was to be buried, policemen circled like hunters on horseback. Fred Rose had cautioned the marchers to ignore their taunts and mounted forays into the procession, not to be provoked. This was the first major demonstration since the beginning of the Great Depression, and it was important not to give the press an opportunity to dismiss it as "a riot." "We are marching in a compact group along a precipitous and difficult path, firmly holding each other by the hand," Lenin had written. "We are surrounded on all sides by enemies…" Our organization is our strength, thought Fred Rose. The working class has no other weapon.

Fred Rose was devoted to the struggle for a decent society—something he longed for but had never seen. His memories of Lublin, Poland, where he had been raised, were shot through with images of Cossacks, antisemitic violence, and carts of wounded soldiers from the Great War. At thirteen he had come to Quebec, where American and English-Canadian interests controlled industry and resources and where the workers—largely immigrant and French-Canadian—were the lowest paid in Canada. He hated the injustice, "the anti-Semitism, and the unequal status of the French Canadians." He remembered the moment at which his socialist reading had struck home…He was supervising women and girls making radio tubes in an American branch plant in Montreal. With windows shut to protect the delicate glass, with no other ventilation, the room felt claustrophobic. Workers, mostly women, fainted at the machines while the manager lived in luxury at the Windsor Hotel. As his anger grew, Fred Rose realized that this, in concrete terms, was what Karl Marx meant by "class exploitation."

At eighteen, welcoming its clear and active program for improving the conditions of workers, Fred joined the Young Communist League. "We believed in the mobilization of the people to improve their lot—by petitions, marches, mass meetings, organizations like the trade unions and the unemployed movement." His knowledge of scientific socialism became part of his life and hopes. He instinctively thought and acted according to its tenets, but "the ultimate, as stated in Party doctrine, was something for the future." Rose fought for practical issues. Whether he organized an electricians' union, or led the broad-based Hands Off China Committee, or recruited and taught French-Canadian militants from the indigenous Association Humanitaire, it was for him all part of one single and indivisible struggle of the working class for power.

Three years before this demonstration, in 1929, four hundred people had gathered on a street corner in downtown Toronto to hear him speak. Other policemen pushed around those who assembled that day. They shoved Fred, ordering him to move, go home. But three young girls placed themselves as a buffer between him and the hefty officers, and Fred made a determined stand. "Like a snowball the crowd gathered from all directions," testified the arresting officer, Inspector Greenwood. As he was taken into custody, charged with disorderly conduct, Fred Rose kept on with his speech: "Fellow workers…" According to Inspector Greenwood, "He was screaming at the top of his voice; you could hear him five or six blocks away."

Fred continued to speak in the face of police harassment: in synagogues and church halls, at relief meetings, anti-deportation meetings, meetings of the unemployed, on street corners, on balconies, at factory gates, at the Labour College, the Université Ouvrière, at Prince Arthur Hall, and to workers everywhere in the immigrant district where he lived. He was emerging as a leader. Five feet four, "short, smart, with a special kind of charm," he believed in what he was doing and did it "for the satisfaction of seeing results." Being a Party member was a calling, a vocation, a way of life. Being a leader meant the front lines. "He was always ready to lead us," said a comrade, "even in song."

Only months before this demonstration, Fred Rose had been arrested a second time at Montreal's first meeting of the unemployed. He had called for emergency measures for those without work. Work and wages! If there is no money because of the collapse of your system, give the victims some security. Money for food. A place to live. Heat. Electricity. Shoes for the children to wear to school. He urged the newly jobless to join the associations of unemployed. This time, he was charged with making "seditious utterances." At his trial three members of the province's Red Squad took the stand in turn and produced little books from which they read the alleged seditious statement: "If necessary we will go down to City Hall and lay down our heads." On the basis of their testimony, Fred Rose, insisting that he loved life too much to have said such a stupid thing, was convicted of sedition and sentenced to one year in Bordeaux Jail.

Now, he was out on bail, marching again, talking exuberantly to those around him, laughing with Joshua Gershman, his body-guard, about the Red Squad's having followed them naked into the fog of the neighbourhood steambath. Policemen, on motorcycles, on horseback, on foot, buzzed about the procession, held in check only by its gathering force. Fred watched them from the sides of his eyes, like a mongoose looking at a snake. The Communist Party was reaching out to unemployed people who had never before been organized. Because Fred Rose was a communist leader, the state had arrested him in Toronto in 1929. They had arrested him two years later in Montreal. Fred and his comrades had no doubt that he would lose his appeal on the latest charge and serve the year in Bordeaux Jail. But he would come out and continue organizing. This was "the New World," but, looking at the cold, stony faces around him, he knew that here, too, was a class struggle. At stake were freedom and life itself. The grail was "a decent society." The jobless and poor standing beside him were broke, desperate, and angry. They had little to lose.

Berlin. 1931
Nothing in Lea Roback's childhood in her home town of Beau-port, outside Quebec City, nothing even in her preceding months in France, had prepared her for the chill when she entered this room. She had written out her request to join the communist student group on fine, onion-skin paper. She had gone to the working-class district in the old part of Berlin and had waited

44

outside the meeting room while a fellow student reported what he had learned about her: no, she had not been in the movement in Canada; yes, she had marched with workers in Paris and in anti-fascist rallies in Berlin. Five feet three, slender, and very nervous, Lea stood stiffly, holding on to what dignity and feelings of good fellowship she could. She was wearing a black coat with a beige fox collar, cloche hat, black dress, and high-heeled shoes. The communist students appraising her were wearing short leather jackets, navy-blue berets, flat shoes. They looked at her as though she were a street-walker. Who was she? What was she? She could speak English, French, German, Yiddish. They could tell by her face that she was a Jew.

Lea's eyes, as she repeated her demand to join the Party, were defiant. She wanted to fight the rise of the Nazi party which, with the support of big business and, to some extent, the aristocracy, had become the leading party of the Right. She told the German communists that she had "got her wits sharpened" at the May Day demonstration in 1929 in Berlin. Law students with swords and swastikas, measuring their manhood by the size and number of their duelling scars, had attacked her and her friends from the university's Linguistics Department. Singing as she held on to her banner, she had seen the police chain their helmets under their chins, readying for action. She watched as they protected the "*provocateurs*," the law students responsible for initiating the violence, and bashed in the heads and broke the noses of her friends. Lea's blood ran colder than the chill in the room at the thought of the Nazi students' favourite chant, "*Wir scheissen auf die Freiheit*"— "We shit on freedom."

In a violent time and place, where the extremes, fascist or communist, seemed the only choice, Lea joined the Communist Party. Pre-Nazi Germany was her baptism by fire. There she began her training: handing out leaflets; selling the communist newspaper *Die Rote Fahne*; organizing "Women in Need," a benefit art exhibit featuring Käthe Kollwitz, whose drawings so dramatically expressed the anguish of the victims of poverty and war. Lea's driving aim

Lea Roback, outside Berlin, early 1930s, on a break from university
and the rise of Hitler.
*Courtesy of the Lea Roback Foundation
and the Jewish Public Library Archvies*

was to "try to get people together to stop the horror I saw growing, growing stronger day by day." It was the beginning of a way of life. There would be no turning back from her absolute conviction that, in the face of inhumanity, "we must act, we must do something."

In 1932, on the advice of Party leaders, Lea escaped Germany—"by the skin of my teeth." By now a relatively seasoned revolutionary, she returned to Montreal and got a job at the Young Women's Hebrew Association (YWHA), where, one again, she heard the faltering pulse of the times in the plaints of young people. She listened to them all, part of a large and growing cohort coming out of schools and training programs, unable to find work. With nothing to do, no place to go, hundreds of thousands between the ages of fifteen and twenty-four saw only unemployment and misery ahead. Not knowing where the next meal was coming from, hungry all the time, they ached with hopelessness and guilt as they ate the food rations on the family table. Lea wondered that they didn't end up in the asylums, St. Jean de Dieu or Verdun, because "there was nothing for them, and so they were nothing."

At the YWHA, she organized a program of dramatic presentations, art classes, and outings. She cajoled and blackmailed the ladies of the board into giving her money for essentials for her charges and, on the side, organized an unofficial Marxist study group. In 1935 she coordinated Fred Rose's first election campaign, braving the hostility of right-wing, clerical Quebec, and later, she travelled to New York to buy Marxist books banned by the Quebec government, smuggling them across the border under her bus seat. From 1936 to 1948 she worked tirelessly as a union organizer, first in the needle trades and then in the electrical industry, becoming the acknowledged mentor of contemporary union leaders of divergent beliefs, such as Madeleine Parent. With courage, earthiness, many languages, and a no-nonsense vision of justice, Lea swept many into the fray, always thankful for the communist movement, which "helped so many people learn that you can't always contemplate your navel; there are things to be done."

Montreal. 1933
In the hall of the Association Humanitaire the air was charged with expectation and thick with the smoke of Kennel pipe-tobacco. Emery Samuel sat stiff-backed among seven hundred other workers, waiting for the French-Canadian communist leader Paul Delisle.

Through the Association Humanitaire, many of the people whom Delisle was about to address had for the first time read forbidden books, discussed philosophy, and taken the drastic step of abjuring their religion. Taking their sons with them, they had banded together to keep the bailiff away from their neighbour's door. In 1928 it had been from this anti-clerical, anarchist association that the original French-Canadian cells of the Third International had been recruited. With the economic crisis of the thirties, militants such as Emery and Delisle had seen the association's anti-clerical activities as a dead end and had formed communist cells separate from the public assembly. Mysteriously, in the night, slogans appeared on construction fences and hydro posts, and Red flags waved from the top of public buildings.

Emery's eyes were now on Delisle as he mounted the platform, tensed, as if for battle. Then, in the grand oratorical style, from the heart, Delisle began, speaking of his people who, during and after the Great War, had come in the thousands from the villages and farms of Quebec to Montreal and Quebec City. Working ten hours each weekday and five hours on Saturday, they bought a small lot, 50 by 200 feet, on the outskirts of the city, along the banks of Rivière des Prairies, remembering the time when they had owned something. All along the river there were trees and children playing Tarzan in the branches. People could build something here. But in 1924 the trust companies repossessed these lots by the hundreds. Without even the dream of a shack in the country—no animals to raise, no garden, nothing to do on Sunday—people were suddenly proletarians. Now they had lost their lots, their jobs, their self-respect. The jobless were evicted, arrested, beaten up, shot. "We are used and abused on our own soil," said Delisle, his string-bean frame hard with hate.

Delisle had become a communist after the First World War. Without even having the time to return home from war, he was shipped in 1918 to the port of Archangel, in northern Russia, a conscript in the Allies' Western Army of Intervention. According to Winston Churchill, the Allied troops were supposed "to strangle the infant [the Bolshevik regime of Vladimir Lenin] in its cradle." Delisle didn't know where he was or where he was going. He had been sent to support the White Russians against the Reds, but even in Archangel, the White Russians' stronghold, the majority of the people were pro-Bolshevik. And the White Russians he met seemed to him morally and physically decayed. Increasingly,

Delisle and his fellow soldiers—Canadians, Americans, British, Serbs, Italians, Finns, Poles, Australians—wondered what they were doing in Russia. Winter came, with sub-zero temperatures and no organized supply system for units moving inland. Each day the Allied soldiers were promised that at the next village they would eat, but when they arrived, all they found was black ash on the snow. The soldiers abandoned their guns. Finally, they abandoned their blankets. They had nothing but despair, and the cold gloom of the Arctic winter.

Delisle hadn't asked to be sent to Russia; he had no interest in reinstating the tsarist regime. Never would he forget the misery he had been tricked into enduring. His suffering led him to an overwhelming conclusion: "They screwed us, the bastards." When, after fourteen torturous months, he was finally shipped home, he became one of the most active young workers in the trade-union movement, then in the unemployed movement. He would soon be one of a number of French Canadians brought into the Party leadership as the Party's activities among the unemployed and the unions increased. Paul Delisle was one of the first chosen to go to the International Lenin School in Moscow, where promising young revolutionaries were trained to be Communist Party organizers and leaders. Since his return from the Lenin School, five months before, Emery and others had talked with him into the night, into the morning, of life, work, the working class. He spoke to full houses at the Association Humanitaire. He had already organized twelve new cells of the Communist Party.

As Paul Delisle denounced the continuing windfall profits of the Redpaths, Molsons, Sir Herbert Holts, and Sir Edward Beatties, Emery Samuel scratched behind his slightly protruding right ear. He pictured these "English" sipping tea at the Ritz while his fellow *Gaspésiens* lined up at the doors of charitable institutions for food. Emery would have liked to break their stupid square heads, but he was now a member of a communist cell and, intellectually, he agreed that his former anarchist militancy would not lead to socialism. Still, there was a certain satisfaction in intimidating the pawnshop vultures and making them back off from the belongings of evicted tenants. Emery wasn't sorry that he and his associates from the Association Humanitaire had taken over bailiffs' auctions so they could buy back beds, desks, pianos, and the rest for sixty-seven cents, and return them to their rightful owners. He hummed the Wobblies' tune to:

> You will eat, bye and bye,
> In that glorious land above the sky;
> Work and pray, live on hay,
> You'll get pie in the sky when you die.
> It's a lie.

This imitation religious tune, with revolutionary words, came from the radical Industrial Workers of the World (IWW), the legendary Wobblies. A hoot of contempt for existing society, it accompanied every strike. Singing it gave Emery something he called "enthusiasm."

> Work and pray, live on hay,
> You'll get pie in the sky when you die,
> It's a lie!

Emery wished he had known the song in 1925, when Ontario Pulp and Paper was paying him twenty-six dollars a month to log on the north shore of the Marguerite River, in Quebec. He and the other lumberjacks had been housed in lean-tos with the horses. They were fed beans and molasses, sometimes butter, depending on transport. Since there were no forks or spoons, the men whittled utensils out of cedar. Their beds were wooden planks which they covered with pine boughs to keep down the vermin. If Emery had known the song then he would have sung it to Leo, the best lumberjack in the camp. Woken him up, maybe, so he would have used his massive strength to change the system of contractors and sub-contractors, rather than trying to beat it by "the dog-work."

Leo had tried to bypass the middlemen by contracting himself out, not only to fell trees, cut off their branches, and saw the trunks into cords, but to harness a sled to his back and haul the cords of wood down to the river. Like other big men before him, he wasn't fast enough in the snow: the large rolling tree trunks had finally overtaken him, crushed his ribs, smashed, killed him. The boss of the jobbers had gone to Leo's widow with a gallon of molasses, a bag of flour, and a small tin of butter, saying "From the goodness of my heart I am taking your interests for mine and give you this for the children." "You will eat, bye and bye."

Maybe he could have sung some sense into Leo and maybe not. To study little books by Lenin and to talk about guts and struggle was, Emery realized, "like being on another planet." Leo was a Catholic and militant talk meant communism. Bourgeois journals had claimed that "*la main noire*," the Mafia, was the cause of communism. Now, they said, it was the Jews and the Bolsheviks. Both would destroy religion and the family. Church and State controlled the people through this kind of propaganda and through an iron web whose strands were political power, education, patronage, economic control: the Catholic Church was the biggest landowner in Quebec.

Emery had been raised on the Church's anti-communist propaganda. He had read its bulletins, tracts, posters, and the Jesuits' *Manuel antibolchevique*, *Le Cahier anticommuniste*, and *La Menace du communisme au Canada*. At church he had heard pastoral letters, sermons, colloquia, calling on the faithful to eschew the spiritual and temporal desolation of the communists. The priests would have told Leo, "Better a crust of bread than no bread at all" and "It's God's will." The priests helped industry prosper. Emery had learned about camp conditions outside Quebec from the lumberjacks who went to work annually in Ontario and Maine. In Ontario the companies had abolished wooden beds and replaced them with First World War surplus iron beds. The men had covers so that they could sleep without the steel touching their flesh. Life for the worker in Quebec was always worse than in Ontario or the Untied States. "We are a cheap, manageable labour force," thought Emery. "With Quebec's rich mines and forests and under-paid workers, the capitalists are in an excellent position to attract investment. Touch one—*curé* or bourgeois—and the whole cavalry is on the march."

From Delisle and Fred Rose, Emery was learning class con-sciousness: "There are two classes: the class of the capitalists and the managers, and that of the workers. I am with the workers." Last Sunday, in the café, where Bolsheviks, anarchists and social democrats argued into the morning, Emery had listened to Delisle teach from Marx's *Das Kapital*. Succinctly, Delisle had explained how capitalist profit is based on the exploitation of labour. The bosses pay as little as they can in wages and pocket the surplus that has been earned by the workers' labour. It was inevitable that capitalism would break down, as it now had, and be overthrown, as in Russia, where workers had fought together and taken over the government. The means of production were now owned by the Russian people, and they shared in the profits. All men were equal. Social Darwinism and classical economics were for the "*maudits*" businessmen. Marxism was the workers' answer to the bosses and "*les jupes noires*," the priests.

Evariste Dubé, Fred Rose and Emery Samuel—the "Secretariat"
(Quebec), 1939.

When he thought about "the class struggle," Emery's skinny, craggy face looked strangely puckish. His time in Quebec's north woods, working like a beast of burden for Ontario-owned logging companies, was etched into his memory. He had left the north to build a new life in the city, only to join his dispossessed countrymen in scrounging for a living in a harsh industrial landscape. Walking the streets on Sunday, looking for someone from his parish, his village, his county, he had come upon the open door of the Association Humanitaire. A voice had called, "Come fill your pipe and sit and talk," and his socialist education had begun. With his chums, he had met in what was first an anti-religious association, later, an anarchist-Bolshevik association, and when Delisle had given him the key to understanding the current economic crisis and his place in a future world, Emery had started down the road that would make him one of the most committed leaders of the French Section of the Canadian Communist Party. He was no longer intimidated by the provincial police; he had exorcised the religious mind-police. The party to which he belonged was bigger than himself, part of a worldwide workers' movement. "The October Revolution is the beginning of a new chapter in the story of humanity." For Emery and the others from small, isolated villages in the Gaspé, it was a heady thought. A world of philosophy and hope unfurled with the Red flags.

Paris. 1931
Stanley Ryerson and his friend were drenched. Rain soaked the streets. Thunderclaps followed their hurried steps. "Just a few blocks farther there's a bookstore," Otto offered. Stanley ran. The decade he had spent at Upper Canada College among the chosen, in the great prayer hall under the portrait of the founder, Lord Seaton, surrounded by the masters in gowns, were behind him. The French government had awarded him a scholarship to pursue his studies in languages and history at the Sorbonne. Stanley felt good. A summer trek over the Pyrenees and into Spain with Otto and another Canadian friend had made his normally phlegmatic body alert and fit. And now he was back in Paris.

From his mother, whose ancestor was the French military commander at Three Rivers in 1636, Stanley had inherited a continental French background and a love of the arts. From his father, dean of the Faculty of Medicine at the University of Toronto, grandson of the founder of the Ontario public-school system, he had inherited an English-Canadian establishment background and an interest in science. Although his eyes were bad and he was no good for cricket, he had been well trained in the tradition of Western European culture and had already written a play, *Abelard*, in Alexandrines. "Wrapped," as he said, "in the cotton batting of middle-class Toronto," his vision was aesthetic and decidedly apolitical. For his final exam in English composition he had submitted a poem on the possibility of the bleak barrens of the Laurentians giving rise to the greatness of a Leonardo, a Michelangelo, a new Renaissance. Now, as he approached the welcoming light of the bookstore, Stanley's face and rain-streaked glasses, shone. He was twenty years old, in Paris—on his own.

"Look, Stanley," said Otto, taking refuge in the bookstore. "There's something in the French communist daily *L'Humanité* about communists in Toronto being arrested." Stanley looked. His "Old Canadian" upbringing had not included mention of Tim Buck, leader of the Communist Party of Canada, nor an awareness of such things as the unemployed movement and political demonstrations. In the left-wing bookstore Stanley bought *L'Humanité*, as well as two pamphlets, *The Cultural Revolution* and *The Communist Manifesto*, which he had never seen before. Most of that night he sat up reading. He was already beginning to have a sense of the crisis in unemployment, along with a disturbing sense of the spiritual crisis in the arts. He had seen Cocteau's highly acclaimed film *Sang d'un Poète* and was surprised by its theme. That Cocteau, a leading literary light, should be fascinated by masturbation at this time of crisis seemed to him "a bit sick." Now, the pamphlet he had bought on the cultural revolution set out an entirely different scenario for the arts, one in which all people would take hold of theatre, poetry, fiction, and painting

as a result of the socialist revolution in Russia. "It hit me"—
the idea of millions of speechless men and women rising from
centuries of silence to express their potential. Stanley made the
intellectual and emotional leap from Cocteau's film being "sick"
to capitalist society itself being sick. The socialist pamphlet on
culture presented an option. But "the illumination that seemed
to come as a flash" was not only fired by the cultural pamphlet.
In *The Communist Manifesto* Stanley found a rational, scientific
explanation of the historical process. "History for the first time
made sense." Art and science, his parental legacies, were fused in a
new vision of a creative, rational world.

For Stanley, as for many Christians, Marxist socialism had
an oddly familiar feel. When he had first started to read, he
read the Bible, and its influence on him was still strong. The
historical perspective he had learned through his Christianity
was chronological, assuming a structure in time that went
from the Creation, to the Messiah, to the Resurrection, to the
Last Judgement. He was brought up with a largely imaginary
concept which gave him a system by which to understand the
world. Marxist science was analogous in that sense, as well as
in its emphasis on the concepts of brotherhood and charity,
which he understood as love, "*caritas*." Engels had said that the
early Christians were precocious communists, and although
Stanley thought the statement could be taken too far, he saw it
as valid, "not merely in relation to the part that is cognitive, the
part that lets you grasp the nature of things...It is at the same
time normative: there is a goal that is good and is urgently to be
sought after because of the way things are; the resultant relations
of comradeship and solidarity implied a sense of responsibility as
well as a sense of belonging."

As Stanley grew older, religious belief had been replaced by
religious scepticism and, finally, in Paris, like the thunderclaps
that had driven him into the bookstore, by communism. Reading
was vital to Stanley, and in a country only five years away from a
socialist government, where Marxism and the communist option

were openly and hotly espoused, he could immerse himself in the literature of the revolution. The Toronto of Upper Canada College, Deer Park, and Rosedale were on the other side of the ocean. He read Lenin's message to the English-speaking world: "Comrades, Greetings from the first proletarian republic. We call you to arms for the international social revolution." And he was moved by John Reed's dramatic account of the Bolsheviks seizing the state power of Russia and putting it in the hands of workers', soldiers' and peasants' organizations, the Soviets. In his first demonstration in Paris, in 1932, people chanted, "*Les Soviets partout.*" Returning home in 1933, he rejoiced to hear the Paris chant echoed in the streets of Toronto: "The International Soviet shall be the human race." [1] Stanley was intellectually ready when, at the summer picnic of the communist movement, a Lithuanian worker asked him to join the Young Communist League. On a park bench just west of the Toronto Public Library on College Street he waited for someone to come and consider his application. He didn't know the importance the immigrant Party leadership would place on his education, background, and native-Canadian respectability; he would be accepted quickly, groomed by Fred Rose, and propelled into the executive leadership. As he waited, hoping to be accepted into the League, Stanley knew only one thing: in Paris, he had awakened to actuality. "Nothing looked the same."

Montreal. December 1931
It was Monday, 8:00 A.M. Stocky, eighteen-year-old Henri Gagnon leaned against the wall in the contractor's basement, where for months he had stood vigil. Since age thirteen, Henri had been an apprentice-electrician. "Get your licence," his father had said before he died. "It's a good trade." Now, Henri's pleasure at having graduated turned to bitterness as he watched older, experienced men waiting days for a two-hour job. Factories, businesses, and construction offices had closed their doors, and the chronic poverty, aptly called the Great Depression, had begun its long, debilitating course. By 1933 almost one fifth of the labour force

in Canada would be out of work. Sixty per cent of the workers in Quebec would be *chômeurs*, jobless. Wages, if there were any, were down. There was no unemployment insurance. Misery, a constant companion, was the grotesque attendant even at birthings: of the astounding 20,300 infant mortalities in Canada, half were in Quebec, a cruel index of a grossly malfunctioning society.

In the eight-room flat on Lagauchetière, Henri and the eleven members of his family, including Grandpapa, fended for themselves. All the Gagnon family received was subsistence relief through charitable institutions. If they hadn't been Catholic, they might have said a prayer at the Salvation Army and gotten a bowl of soup. They went instead to Saint Vincent de Paul and got potatoes and molasses. Henri did the electrical work for the landlord in lieu of rent. He jumped the cables, bypassing the electrical company's meter to get light, and reconnected the stove into the main line to heat the house. Eventually, the government gave destitute people coupons for food. With judicious shopping, Maman might find twenty pounds of barely edible meat for one dollar. "We hung on," said Henri. "It affects you profoundly, but you get used to it."

In 1930 the Catholic clergy and the Liberal government tried to convince unemployed Quebeckers that they would be happy returning to the farming land of their pioneer ancestors. Fifty thousand unemployed men duly left the cities as part of *Le Retour à la Terre*. Henri and fifty men went to Abitibi, in the far north, where one group was designated to clear the land, another to make a road to the gold mines in Chibougamau, a third to build houses for the families that were supposed to join them. "The first promise that they broke was that we would go by horse with everything we would need. Finally, we were sent with rudimentary tools and our bare hands." They were paid twenty cents an hour. "At the end of six months, I received a cheque from the government for all the money they owed me after deductions—ten cents, the price of a package of tobacco at that time."

Returning to Montreal, Henri played softball three hours a day with the Unemployed League at Lafontaine Park. On Sundays he went to church and heard the pastoral letters from the bishops of Quebec warning against communism. "It is incumbent on the public powers to stop the message of these agents of spiritual and temporal desolation," they said, "but all citizens must participate in this work of protection, at the very least through prayer." Henri laughed at the leftists in the softball league. Everybody did. As the depression wore on, however, the laughter stopped. In time Henri undertook a study of Marxism that would change his life. In time he would seek out "the Third International," hoping to join the only organization he knew that would do something about his sad, desperate, angry ache.

CHAPTER TWO

The Third International

FRED ROSE, PAUL DELISLE, Lea, Emery, Stanley, and Henri joined a growing, worldwide revolutionary movement, an offshoot of the Russian Revolution. With the fall of the Russian monarchy, history had changed. The new Soviet order signalled a fresh beginning and the end of old imperial regimes. "Come the revolution…" was an invocation of hope—lands in the hands of farmers, factories owned by those who worked in them. It was believed that finally, at least somewhere, working people were free from every slavery and every exploitation. "There is only one master of the Russian land: the union of the workers, soldiers and peasants," declared Leon Trotsky, on November 16, 1917, at the triumphal session of the All-Russian Congress of Soviets. "All workers' movements in the past have been defeated," said Maria Spiridonova, the most loved and powerful woman in Russia. "But the present movement is international and that is why it is invincible. There is no force in the world that can put out the fire of the Revolution! The old world crumbles down, the new world begins." In nine historic words, Lenin proclaimed, "We shall now proceed to construct the socialist order."

In 1918 people crowded into shabby ghetto halls in Montreal to hail the Revolution. The distant storm signals promised change at home. Would they be heard in the crowded sweatshops, in the factories, the mines and railway yards? Would the bosses hear in Montreal? Would life become a little easier for poor people?

As workers cheered, British ships carried the Western Army of Intervention to Russia. Sixteen countries attacked the newly formed Bolshevik government, come to power on a "stop the war" platform. The invasion that was to leave Paul Delisle bitterly angry convinced the Soviets and their supporters that socialism must always be ready to defend itself. In 1919 the lone socialist state created the Communist International, a global federation that was to provide the Soviets with support from working people around the world.

The destiny of communists everywhere quickly became intertwined with that of the Communist International. All national Communist parties joined this Moscow-based federation; and communists in Canada, as in other countries, inherited a two-fold allegiance: to the Communist International and to their national party. The application for membership in the Communist Party of Canada's original constitution read: "I, the undersigned, declare my adherence to the programs and statutes of the Communist International and of the Communist Party of Canada, and agree to submit to the discipline of the Party and to engage actively in its work." As Nikolai Bukharin, Soviet Politbureau member in charge of press and propaganda, wrote in the *ABC of Communism*, "It is not surprising that all who are live, trusty and revolutionary-minded members of the international proletariat are turning more and more eagerly toward the new International and are joining forces to form the workers' vanguard." It seemed as if the possibility of revolution anywhere in the world depended on the fate of the experiment in the U.S.S.R. In Quebec the communist newspaper warned each worker to prepare for the defence of the Soviet Union against imperialist attacks. The defeat of the workers' government in the Soviet Union would mean the defeat of the working class. International workers' solidarity would protect the socialist dream. "At the beginning we were small sects and we stuck close to the Party line," said Fred Rose. "We inherited ideas."

But international solidarity was not only a defensive concept; it was, in Henri Gagnon's words, "an opening to the world." As members of the Communist International, Emery, Lea, Fred Rose, Stanley, and Henri became the comrades of people in many countries. "The Canadian party was part of the Third International and that meant part of the great internationalist ideal," recalled Henri. "You could serve on the Provincial Committee, on the National Committee, or even go to the Congress in Moscow. It was very democratic." The possibilities for someone from the working class seemed enormous. There was no school in Canada to train Party leaders, so promising young communists, including Paul Delisle, his wife Berthe Caron, and later, Emery Samuel, were sponsored by the CPC to study at the International Lenin School in Moscow. For Emery, who could barely read when he joined the Party, the wonder was that "they opened to us libraries the size of which we had never seen before. Depending on how lazy or brave you were to stay up and burn the oil, there was nothing you couldn't learn."

The International became the motor of early social change, the organization to which North American labour leaders, working with unskilled, non-unionized workers in the mines, mills, and sweat-shops, could look for help. The fledgling Canadian party could count on it for practical support—training, literature, some money. Local communists gained force and credibility because Marxism was no longer only an intellectual construct; it had been realized. Canadian communists were thus inextricably bound to the Soviet Union because, as Fred Rose would later say, "We needed it for survival."

For the Canadian government, the Winnipeg General Strike brought the bogeyman of the Russian Revolution home to roost. In 1919, 35,000 working men and women, of whom very few were communists, took over the city of Winnipeg for a month. Suffering from the post-First World War economic collapse, they demanded a living wage, an eight-hour day, and the right to organize. Government reaction was unequivocal and violent: a deputized "special police," vigilantes with lead-filled wagon yokes and baseball bats, an armed charge of the Royal Northwest Mounted Police, one striker murdered, hundreds injured.

Arrests, accusations of seditious conspiracy, and the imprisonment of strike leaders followed the Winnipeg General Strike, as
did new and repressive legislation. The duties of the federal police
were greatly extended, with the newly dubbed Royal Canadian
Mounted Police reconstituted as a "bulwark against Bolshevism."
The government also passed the Unlawful Associations Act which,
in 1924, was incorporated into the Criminal Code as Article 98.
Under Article 98 it was illegal to attend a meeting of an association
deemed to be revolutionary, to pass out radical literature, even to
carry an insignia "intended to suggest" membership to such an
association. The penalty for breaking this law was up to twenty years
in prison. "Up to 1926 we had the right to organize labour parades
with unions and different organizations. After that, parades were
banned," remembered Fred Rose. "May Day, 1927, we gathered at
Prince Arthur Hall in Montreal. They brought out practically the
whole police force, and we saw them coming from downtown to
Prince Arthur. They walked up like an invading army, blocked the
street, surrounded the building, created a situation as if a revolution was about to happen. No parade took place because we
didn't want a blood bath." From 1931 to 1935 militant Canadian-
born labour leaders were jailed under Article 98 of the Criminal
Code, and sections 41 and 42 of the Immigration Act took care of
the foreign-born agitators by deporting them. As Fred Rose saw it,
"The Red scare started immediately following the Russian Revolution. Increased lies and slander about the Soviet Union coincided
with the General Strike in Winnipeg. It stepped up in the thirties,
with the crisis in unemployment."

The tattered, dispirited jobless were the litter of the depression.
In answer to their cries for help, established leaders expounded their
theory of social Darwinism, that "natural selection" had chosen
them to succeed economically and rule socially. They pontificated
on the inevitability of periodic depressions under capitalism and
the corrective mechanism of the "natural laws" of economics.
"The dole," they asserted, was economically unsound and morally
offensive; it would sap the initiative and independence of the

working class. They urged patience and fortitude. "Work and wages!" answered the communist speakers. "There's no unemployment in the Soviet Union, comrades," they added, "and there wouldn't be any here if we workers owned the means of production." Provoked by this impertinent foreign movement, capitalist leaders instituted economic sanctions against the Soviet Union and intensified anti-communist measures at home. In 1931 Fred Rose and four others were arrested at the Labour Temple in Montreal as they addressed the first meeting of the unemployed. Soon after, all the national leaders of the Canadian Communist Party were rounded up and jailed under Article 98 in an attempt to behead the Communist Party and thereby remove its influence from the increasingly desperate and militant organizations of the unemployed.

The consistent attacks on the Soviet Union, starting with the 1918 economic blockade and the War of Intervention, as well as harsh local persecution, reinforced the communist concept of "the new model" party as "a weapon, not a vote-getting organization or a debating society." Lenin's pamphlet, *What Is To Be Done*, discussed the necessity of the Party's having an illegal underground apparatus and a vehicle for using legal means, depending on the regime. The Canadian party was, at best, quasilegal: it was begun in 1921 in conditions of illegality, under the War Measures Act,[2] infiltrated at its founding meeting; hounded under the Unlawful Associations Act; banned under Article 98 from 1931 to 1936; illegal in Quebec under the Law Respecting Communist Propaganda from 1937 to 1956; banned under the War Measures Act from 1939 to 1942; the object of a secret witch-hunt after the Second World War; constantly under police surveillance. Party members always retained the option of going underground and, for security reasons, were grouped into what they themselves called branches and what the public called cells, a structure still used by revolutionary organizations around the world. Whenever necessary, contact between groups was minimal and membership was secret.[3] The model for the Party came from pre-revolutionary Russia, where it was created under a tsarist autocracy that had banned it for all but two years—where the construction of a formally democratic party would have meant imprisonment by the tsarist police.

The Canadian Communist Party maintained this clandestine option for times when repression was severe, but it functioned openly and through parliamentary channels whenever possible. When the Party was legal, most secret underground functions disappeared and the members of these units of six or seven people were publicly communists; they handed out leaflets, sold the communist newspapers door to door, and campaigned as communists in federal and provincial elections. They knew each other from educational meetings, women's meetings, trade-union meetings, demonstrations, picket-lines, and Paul Robeson concerts. They learned to live with constant intimidation and to joke about the omnipresent undercover policemen from the Red Squad assigned to their surveillance. Being members of a party that was always infiltrated, legislated against, and persecuted, they developed a reflex sense of survival: never talk Party business on the phone or talk elliptically or, if Jewish, in Yiddish; notice if you're being followed; identify members of the Red Squad. The actual clandestine activities of rank-and-file members might be to print and distribute communist literature when it was illegal to do so. Bella, a Party member active in the Canadian Labour Defence League and, later, in the Canadian Seamen's Union (CSU), explained the meaning of "underground" for communists: "Underground meant that the Party was illegal and could not work above ground openly. Any time you did, you were taking a chance."

For militant immigrants, Canadian anti-labour legislation, state surveillance, and police attacks differed from the state repression of their old countries only in kind. A Party member reported that, at an open-air meeting in 1926, at the Place Viger in Montreal, the provincial police "came pounding down like Cossacks, bashing everyone." In other provinces similar policing was handled by the RCMP, who viewed all immigrants with dark suspicion and reserved their special enmity for immigrant labour-organizers. In 1931 RCMP officers rode into a miners' strike at Estevan,

Saskatchewan, with rifles, clubs, and machine guns, killing three men and wounding a score of others. That year alone they helped deport seven thousand immigrants. In the thirties strike-breaking and open-air attacks became RCMP specialities. Their routine tactic of riding into a demonstration or a meeting, separating out small groups and beating them senseless was personally known to everyone who had ever taken to the streets in protest. A deep inner hatred of communists distinguished members of this force from ordinary policemen. Their quarterly magazine spoke of "tearing the camouflage from the Red beast;" it anguished over "the ugly cancer gnawing at the vitals of the Dominion;" and, betraying another deep-seated prejudice, that of anti-Semitism, it warned against the "dark Jewish conspiracy."

Communists, in Canada and elsewhere, in what they saw as their "colossal task of restructuring society," adopted the Bolshevik principle of organization known as democratic centralism. "It is democratic in that the central body...is democratically elected. It is centralized in that during its period of office this Central Committee...has power to make decisions which are binding on the whole party, and to use the whole strength of the organization, unimpaired by inner disputes, in the most critical phases of the struggle at any given moment."[4] Theoretically, all members were required to study, discuss, and vote on all matters of policy. The democratic discussion would then be distilled and implemented by the Party centre. Once its decision was made, members were bound by it, whether they liked it or not. "We were under attack all the time," explained an early militant. "If you are fighting for your life, you can't stop to take a vote. You have to have a central authority." Because communism threatened those with large property holdings, often the same men who controlled capitalist governments, communists were in opposition to and opposed by the existing state. Their political choice became a sectarian way of life—a close-knit circle of friends who were comrades, daily Party tasks, and Party discipline. The sense of personal responsibility that had motivated them to join the Party was overlaid with the conviction that the Party was the vehicle of change. And the power of the Party over its members was reinforced by state repression. In the words of writer Jessica Mitford, "It was indeed a matter of conform or get out, but this did not particularly bother me. I had regarded joining the Party as one of the most important decisions of my adult life. I loved and admired the people in it, and was more than willing to accept the leadership of those far more experienced than I. Furthermore, the principle of democratic centralism seemed to me essential to the functioning of a revolutionary organization in a hostile world."[5]

It would have been difficult for early communists to see any danger in disciplined action. "Long live the iron firmness of the Proletariat!" Lenin urged. Discipline seemed a logical exigency, as did Soviet leadership and Soviet organizational models. The members who joined the Friends of the Soviet Union and the leaders who conferred with representatives from the Communist International, who worked in the Communist International in Moscow, who studied leadership at the International Lenin School, and who accepted subsidies for their struggling Party would have found this necessary and ideologically sound. The first socialist country in the world, especially in the context of the depression, was an ideal. All people worked, all had a right to an education, everyone ate three times a day. The home of communism was mythologized by intense belief. Stanley Ryerson thought of the Soviet Union "more abstractly than actually. It was a model more than an actual place." He would believe in it, long for it, and defend it for twenty years before actually seeing it. By the 1928 Sixth Congress of the Communist International, national parties outside the Soviet Union had accepted "the subordination of partial and local interests to general and permanent interest, and the strict application of all the decisions of the ruling bodies of the Communist International." It would have been difficult, then, to foresee that in time habit would make the defence of the revolution at home secondary to the defence of the revolution in Russia. For the executive leaders of the Canadian Communist Party the distinction between the needs of the Canadian working class they represented and Soviet needs would blur. Ultimately, when there was a critical conflict of interest, they would, most unfortunately, not be able to distinguish whom they should serve.

In the early thirties, however, unionization was the communist rallying cry. It was an essential struggle that had to be carried on, leaving little time for theorizing. As Fred Rose remembered, "We had our own ethics, principles. We were involved in very practical issues of fighting for the people. Issues of the day. Theory was very superficial. We knew very little of the faults. We believed." Communist militants were concerned "first and foremost with the problem of unionization." In most of the industries that didn't involve highly skilled labour, there were no unions; in Quebec, in 1931, only ten per cent of salaried employees were unionized. The Party was organizing workers, in the needle trades, in the mines, whom no one else would touch. Workers who found the American Internationals conservative and the Catholic unions reactionary joined the communists and took the consequences. "The boys were in the streets," Emery Samuel recalled, "and those who bled, bled, and those who were lucky enough to be hit over the head congratulated themselves and hoped their luck would continue." The Communist Party was the only party actively fighting for unskilled, unorganized, unemployed, and French-Canadian workers, reaching out to people never before in contact with organization. Bella, an early communist, said that the best thing was the feeling of solidarity between people and their support for one another. "It was a closeness that doesn't exist today. It was a bread-and-butter thing. These were very hard times." If a worker didn't have a job there was no unemployment insurance, no welfare. "It was a different world. People understood and worked with you and tried their best. Great friendships were formed."

Join the Union Fellow Workers
Men and women side by side
We will crush the greedy shirkers

Like a sweeping surging tide
For united we are standing
But divided we will fall
Let this be our understanding
All for One and One for all.[6]

[CHAPTER THREE]

Seditious Utterances,
Unlawful Associations

As CANADA SANK DEEP into the Depression, broke, jobless men rode the freights, hoping that somewhere they would find work. They were hounded by police, escorted out of town, often arrested as vagrants. Weekly trains came west, jettisoning more unemployed into the cities rumoured to have work. The glut of hungry, homeless people grew, and single unemployed men applying for relief were shipped out of urban areas to "relief camps," the government's answer to the problem of unemployment.[1] These camps were administered and run under the jurisdiction of the Department of National Defence. The men were made to do heavy labour, clear land and build airports and roads—for twenty cents a day. There were no mattresses, no sheets, no books, no sports; only the gruelling work and the rough, crude, and bitter isolation of men without prospects. Secretly, so that the supervisors and police spies sent to infiltrate the camps couldn't arrest them as "agitators," communists organized unions among the unemployed workers. For five cents a month, a man could be a member of the Relief Camp Workers' Union, set up on a genuine trade-union basis. A member paid dues, attended meetings, elected officers, and put forward grievances. He could read the abundant working-class literature, join with others and strike, if necessary. "We had to organize the camps," said Red Walsh, a leader in the Relief Camp Workers' Union. "It was our only hope. We couldn't see any future.

It seemed we'd be in those camps for 8 or 10 years."[2] In the study sessions "slave labour" was condemned. There was talk of a future in a new kind of society.

Communists also organized clubs of unemployed workers in cities across Canada. Lucien Dufour, a young unemployed married man, became a militant organizer of the Montreal unemployed. "Workers had to go to public charity, mostly religious charity, to give food to their families. We couldn't take it—the poverty and the degradation. In all the neighbourhoods of Montreal, unemployed workers' associations were formed." The associations made sure that families were fed, organized round-the-clock pickets to protest evictions, and collected signatures for a trans-Canada petition demanding national non-contributory unemployment insurance. "We didn't believe the workers were responsible for the economic chaos," said Dufour. "We asked the government, not charity, to assume responsibility for the unemployed." Neighbourhood workers' associations sent representatives to larger organizations of the unemployed, such as the Conseil des Chômeurs de Montréal, which made demands to the various levels of government. Eventually, the Conseil forced the municipality to give some relief to the unemployed heads of families. "We got direct help after fights and imprisonments," said Dufour, recalling his experiences, "but not electricity, heat, or boots for the children for school." The Workers' Unity League, a strong, communist-led union in the forefront of trade-union struggles from 1929 to 1935, supported the Conseil's demands for unemployment insurance and, in 1935, helped organize the On-to-Ottawa Trek of the unemployed. Headlines in the communist newspaper *The Worker* read: "Fight Don't Starve," "Masses Pour into Streets in Nation-Wide Unemployment Demonstration in Spite of Police Terror," "300,00 Sign Insurance Demand." "The unemployed were a new stage of work," said Fred Rose. "The Communist Party was the only organization to take up their cause." For the working poor and the unemployed, communist courage and communist tactics were heartening. For members of the Canadian establishment, rabble-rousing attacks on their God-given right to govern as they saw fit were unlawful and seditious.

When Fred Rose and the four others arrested in 1931 at the unemployment meeting in Montreal appealed their sedition sentences, there was a demonstration held at Montreal's Prince Arthur Hall to protest against their imprisonment. Among those arrested at that meeting was Leslie Morris. He had said, "All those in favour of the resolution raise your hands." At his trial police testified that he had said, "All those in favour of the revolution raise your hand." He soon after joined his comrades in jail.

The sedition frame-up in Quebec was a prelude to the infamous 1931 communist trials, the government's bid to break the Communist Party and stop the unemployed movement. The logical instrument for an all-out legal offensive against the communists was Article 98 of the Criminal Code. Since proceedings under Article 98 had to be instituted by a provincial attorney general, and since the headquarters of the Communist Party of Canada was in Toronto, Ontario was to spearhead the attack.

Mayors, crown attorneys, local police, RCMP officers and police informers were asked to scour their districts for anything that could be the subject of a prosecution under Article 98. The attorney general of Ontario, Lieutenant-Colonel William Price, amassed pounds of paper in preparation for the crackdown: Edward Bayly, deputy attorney general of Ontario, wrote offering to do his best in Hamilton to prosecute the left-wing Hungarian-Canadian newspaper, the *Kandai Magyar Munkas*, under Article 98, the commissioner of police for Ontario sent a report on communist-led meetings in the town of Cochrane; Major Knowles of Barrie, in charge of two relief camps, had a list of seventy-three people he considered communists; the police department in Toronto contributed the names of all the members of the National Unemployed Workers' Association, Ukrainian Branch. An excerpt from *The Worker*, March 21, 1931, was included in the attorney general's file as evidence of the communists' violence, but it in fact mocked its intended purpose: "The steadily increasing attacks of

Police and organized fascist bands on workers' demonstrations and gatherings places before us, now sharper than ever, the necessity of building the Workers' Defense Corps. One of the outstanding weaknesses of the demonstrations on February 25 was the fact that with very few exceptions there was no organized body to protect speakers, supervise the order of the demonstration, and *repulse the brutal attacks of the Police in an organized fashion*" (italics added by the Attorney General's Office).

The search for something to prosecute became farcical. The following vital security information was respectfully reported by J. Chisholm, assistant inspector of detectives, to Major-General V.A.S. Williams, commissioner of the Ontario Provincial Police:

Dear Sir:
We are informed that a number of girls have arrived from Montreal and other towns to attend the Training School at Camp Kindervelt. The students there pay $8.00 weekly, and we are in receipt of information that girls and boys are sleeping in the same tents.

This for your information and whatever action you may deem fit.

On August 11, 1931, at 6:50 P.M., six police cars, their tires squealing, pulled away from Queen's Park. So secret were the raids that Commissioner Williams had only just advised his eighteen arresting officers of their mission: "Gentlemen," he had said, "we are going to strike a death blow at the Communist Party—we hope."[3] Party headquarters, the office of *The Worker*, the offices of the Workers' Unity League, and the homes of every member of the Political Bureau were raided. Doors were broken open; clothing, linen, kitchen cabinets were ransacked and personal libraries confiscated. In a precedent-setting case, the attorney general of Ontario, with the help of the RCMP, local and provincial police, miscellaneous informers, and small-town prosecutors arrested communist leaders and charged them with being members of an unlawful association as defined in Article 98(3) of the Criminal Code: "Any person who acts or professes to act as an officer of any such unlawful association, and who shall sell, speak, write or publish anything as the representative or professed representative of any such unlawful association, or become and continue to be a member thereof...shall be guilty of an offence and liable to imprisonment for not more than twenty years."

But Chief Justice Rose would not accept the proposed indictment. According to his reading of Article 98(3), "mere membership" in an unlawful association was not an offence. In Justice Rose's interpretation, the first "and" in the wording of the law was conjunctive: that is, one had both to be an officer of such an association and to commit the actions specified to break the law. When Joseph Sedgwick, inspector of legal offices in the Attorney General's Office, was unable to convince Justice Rose to read the "and" as "or," thus stretching the interpretation of the law to include Party members as well as officers, he took the matter up with officials in the Department of Justice in Ottawa. The indictment was changed to charge the accused with being both officers and members, with the understanding that the necessary amendment of the act would be passed at the next sitting of Parliament, so that, according to Sedgwick, "the fruit of it [Article 98] would be saved in that it would establish the unlawfulness of the association and future proceedings could be taken against those who are mere members of the association, as was always intended."

Despite a lack of ballast, the 1931 communist trial sailed along. *The Communist Manifesto* of 1848 and the 1919 program of the Communist International, standard evidence for the prosecution in trials of communists, were used to prove that the Canadian Communist Party was part of an international organization advocating violence. RCMP Sergeant Leopold, a police spy who had infiltrated the Party in the 1920s, took the stand, dressed in full Mountie regalia, to clarify the danger, and the judge reminded the jury that the fundamental and first responsibility of the state was "to protect itself." In Communist Party leader Tim Buck's final

73

address to the court, he spoke of the "immediate struggles against starvation and wage cuts" that needed to be led by a strong and disciplined revolutionary party "armed with working-class science." "Guilty," said the jury; "a species of treason" contrary to "the spirit of Canadianism," said the judge. "People who come to this country must and ought to learn to submit to the laws and institutions that exist here." The judge thanked both the city's police and the Royal Canadian Mounted Police for enforcing the law and gave all the books, correspondence, documents, papers and memoranda seized both at the homes of the accused and at the offices of the Party, *The Worker*, and the Workers' Unity League, to the Crown. That done, the attorney general of Ontario announced to the radio public: "Communism will never raise its head in Ontario again."

On November 14, 1931, seven members of the Political Bureau of the Communist Party of Canada were sentenced to five years' imprisonment, as Party organizer Sam Carr said, "for communism." In the same year Fred Rose and four of his colleagues in Quebec were sentenced to a year of hard labour in Bordeaux Jail for sedition. While sedition charges were old hat, the five-year jail sentence for expressing communist views was a first for Western democracy. The jailing of the Quebec communists and of seven of the "Kingston 8" became a *cause célèbre*, inflaming anger against Article 98 and broadening the fight for civil liberties. Letters flowed into the Attorney General's Office, calling Article 98 a law against freedom of speech and assembly, a threat to workers on strike, and an attempt to force Canadian workers to accept "greater exploitation in the form of wage cuts and forced relief work at miserable rates of pay." Protest letters from the Electrical Trades' Union, the Finnish Association, the Mine Workers of Canada, and other working-class organizations were duly filed by the ex-military enforcers of law and order: Brigadier-General Draper, Major-General Williams, and Lieutenant-Colonel Price. Although the communist-led Canadian Defence League organized the fight for the release of the Kingston 8 and the repeal of Article 98, the campaign crossed political lines. As a non-aligned union man said, "Communists were only a tiny group, but they were the target to scare everyone. The unemployed movement and labour organizing were the real targets of Article 98."

The clamour for the release of the communists increased in 1932 when a penitentiary guard, in the confusion of a prison riot, fired a rifle at Tim Buck in his cell. Buck saved himself by hiding behind a narrow strip of concrete, but the eleven bullet holes on the back wall of his cell told the tale. The shot that was meant to eliminate the leader of the Communist Party made him a labour hero, almost a martyr. Within a year and a half membership in the Canadian Labour Defence League grew from 25,000 to 43,000. The government flexed its muscles and used its extended powers, increasing arrests and court convictions under Article 98. The broad mandate given the government by sections 41 and 42 of the Immigration Act were used to intimidate and deport European and British-born labour organizers. Under this law any immigrant who was "a member of or affiliated with any organization entertaining or teaching disbelief in or opposition to organized government" was liable to deportation. When David Chalmers was released from Bordeaux Jail after having served his sentence for "seditious utterances," he was promptly prosecuted under sections 41 and 42 and deported to Scotland, one of seven thousand immigrants deported in 1931. Yet, despite Conservative prime minister R. B. Bennett's exhortation to Canadian men and women to support the government and "put the iron heel of ruthlessness on propaganda of that kind," trade unionists, farmers, civil libertarians, and leaders of the newly formed Cooperative Commonwealth Federation (CCF) joined the communists in condemning the authorities. In 1932, 459,000 people signed a Labour Defence League petition; and by 1934 public pressure was such that the government was forced to free Tim Buck. After an underground conference of his outlawed Party, Buck celebrated his release by addressing 17,000 people in Maple Leaf Gardens, the kick-off to a cross-country tour he would then make in defiance of Article 98.

Imprisoned, communists had been pinned gadflies, symbols of the country's repressive laws. Freed, they would begin to build a party, organizing a base in the unions and gathering mass support for their militant stand against racism and fascism.

CHAPTER FOUR

Inroads

JOSHUA GERSHMAN, PRESIDENT of the communist-led Needle Workers' Industrial Union, had a pleasant problem. Strike headquarters, the big dance hall in Montreal's garment district, was over-packed. Desperate conditions in the *shmata* trade had culminated in the Dressmakers' Strike of 1934, the first large strike of low-paid workers in a largely French-Canadian industry. Even though the Catholic unions pressured these workers to get along with their bosses and the priests said that striking was a sin, Gershman saw before him more women than had ever before demonstrated in Montreal. But, just as Stanley Ryerson was about to try out his fledgling talent as a public speaker, a messenger warned Gershman that two strange fellows outside the building were looking for him. Gershman went outside to meet them and for half an hour sat in the strangers' car. One of the young boys was called "George the Payes." His hair, curled in the sidelocks of the Orthodox Jew, was white. In Yiddish he told Gershman that he didn't personally have anything against the union, but that he and the boys had contracted with the management association to do a job on the union organizers. Gershman thought fast. The Jews who owned most of the needle-trades establishments were an obvious class enemy—largely conservative, exploiting capitalists who wanted to be as delicately English as possible. He knew the gentry type from his native town in the Ukraine, where he had first joined a group of young revolutionaries. George the Payes, however, was a working-class kid who, like so many other poor immigrants, had found some of the only work available in the depression: he was a hood. Luckily for Gershman he was a hood with a big heart. Gershman arranged that he and another organizer would appear at the next assembly bandaged and "looking beat-up." After they had done so, George the Payes collected. He and the boys threw a party for Gershman at the Lasalle Hotel.

Gershman hadn't foreseen the proportions that the Dressmakers' Strike would take on. Before this general walkout, only the Jewish craftsmen of the dress industry, such as the cutters, had taken strike action. For the most part they were from Eastern Europe where even small towns had unions and where, when the labour organizers came to the synagogue to talk shop, prayers stopped. "The Jewish needle-trades workers from the old country brought with them the militant traditions of the trade-union movement and helped build the trade-union movement in Canada," said Gershman. "They were outstanding fighters because they had it in their blood and in their bones."

Thus, within an industry of largely unskilled French-Canadian women was a core of skilled militant immigrants, and with their support, communists concentrated on organizing the appalling sweatshops of Montreal—the worst in Canada. Lea Roback was sent by the Party to help organize workers in the garment industry. Because of she spoke fluent French and had organizing experience, she was to be the education director. At the same time, she was to make contact with workers in their homes and take charge of shop grievance-meetings. Lea was shocked at what she heard and saw: "Cockroaches, filthy dirty washrooms, no place to have your lunch and no time anyway because you had to work all day to make your pay. Workers logged seventy hours a week for five or six dollars, despite the minimum-wage law. Often three workers, a mother and two daughters, were made to punch in on the same card so the boss could pay only one salary. On piece work, if you were nice with the boss, with the foreman, and with the designer, you'd get a big, big bundle. Others would get nothing. There was no division of work at all. No protection. It was a dog-eat-dog situation." In the summer time the heat and vapour from the pressing tables would make the pregnant women and the women who had just had babies lactate. The milk flowed into the filth. Lea was furious. "You know it is disgusting and inhuman to dare to use human beings like that. That's cannibalism. They didn't put them in a hot pot to boil and eat them, but work in the sweatshops was cannibalism."

When Lea went from house to house to see workers privately, she talked about improving working conditions, a shorter work week, increased wages, convincing with economic rather than

Lea Roback, Montreal, c. 1936.
*Courtesy of the Lea Roback Foundation
and the Jewish Public Library Archives*

political arguments. She and the other *shmata*-trade organizers were at the door of the factory handing out leaflets in the early morning as the workers were going in, and calling them to meetings in the evening. "The leaflets spoke very clearly about conditions and what they were getting and that it was time for an improvement. We had an educational department, we had a library with French and English books, and we had lectures on the question of wages and surplus value, and how the surplus value goes into the boss's pocket and not yours."

The day of the first Dressmakers' Strike in Canada, four thousand men and women were in the street, three abreast, forming a column a mile long. One hundred and twenty-five shops in the garment district were paralysed. Bella, in the movement several years, watched proudly: "That was something to see. Can you imagine pickets, side by side, walking all the way from Bleury to Peel and back again, a constant stream of marchers?" The young girls fended off the whips of the police on horseback by sticking hat pins in the horses' flesh. The ethnic organizations collected money and fed the strikers. Weeks stretched into months and still they held on. But, as Gershman recalled, "we underestimated how big the strike would be. We didn't have sufficient money for such a prolonged strike." Slowly the workers returned to work.

The results of the strike were mixed; the majority of shops gave salary increases of twenty per cent, but this was less than the strikers had demanded, and most establishments still refused to recognize the union. Bosses purged factories of Jewish women workers, whom they held responsible for the agitation. Gershman remembered the situation with irony: "Jewish girls had to put on crosses when they asked a Jewish boss for a job." Yet the Dressmakers' Strike was the beginning of labour unity in Quebec: it gave proof of a militancy supposedly non-existent among French-Canadian workers, especially women, who by 1936 made up almost all of the labour in the large needle-trades industry. Despite the official conservatism of the American Federation of Labor (AFL) and the Catholic unions, it showed that strikes could have an effect even during the depression. By involving unskilled workers, the way was paved for other union campaigns, like that led by the Congress of Industrial Organizations (CIO), which communist organizers joined after the dissolution of the Workers' Unity League in 1935. For the communists, whose much-quoted dictum was "One step backward and two steps forward," it was progress. So carried away was Lea with her description of the early struggles that, in all seriousness she announced, "Two steps backward and one step forward—that's how we progressed."

As wages dipped and the number of unemployed grew, the flood could no longer be dammed with repressive laws, social-Darwinist pontificating and religious platitudes. "*Ecoutez, pour gagner votre ciel, vous allez voir, le bon Dieu va vous aider,*" said the priests, but fewer and fewer were willing to wait for the Lord to show them the way to His Kingdom. Communist organizers held kitchen and back-yard meetings of small groups, five women, four men, where they encouraged questions— "and in that way there was a possibility of putting a bit of nerve into them," said Lea. In 1935 several thousand unemployed gathered in front of Montreal's City Hall for a landmark demonstration up The Main. "It was a tremendous, tremendous demonstration," Lea remembered. "People that were on the sidelines had tears in their eyes; they said, 'Good, good, *merci, merci,*' because at last someone was taking up this thing with banners and saying, 'We need jobs, we need help, this can't go on, down with the government.' People had the guts to stand up. They were tired of being a piece of shit in the eyes of the privileged."

By chance, Dr. Norman Bethune, Canada's legendary revolutionary hero, was one of the onlookers. The brutal police attack he witnessed that day was one of the reasons he would break with his middle-class, Anglo-Canadian past and join the Communist Party. And it was at this time, in the streets, that Henri Gagnon, back from the Liberal government's *Le Retour à la Terre*, stumbled, almost literally, onto the communist movement. Walking through the centre of the city, he chanced upon the speakers from the Front Populaire, a mass organization run by Jean Perron, a respected "engineer of the City of Montreal," under the direction of the Party. Curious, Henri attended one of its weekly open meetings at the Labour Temple. He listened to Perron lambasting the sky-rocketing poverty and evils of fascism, and extolling the good works of socialism in the U.S.S.R. When he urged all those listening to join him in the fight for peace and people's rights, Henri knew that he had never before heard a speaker so powerful, yet so simple and clear. "It was like an open organization," said Henri. "Some came once and some, like me, came back."

Henri also sought out the films shown by Louis Kon at the Friends of the Soviet Union, glorifying "*la force ouvrière*" in the reconstruction of Russia, and he discovered the Marxist bookshop on Bleury Street. He began an intensive period of reading that, he said, "opened my eyes to other dimensions than I had ever seen." For five cents he bought *The Communist Manifesto* and the *ABC of Communism*, clearly written books that corroborated what he had before only sensed. He read seven, eight hours a day, through the night, into the early morning. For Henri, as for many new recruits, the rigorous Marxist ideas were personally transforming. "You find philosophy, then you find one that you identify with because you are there in it. Materialism, the primacy of matter in this world, not the next, was a big thing for me, who had wanted to be a missionary at twelve years old. It breaks everything. It is a weird impression. This occurred over a period of months. Even then I would ask myself if the Little Jesus idea was true." After reading and questioning, Henri decided to join the Communist Party. "It depends to what extent you are imprisoned. In my case, it was a long soul-searching."

The Party, because it was illegal under Article 98, was difficult to contact. Henri went to Boutin, who had sold him some pamphlets and the Montreal-based communist paper *Clarté*. He told Boutin that he wanted to join the Party, and Boutin, thinking he was an informer, disappeared. Henri then found an old leftist who took him to the Association Humanitaire, where there was a group of atheists sitting around making declarations such as, "Let Him come down to earth and we'll take care of Him." Henri kept reading, and after awhile his friend said, "Listen, there is a Third International, and I know some guys in it." The first evening Henri attended a communist cell meeting seven people were there, including Willie Fortin and Philippe Richer, both of whom had been to the International Lenin School. There were pamphlets to hand out. For Henri it was an initiation by fire. He was scared: "A hell of a fear. But I had to do it. The Party at that time was made up of workers, the best workers, the ones ready for the fight and ready to answer the call. It was no joke at the time. There was pretty heavy police repression. There were demonstrations. There was a need."

Petitions, demonstrations, and all attempts to negotiate with the government failed to affect its position of cruel disdain. Formal requests from the National Council of the Unemployed and from the Relief Camp Workers' Union argued for an end to military control of and adequate first aid in the relief camps, the repeal of all anti-labour legislation, and a system of non-contributory unemployment insurance. These carefully worded, neatly presented appeals were as futile as strikes, rallies, and the occupation of public buildings. Prime Minister Bennett, the Tory millionaire, held firm to a policy of *laissez-faire* economics. "Neither this government nor any other government that I am a member of will ever grant unemployment insurance," he declared. "We will not put a premium on idleness."

In 1935, with the exigency of a group of striking relief-camp workers at the end of their resources in Vancouver, the Communist Party, the Workers' Unity League, and the Relief Camp Workers' Union called on the one million unemployed to take part in an On-to-Ottawa Trek. "Work and wages—that's what we were going to Ottawa to ask the government for," said organizer Red Walsh. "The only way we could get to them was to go down there."[1] More than one thousand men from British Columbia and Alberta piled into freight cars to get to Ottawa, and thousands more gathered at the station to see them off. Squeezed under the carriages, hunkered down on the roofs, it was clear after the first stop that the trekkers would stay together. They were disciplined and determined. All along the one-thousand-mile route, across the interior of British Columbia, through the cold Rocky Mountains, on the prairies, people fed them and gave them money. Supporters joined them until their numbers had doubled. When they arrived at Regina, the half-way point, a cheering crowd of fifteen hundred waited in welcome. "I thought we were making history," said Red Walsh. "No doubt about that."[2] There was a growing feeling that the march would compel the government to take other measures and close the camps.

Emery Samuel was on his way from Montreal to rendezvous in Ottawa with the unemployed workers from the West. He was nearing the Victoria Bridge, one of the two bridges out of Montreal. The contingent with him had heard about a terrible new invention called tear gas that would be used against them. The anarchists warned them to cover their noses with a handkerchief. "But when they threw the tear-gas bombs," Emery recalled, "we remembered how people behaved in the movies, and we understood that hand-kerchiefs weren't enough and that the anarchists weren't seasoned warriors. Half of the people who tried to get out of Montreal were continually pushed back by the gas and the threat of the machine-guns, which we had never before seen used in demonstrations." Towards nine in the evening, the groups that hadn't been able to get out of the city returned home.

In Ottawa, Prime Minister Bennett had decided that the trekkers from the West had also come close enough. He summoned their leaders to the capital and threatened to deploy forces to stop "the trouble." When the would-be negotiating committee returned to Regina to report to a large open-air meeting of Regina citizens, some with baby carriages, Bennett was as good as his word. On instructions from Ottawa the RCMP, mounted on horseback, attacked. Citizens were beaten and shot at, chased into alleys, and clubbed down. Red Walsh, who was in the Unemployed Hall preparing a press release, went out to see what was happening at the meeting. "I see people running in every direction. The police were running too. There was smoke and dust and glass. Scarth Street where the meeting was held on Market Square—it looked like a tank had went [sic] through it...They were firing til midnight."[3] It was a desperate, unequal confrontation, one of the most vicious in modern Canadian history. Public sympathy was with the protestors, but brute force was not. The day following the rout, Trek leaders, on their way to arrange food and trains for the men returning to the west coast, had to pass by policemen with machine-guns. Many, with no alternative, went back to the relief camps. The leaders did their best to avoid the warrants for their arrest.

After the police attack in Regina, the unemployed movement became more militant. In Emery's estimation, the On-to-Ottawa Trek was a turning point. "Everyone understood that the concepts of goodness and honesty and 'Look at us, we're suffering, we and our families,' counted for nothing in the heads of the criminals who were attacking with tear gas, machine-guns, and even murder. From that moment on, the movement took means to defend itself, used other tactics, other methods. In order to continue our activities in Canada we began treating the bourgeoisie as a military enemy. This was the great lesson produced by the unemployed movement."

[CHAPTER FIVE]

Vortex

IN 1935 PRIME MINISTER R. B. BENNETT and what he himself called his "iron heel of ruthlessness" were rejected by an electorate increasingly fed up with the Conservative government's harsh and repressive politics. Yielding to pressure from civil libertarians, socialists, workers' associations, and the new Liberal government, the Senate agreed to repeal the unpopular Article 98 of the Criminal Code. In Canada it was no longer illegal to join an association "whose purpose was to bring about governmental, economic or industrial change," a hard-fought-for right.

Communists were by now a seasoned and integral part of the labour movement and would soon have a growing constituency among the middle class. There was a network of communist-led unions in the merchant-navy and in the automobile, rubber, steel, textile, and transportation industries—over one hundred communist groups in the factories and mines, compared to none in 1929. Communists led 100 of the 189 strikes in Canada in 1934 and of these 84 were won. And the Party had led the most important workers' protest since the Winnipeg General Strike: the On-to-Ottawa Trek. With the repeal of Article 98 by Prime Minister Mackenzie King in 1935, Fred Rose, leader of the fifteen hundred Party members in Quebec, ran for the first time as a federal communist candidate in his home riding of Montreal-Cartier and received 3,378 votes. In 1936 he ran again, this time as a provincial candidate in Montreal-St. Louis. The Party published a pro-peace, anti-fascist programme and set up an election centre on Prince Arthur Street East, where *Clarté*, the province's only openly anti-fascist paper, was published.

"Freddie asked me if I would work as his manager and so I said, 'Sure, I'll be glad to,'" said Lea. "We opened up a place and there we had people come in—lots of police informers and all that crap." Money for the campaign was gathered mainly by members of the ethnic organizations—by Finns, Hungarians, Italians, Czechs, Poles—who had seen war and fascism first-hand. They and the Jewish refugees from Eastern European pogroms and from the violence of Hitler's Germany knew what fascism meant and were determined to stop it. "People say, 'Moscow Gold, *l'argent de Moscow*,' and all this blah, blah stuff," said Lea. "They should have seen these people come in." Lea described a Finnish immigrant as strong and powerful as the white birches of his homeland: "This man would come in with a package of their language paper and in it were lots of big brown pennies, the little wee nickels we had in those days, and once or twice a dollar bill. He would say, 'Not much money today, Comrade Roback, but tomorrow we bring more.' It rings in my ears with a smile—and such modesty." The ethnic members went from house to house, saying, "We have to publish programmes, we have to see that Comrade Rose gets in." For them, said Lea, "it was just as important, just as matter-of-fact, as you put on your pants and your suit before you go outside."

Young people were mobilized to put up posters and hand out leaflets at factory gates. Emery Samuel, Henri Gagnon, and the other members of the French Section, who knew and admired Fred Rose's work and who liked his warmth and "his big bad jokes," campaigned in the communist style, canvassing door to door, handing out programmes in shops and at factory gates, and hosting private kitchen and back-yard meetings for small groups of people. "Yet, even when the Party was legal, whenever we tried to do anything we were up against different laws," said Fred Rose. Lea was becoming more intimate with the Red Squad than she would have liked. "You could smell them. Anyone who can't smell a dick should take a course; there should be a course. You'd smell them and you'd say, 'That's it.'" University students, encouraged by senior religious officials, also paid visits to the election centre. One day, towards evening, a procession of hundreds of students, many of them members of nationalist youth leagues came marching down Ste. Catherine Street to do a job on the communists. Led by Monseigneur Emile Chartier, whom Lea described as "a myope with red, red hair, red skin," they smashed in windows, threw leaflets on the ground, hit Lea over the head. She appealed to a policeman standing in the room, and he told her to get out of the Party. She asked him what to do about her bleeding head, and he answered, "Go see a doctor."

The marauding students reflected the prejudices of the majority of Catholic Quebec's middle class. For the most part, they subscribed to a clerically led, right-wing nationalism, with anti-Semitic and pro-fascist overtones. "Nationalism was basically middle class," said Fred Rose. "Church, professions, law and order, status quo, and the youth followed suit." Raymond Boyer, raised in an upper-class French-Canadian home, remembered that "it wasn't considered subversive to support Mussolini, Franco, or Salazar." Hatred of communists and Jews, terms often used interchangeably as invectives, was almost a Church tenet. The Church supported both Mussolini and Montreal editorialist Paul Bouchard, a pro-Italian fascist who was "a very influential guy." Rabid nationalism held sway. Its racist theme was heard in Abbé Lionel Groulx's "*l'appel de la race*," an atavistic doctrine of blood purity. "It turned against the Jews," said Fred Rose. Slogans were directed at Jewish shopkeepers— "*Achat chez nous*"— "Keep money at home"—and the nationalist St. Jean Baptiste Society collected 127,364 signatures in support of the federal government's policy of keeping European-Jewish refugees out of Canada; the petition was presented to the House of Commons early in 1939 by a Liberal member from Quebec. André Laurendeau, one of Quebec's most respected humanists, recalled the racist reflex of old-fashioned Quebec nationalism in a moving confession of his own youthful anti-Semitism. Even Gratien

Gélinas, a cultured, compassionate man of the arts, always included an anti-Semitic sketch in his popular yearly revue of the thirties: French Canadians are seen trying to get ahead; they are alone until a gang of Jews move in and take over. A senior Canadian public servant from Quebec recalled pelting Fred Rose with tomatoes and painting crosses on a synagogue. His family supported Adrien Arcand, the local Nazi leader who was Hitler's contact in Canada. "My family were in sympathy with Arcand's plan to eliminate the Jews," he recalled. "We had been told that Jews would take over our jobs. We read books that said Jews killed the Christ who came to save us." Although Arcand, the pro-German fascist, wasn't as respectable as the pro-Italian fascist Paul Bouchard, his Nazi-style party, based on anti-communism and anti-Semitism, had 18,000 paid-up members by 1938.

The economic line of Quebec nationalism was corporatism, a doctrine borrowed from Mussolini's Italy. Representatives to government from the various economic classes were not to be elected by popular vote but selected by government leaders. Strikes were illegal, and real power rested with the state, which settled all disputes through compulsory arbitration. "Many of the middle-class French Canadians supported the *Mouvement du Corporatisme*," said Lea. "They wanted to keep what they had, they wanted to be the big guys." And just as the Catholic Church praised Mussolini and his allegiance to the Pope, so the Catholic unions for many years advocated his doctrine of corporatism. "The change came after the war, with the Asbestos Strike," said Fred Rose. "It saw a militancy in the Catholic unions that had nothing to do with their former position." The civil servant who had pelted Fred Rose with tomatoes added, "Quebec was fascist until the Second World War, when the Anglo-Saxons said, 'Go fight the fascists.'" In the latter half of the thirties, Harry, the child of Jewish immigrants, might well have felt that "there was an enemy in Italy and Germany, and it wasn't very different here." Harry knew that Park Lafontaine was French-Canadian territory and Fletcher's Field was Jewish. He saw windows on The Main smashed, streetcars stopped, pedestrians assaulted, as

Arcand's thugs shouted, "*A bas les juifs, à bas les communistes.*" He knew that English-Canadian discrimination against Jews existed in unofficial quotas in the administration of schools, professions, and the corporate Protestant élite, and that there were official quotas for Jews at McGill University. He had read "No Jews, No Dogs Allowed" signs in Laurentian resort towns. In everyday anti-Semitic gestures and rhetoric, he recognized what the Montreal poet A. M. Klein called "the body-odour of race." As Raymond Boyer, an upper-class French-Canadian Montrealer knew from experience, confirmed Quebec nationalists were, of course, anti-Semitic and pro-fascist: "I was used to it."

In this climate the 1936 communist pro-peace, anti-fascist program didn't have a chance. Fred Rose got 538 votes in his second campaign, and Lea got hit over the head and "treated like a cockroach" because she was a woman campaign-manager. "The Liberals," according to Lea, "had St. Louis all tied up. The prostitutes in the area, not only the Jewish, the French, would come in with a different hat; they got two dollars from the Liberal party for each vote, and each one had about six hats. We'd try to stop the vote, and their lawyers—some of our Westmount *Yiddishe* boys—would be there doing the bidding of the Liberal party. The cops would just throw us out." Still indomitable, she concluded, "Cast your bread on the waters and sometimes something comes back." Despite Lea's communist-style optimism— "We only got 538 votes, but just wait until we find those guys"—legality for the communists in Quebec, such as it was, would be short-lived. The right to organize workers' associations or even read what one pleased was soon outlawed under Quebec law. The Party was forced to operate clandestinely, and Fred Rose would be prevented from running for political office again until 1943.

Contemporary Quebec historians and poets refer to the period from 1936 to 1943 as "*la grande noirceur*"— "the great darkness." Premier Maurice Duplessis, elected in 1936 on a platform of socio-economic reform that promised the elimination of slums and the inauguration of health insurance and of a labour code, quickly showed his true colours: conservative blue, fascist black. He refused to establish a government-controlled hydro-electric system, abandoned the fight against the trusts, began the wholesale selling out of Quebec's natural resources to American interests and passed Bills 19 and 20, which allowed the state to annul or modify collective labour agreements. In 1937, in answer to King's repeal of Article 98, he passed an Act to Protect the Province against Communistic Propaganda—the Padlock Law—the most notorious piece of legislation in Canadian history. It gave Duplessis, wearing his attorney-general's hat, the power to padlock any house, school, and building, and to imprison whoever participated in "communist" or "Bolshevik" propaganda, neither of which the act defined.

In keeping with the anti-communist climate in Quebec, the Padlock Law was passed unanimously, sailing through the Legislative Assembly with three readings in half an hour. Exploiting anti-communist sentiment at a time when communist agitation was palpable in the unions, in the regular publication of *Clarté*, in elections and public anti-fascist assemblies, the law satisfied conservative Church elements and provided a means of opposing the radicalization of workers. As well, it attempted to obstruct the alliance of progressive forces as embodied since 1935 in the Front Populaire.

Rather than frightening the communists into submission, however, the Padlock Law made them angry and determined. Lea was "visited" five times. "We had them coming up to the house in droves. The whole of Querbes Avenue had to know the police were coming to the Robacks." They took Lea's leather souvenir case from Grenoble, her address book with notes from friends in Europe, her fine library of Marx's works, which, because the books were in German, she knew they couldn't read. "I felt: these bastards, what are they going to do with my books? It made me very angry and it made Mama very angry, too. She wasn't a communist, but it made her stand up. She'd take my father's prayerbook, the *Chummash*, and she'd stick it up their nose, saying, 'Take that, it's communist.'"

Lea wouldn't buckle under, but she didn't like it. "With such things we don't get stronger; they frighten the children; but it showed how they feared us, and through my anger I was able to continue working. They had no right to do that when they spoke of democracy."

Despite the Padlock Law the Party continued to function and grow. As well as organizing within the unions and among the unemployed, it focused on the rise of fascism in Europe, warning that international collective security was the only defence against war. When the 1935 Seventh Congress of the Communist International recognized the need for a united front of all anti-fascist forces to prevent war, communists were no longer cut off from other progressive forces. They had greater autonomy than before in referring Canadian matters to the Comintern and they were able to increase their influence through united front organizations. The Workers' Unity League was disbanded, and Lea joined the International Ladies Garment Workers' Union, "because it was there and powerful and we didn't want to make splits." Emery remembered the period as one in which "communists extended their hands to social democratic workers, to anarchists, liberals, conservatives, to the Christian unions, to Catholics, to all religious organizations; all were included in the anti-fascist front." Communists were the most vocal anti-fascists, and the Communist Party virtually the only unequivocally anti-fascist political party. Jews who lived with anti-Semitism, students who had seen fascism in Europe, and Christian humanists who believed in the equality of man were attracted by the communists' anti-fascist stand and impressed by the example of the Soviet Union. Canada was five years into the massive unemployment of the Great Depression, the Soviet Union five years into the full employment of its second five-year plan, and it seemed to many that Western economics were disintegrating while a feudal economy was being transformed, through socialist planning, into an advanced industrial state. Thus, in reaction to both the obvious failure of capitalism and the rise of fascism, more and more middle-class people were joining the Communist Party.

Stanley Ryerson was uniquely qualified to teach the new

recruits. He had begun his pioneering history of the 1837–38 Canadian rebellions, the early struggle for freedom from Britain and equality for French Canada. Under the pen-name "E. Roger," he was assistant editor and a regular contributor to *Clarté*. He was the Party's protégé: spending a lot of time at Fred Rose's house, getting a bit of the starch knocked out of him by speaking at workers' meetings, on his way to becoming the Party's expert on French Canada and its theoretician, par excellence. Stanley, for people such as Raymond Boyer, who would join the Party in its united-front days, was "a very intelligent person who could have had an outstanding career, but chose to do what he could to bring about a better society." As education director, he met with people in the professional groups—school teachers, artists, architects, scientists—and, along with Fred Rose, taught the French-Canadian groups. It was Stanley who explained Marxist dialectics to Norman Bethune in terms that could not fail to touch the young man's soul. He spoke about Engels' "science of interconnectedness," the conflict and unity of opposites, the simultaneity of process and structure in movement. When Bethune encountered these concepts, "he practically shouted his delight," Stanley wrote, "at the recognition of things sensed and now set forth in a fuller, more meaningful frame of understanding."[1] Painter Fred Taylor, who also became part of the communist movement at this time, said, "Stanley was the best Marxist I've known. Sometimes I couldn't follow his rationalizations, they were too involved, but he made them stick better than Tim Buck."

Fred Rose coordinated the fifteen-hundred-member Quebec branch of the Party. Its Young Communist League was one of the strongest Leagues in Canada, with four hundred members, two hundred of whom were French-speaking. Fred Rose had seen for himself that "French Canadians were underpaid people," and he believed that "the future of the Party lay with building it up among the French Canadians." With increased Party activity among the unemployed and the vigorous promotion of unions, French Canadians had been brought into the leadership. Henri Gagnon led the dynamic Young Communist League and Emery Samuel was one of those sent for leadership training to the International Lenin School in Moscow. As a senior, experienced Party leader, Fred Rose spoke and taught in French, Russian, Polish, German, English, and Yiddish. His classes, according to Lea, "enticed you to think. He had a class, but it was a conversation. With the French groups, he started from nothing and gave them the ABC's." Henri added, "The guy who carried the torch at the time was Fred…We were schoolboys."

Fred Rose was particularly interested in the unequal status of French Canada in Confederation, and the alleviation of economic disparity in the country was one of his main themes. The latter preoccupation was fueled by the 1935 Royal Commission on Price Spreads, the Stevens Report, which proved how far Quebec was behind the other provinces. One profitable Quebec factory showed apparent minimum-wage infractions in February 1934 for 101 out of 265 female workers. The natural silk industry provided a graphic illustration of the general condition of wage-level variations between Ontario and Quebec: "The average wages of all employees in the former province," the report specified, "are 18 per cent higher than in the latter." According to Fred Rose, "The most important thing was not only talk about unionization, but to bring the workers' standard of living closer to workers in other provinces." In pre-convention discussion, committee meetings, and in the Party press some months before conventions, the needs and rights of French Canadians found expression. French-Canadian militants, like many Jews, saw the Communist Party as a champion of their people. Fred Rose was "*un bon gars*", "*un des nôtres*", "*un homme*", "*un ami*."

On his return from the International Lenin School, Emery Samuel became "*un permanent*," a full-time Party functionary, and was put in charge of the French Section. He had not only developed "a great respect for the Russians" and an emotional attachment to international communism, but he was familiar with Marxist theory, Russian labour history, and the heroic exploits of Soviet leaders. Emery's favourite hero was Vasily Ivanovitch Chapayev, the great division commander of the Civil War, who had dragged the first enemy tank he'd captured to the Russian trenches with ninety horses because he didn't know how a tank operated. Chapayev, an illiterate, argued against all theoreticians about the art of military warfare and won most of his battles, plotting his strategy with potatoes and turnips. "What did I get about the art of revolutionary warfare out of that?" asked Emery. "I got more romanticism than concrete things on what to do when I returned to my own country. They trained me as a polemicist, a man who would understand what I was reading and would say some good words for socialism, the socialist world, and the national liberation movements."

Back home, in the spirit of the popular front, Emery proposed that Quebec communists, collaborating with other groups, should lead the Quebec nationalist movement in a working-class, socialist direction. The suggestion was contrary to all Communist Party policy on nationalism, especially Quebec nationalism, which was despised as church-controlled, anti-Semitic, and irrevocably anti-communist. Although the Communist Party espoused French-Canadian rights, it had always done so in the context of a worldwide workers' movement. The Party was against ethnic discrimination and against autonomous nationalism, which it saw as two sides of the same chauvinist coin. In 1925 a move had been made to unite the Party membership, especially among those ethnic groups who had their own organizations. The Party wanted to break down the isolation that they thought unproductive and bring all national groups—Jews, Finns, Ukrainians—closer to the Party centre. "It was an important step," said Fred Rose. "We could take advantage of the potential that was there to be used properly." Under the banner of the Party's revolutionary internationalism, Fred Rose responded to Emery's suggestion by warning in generalities against those who work to create a split between races, classes, and religious groups, against those who stir up hostilities. Without underestimating the deep-rooted nationalist sentiments of French-Canadian workers, he predicted that "nationalist separation can bring the French toilers only one thing: increased misery."

But Emery Samuel, Henri Gagnon, and other French-Canadian militants, attuned to the natural aspirations of the Quebec people, were developing a thesis of national affirmation unacceptable to the Party leadership. Emery claimed that the French Section could and should influence existing nationalist movements, a claim and plan that met with leadership disapproval. Defining French Canada as a nation, Emery and others in the French Section would eventually go farther, demanding the right to determine their own position in Confederation, up to and including Quebec's separation from Canada. As long as the Party leadership in Quebec was represented by Fred Rose, there was both an acceptance of an overriding internationalist principle and a mediator between the Central Committee in Toronto and the French Section. "Even though Fred didn't share our opinion on the national question," Henri explained, "it was difficult to have a fight with him. He would just say, 'Aw, you guys.'"

The underlying problem would finally emerge full-blown in 1947, when the Party position on Confederation had to be decided and when Fred Rose, in St. Vincent de Paul Penitentiary, was no longer on the scene to mediate. But now, the ball was rolling too fast; there was too much to be done. Popular-front governments were elected in France, Spain, and Chile. Socialist and anti-fascist organizations blossomed around the world. In Canada, broad-based, socially committed groups would have their heyday: the Civil Liberties Union, the Canadian League Against Fascism and War, the Progressive Arts Club, the Workers' Theatre, the Friends of the Mackenzie-Papineau Battalion, the Canadian Youth Congress, the Committee to Aid Spanish Democracy. These organizations would support trade unions, express sympathy with the Republicans in Spain, protest anti-civil-libertarian laws, and favour an alliance with the Soviet Union to contain the threat of the Berlin-Rome axis. Between 1934 and 1939, Party membership would increase three-fold. As the vortex churned, as the line between fascist and communist was drawn, many would be left with no choice but to choose.

CHAPTER SIX

The Second Contingent

Montreal. Winter. 1937

THE GOOD THING ABOUT Ben's restaurant was the crackers, as many as you could eat. Having warmed his hands around the steaming bowl, Sydney broke open five packets and quickly crumbled them into his soup. He needed the sustenance. He had left home early that morning to walk to the business section of Montreal. He was apprenticing in the offices of a chartered accountant he had met while waiting on tables at a Trout Lake summer resort near Ste. Agathe. He would eat and then walk to McGill University to take his accounting classes, the only professional training given at night and, therefore, the only profession open to a student without money. After classes he would walk home to St. Urbain Street to study, bundled up in an overcoat, warmed by the coal his mother had managed to save. Out of four children Sydney was the only one going to school, the chosen one. His sisters, Sarah and Katie, skilled and nimble with their hands, made hats and finished lampshades, and his tough older brother Nat lived in the pool halls and on the street. His blacksmith father, the forger of the Canadian Pacific Railway (CPR) ties, was out of work, and his mother made do by sewing at home. She, who had taught herself to read and write Yiddish and to speak English, who treasured books and conversation, was his muse. She believed in education and in him.

It was a short walk to McGill and a longer walk home. Sydney was tired, but at least the exercise reminded him that he was only twenty-three years old, an athlete who had played for his high school basketball team and had flown through the air in gymnastic competitions. Sydney loved sports, but even more did he love Annette, whom he had courted since they had met in the Baron Byng high school gym when they were fifteen. When he got home, she would be visiting, waiting for him, a round-faced, dark-eyed beauty. She would look at him, giving value to his manhood, reinforcing his discipline. At the end of the year, when he graduated, he would ask her to be his wife. They would have children and be together always. The prospect made him feel as good as an hour's workout on the parallel bars. It was bliss.

Yet, in the Jewish working-class district around St. Urbain Street, the frightening blasts of Nazi power and the weak whimpers of Western compliance were discussed daily. In cafeterias on The Main, not far from his home, workers and intellectuals met after work or, if they were unemployed, during the day. Along the neighbourhood streets, in the pool-halls and corner stores, laid-off workers gathered and talked. The community was made up of people who had come to Canada ten to thirty years earlier, who had gone through hard times; some of them had taken part in the 1905 Russian uprising, such as Sydney's own mother, who had seen a brother killed. Many had been members of left-wing political parties in the old country and they now found a support system in fraternal socialist organizations in Canada—in Ukrainian, Russian, Lithuanian, Polish, and Hungarian cultural groups, or in the United Jewish People's Order (UJPO)—which were pro-Soviet and pro-Communist. At all times in the St. Urbain Street area there were at least five widely read communist papers, in French, English, Yiddish, Russian, and Polish. The communists were actively engaged in the neighbourhood, trying to link the struggle for better wages with the need for social change, warning of the rise of fascism and the danger of another world war. Sydney's mother belonged to the Consumers' Association and to the UJPO. With the Consumers' Association she led a meat strike which cut the cost of kosher beef. In the UJPO she organized food and rummage sales which subsidized concerts, lectures, plays such as *Waiting for Lefty*, in Yiddish, and a mandolin orchestra. On her evenings out, she sang with the UJPO choir. Working-class songs and songs of freedom were Sydney's lullabies.

Sydney graduated in 1937, and he and Annette were married. By this time Hitler had deprived German Jews of their civil liberties and their citizenship, and Brownshirts marched in the streets of Montreal. The young couple heard about regimented Sieg Heils, about plunder, insult, torture, murder, and bombs. Visiting her parents in their rented cottage in Val David, fifty miles north of Montreal, Annette saw "Restricted" notices in the whole area around Golden Lake, where she had played as a child. Down the road from the cottage, the little wooden synagogue stood empty, swastikas covering its white, freshly painted walls, the Torah sinking, where it had been thrown, into the river. Annette now escorted her parents to the village to buy supplies, running a gauntlet of hostile eyes. If she and Sydney were to have children, they would be born into a world that was killing Jews or, at best, was indifferent to their persecution. "Before we could have a family, fascism had to be stopped."

There was little help Sydney and Annette could expect from the Western powers. Fascism and Nazism had established themselves in Germany, Italy, and through Germany's occupation of the Rhineland. Britain, France, and the United States, protecting their share in the West's world-market system, favoured Hitler over the alternative military power, the Soviet Union, and aimed to join in a bloc with the Berlin-Rome-Tokyo axis. Sympathetic to Hitler's objective of destroying "Bolshevism," they expected that his intensive war-arsenal would be directed not at them but at the Soviet Union. Thus, fascist aggression went unchecked. Mussolini had invaded Ethiopia and, in Quebec, Abbé Lionel Groulx had described the attack, which included saturation bombing, as "an exploit of genius." Japan had invaded the Republic of China, and, finally, in 1936 Hitler and Mussolini, in support of their ally, General Franco, had tested their murderous weaponry on the newly elected Republican government in Spain.

The Spanish Civil War, its cruelty and destructiveness escalating rapidly, horrified Sydney and Annette, for whom Franco was yet another vicious, unrestrained fascist dictator. Their fears were fuelled by the pro-Franco response of most French-Canadian Catholics for whom Franco was the saviour of the Church. The 1936 Christ-Roi Fête in Montreal became the platform for Church support against communism and for the "crusade" of General Franco; one hundred thousand men—no women allowed—heard the religious authorities denounce the Republicans, "the blasphemers who destroy the marvels of Spain and massacre nuns and priests." Two thousand Franco supporters gathered at Montcalm and Ste. Catherine streets to shout, "Down with the communists! Down with the Jews!" Around the world the Spanish Civil War provoked equally intense partisan reactions. Like Sydney and Annette, many, when they saw the battle-lines drawn, agreed with the historian Philip Toynbee that "the gloves were off in the struggle against fascism."

As the Spanish fascists, with the moral support of the Holy See and the active military support of the Nazi and fascist dictators, provided a preview of the greater conflicts to come, Britain, Canada, and a group of European nations closed their eyes and made a ludicrous non-intervention agreement with Germany and Italy. Sydney's and Annette's disillusionment with Western democracy deepened as totalitarian war experiments, more saturation bombing, continued without censure from the West. For them the bloody conflict was an ideological war between the forces of freedom and the forces of repression. "Yet the Western democracies were sacrificing Spain like they would sacrifice Czechoslovakia."

The only country openly supporting the republican form of government in Spain was the Soviet Union. In the League of Nations, Maxim Litvinoff, the Soviet foreign minister, was a lone voice speaking on behalf of Spain and in support of a collective front against Hitler. "The events in Spain have created one of the greatest dangers to European and world peace," he warned. If this attempt succeeded and went unpunished, there would be no guarantees that it would not be repeated in other countries. Litvinoff called repeatedly upon the League Council, in the interests of international justice and the preservation of peace, to "render all possible support to the Spanish people." Just as the Soviet Union was the only country openly supporting the Republican cause, so the Communist Party was the only political party openly committed to aiding the Republicans in Spain. The 1936 CCF convention had insisted that in any war Canada should remain neutral, no matter who the belligerents might be. At the 1937 CCF convention the word "imperialist" was inserted before the word "war," but the basic position in favour of neutrality was not changed, even by 1938. "We felt," said Sydney, "that the only political party in the world that was taking an active stand against fascism and the possibility of the outbreak of another world war was the Communist Party." The communist call to action on behalf of Spain crossed all dividing lines, mobilizing people as nothing would, ever again. As the news from Spain became more urgent, the Committee to Aid Spanish Democracy collected more money, and asked Dr. Norman Bethune to go to Madrid as the head of a medical unit. While Bethune deliberated, fascist groups at home exercised their legions, distributed German racist propaganda, and celebrated their ascendency by breaking shop windows and bashing Jewish heads. "The insanity is spreading too quickly," said Bethune to friends. "They've begun in Germany, in Japan, now in Spain, and they're coming out into the open everywhere. If we don't stop them in Spain while we can, they'll turn the world into a slaughterhouse."

So compelling was the battle of the Republic that Bethune soon left for Spain, where he was joined by 1,239 Canadians, who formed the Fifteenth International Brigade, the Mackenzie-Papineau Battalion. They too had volunteered their lives "for liberty." Some were intellectuals, but the largest single group was made up of the militant veterans of the relief camps and the On-to-Ottawa Trek. When the Canadian government passed the Foreign Enlistment Act of 1937, making it illegal to join the International Brigades, Communist Party organizer Sam Carr, from Toronto, printed thousands of passports for volunteers, and Fred Rose took charge of those who had left for Spain from Montreal. "They believed that what was happening in Spain could happen in Canada," said Fred Rose. "They were going to fight for Canada."

Embattled Spain had become the symbol of world freedom, and young people from many countries set out to fight for the Republicans. They were housed for several weeks in a centre in Paris, then taken in covered trucks to the Spanish border, where they crossed the treacherous Pyrenees on foot. "They were carrying our flag," said Sydney. "The emotions of their countries went with them. The battle was internationalized." It was as if the future of the world was being decided on the barricades in Spain. "Madrid will be the tomb of fascism!" shouted the Republicans. "They shall not pass! *No pasaran!*" A *"Lettre du Front"* from members of the Mac-Pap Battalion, published in the French-Canadian communist paper *Clarté*, May 1937, read: "We can already see that the cause of democratic Spain is the cause of humanity. If fascism is victorious here, there will be a generalized attack against the democracies of Europe...We call on all Canadians who cherish peace and democracy to launch an appeal to save humanity from the barbarism of fascism." Leading intellectuals, writers, and poets, such as George Orwell, Stephen Spender, Arthur Koestler, André Malraux, Ernest Hemingway, Dorothy Parker, and John Dos Passos, were drawn to the scene of the epic battle, and out of Spain came reportage, poetry, music and songs that stirred the soul with a hatred of fascism and a fulsome, strong commitment to freedom and justice.

Spanish heavens spread their brilliant starlight
High above our trenches in the plain;
From the distance morning comes to greet us,
Calling us to battle once again.

Far off is our land,
Yet ready we stand,

We're fighting and winning for you:
Freedom![1]

"We all sang the songs," said Sydney. "They were part of us."

One evening, Sydney and Annette, along with 15,000 others, packed into the block-long Mount Royal Arena to hear Fred Rose, Stanley Ryerson, and Norman Bethune, who had just returned from the Spanish front. Bethune described what he had seen: "...the refugees on the road from Malaga, the bombing of the evacuees, the people falling by the roadside, and then the attack on Almeria, the entombment of the dead and the living...the agony of a people which international reaction condones and sanctions under the guise of non-intervention."[2] Stock-still and straight, Lea listened: "It got right into your guts. The election had been held, the Republicans were in, everything had been done according to Hoyle, and then we were powerless, fighting airplane bombs with brooms." Bethune ended his lecture with an exhortation: "Spain can be the tomb of fascism. History will some day take full revenge on those who fail her." In the Mount Royal Arena, the audience stirred, rose as one and cheered in a tumultuous ovation. "I remember that meeting convinced us," said Sydney, "that our place was in the Communist Party, too. After the meeting we went up to Stanley Ryerson and said that we were just two ordinary people who wanted to do whatever we could, and we wanted to join the Communist Party." It was the height of the political repression under the Padlock Law and the couple's candour was unheard of. Sydney and Annette were checked out for several weeks and then formally asked to join the Party.

For Sydney, raised in a working-class neighbourhood by a mother who was an old-time revolutionary, socialism represented the chance for everyone to develop and achieve equally in society. It was obvious to him that under capitalism many people didn't have a chance. "If you were poor, you couldn't possibly go to university, you had to work. If you were Jewish, you couldn't go to universities of your choosing, you couldn't go to hotels you might have liked, you and other minority groups were excluded." Etched in his mind was the memory of his mother, holding him in her arms in the overcrowded poor people's ward of the hospital, crying and begging for a doctor to attend his broken wrist. "Because we didn't have any money, my mother was turned into a less dignified person than she was. It was one of the few times that I ever saw my mother cry, and she didn't cry for herself. She cried for one of her children." Under socialism, the ills of his childhood would be eradicated. There would be no poverty, no exploitation of man by man. No child would have to see his beloved, proud, and dignified mother humiliated. Under socialism, a planned, balanced economy would mean an end to imperialist war. "The thought of a society where everybody would live in a peaceful, dignified way was vitally important."

Sydney and Annette at the country cottage built by Sydney, his father, and his brother, 1939.

Traditionally, people from working-class ethnic backgrounds had joined the Communist Party because, in the words of the leader of the Canadian Seamen's Union, J. A. "Pat" Sullivan, the communists "were the only people that had shown any concern about my welfare or that of my mate…They had given practical evidence of their willingness to help." Or, as someone who had grown up in the Jewish working-class district of Montreal, recalled, "During the Depression when everything was so hard, I met communists who said, 'Comrade,' and helped people." In 1936 political forces polarized for many others, as well, and on the battlefield in Spain, the opposing forces appeared in black and white—the war a classic struggle between good and evil. Ethnic and working-class Party members, who had been in the majority, were now outnumbered by Canadian office workers, students, professionals, intellectuals, and artists, who joined for ideological solidarity and not only economic imperatives. One such, Allan, a respected painter brought up on the spirited poetry of Robert Burns and the political values of Abraham Lincoln and American socialist Eugene Debs, put the motivation of the new recruits succinctly: "I was enraged with fascism. I was eighteen when I heard of the riots between the communists and the Nazis. All the Nazis had 'Von' in front of their names. I said, 'The German aristocracy is coming back.' Franco was too much for me. That's when I joined up."

With Spain as the rallying point, communists around the world became, as Allan remembered, "an international web of comrades. Being a communist was like an open sesame. It was wonderful, made you believe in people." Allan recalled the voyage he made from Europe back to Canada during that period. "It was after Mackenzie King had passed a law to deport all those born outside Canada who had fought in the Spanish Civil War." Canadian immigration officers did their work at sea. A Polish-Canadian working-man was being questioned in front of Allan.

"Why were you in Paris?" the immigration officer asked.

"To visit my sister."

"Did you visit your sister for a whole year?"

"Yes."

"Come on, you were in Spain."

"No."

The man continued with his denial. After he was dismissed, Allan overheard the official say, "We'll pick him up later." He found the worker on deck, staring at the water. Allan looked straight ahead, as if out to sea, and whispered, "You will be picked up."

"How do you know?"

"I heard them talking."

"I don't know you."

"I'm a friend," Allan said, mentioning the names of friends known to them both.

The worker went to his cabin and Allan, half an hour later, followed. The Spanish veteran was pacing, frightened. He showed Allan one thousand Spanish dollars, battle photos, discharge papers. "What do I do?"

"If they catch you, they'll send you back to Poland. You'll be shot," Allan answered. "Throw it all overboard."

"I can't. It's all I have."

Finally, Allan decided. "I'll take it for you."

"How will I get it back?" the man asked.

"I'll give it to the people who sent you to Spain."

Allan hid the money, photos, papers, behind the metal back of his paint box. Five weeks later he met the Spanish veteran on the street in Montreal. He had retrieved his belongings.

"You saved my life," the man said. "They knocked down the door in my cabin at three A.M. that morning. They pulled apart the luggage, drawers, mattress."

When today Allan asks, "Why did I take the risk? What did a third-generation WASP have in common with a Polish working-man?" his answer affirms the solidarity he knew: "It was because we both loved the Spanish Republic so much. Those were wonderful times to be alive."

Montreal. 1937

Irene pulled on her sheer nylon stockings, tucked in her blouse, and adjusted her hat. Dressed to waltz into her high-powered ad agency job, she had first to walk through an intense political discussion in the adjoining room. The meetings went on from morning to night. Today, she would fly to New York, eat a fifty-dollar supper with executives from Young and Rubicam, then return home to yet another meeting in this two-room cold-water flat, where she lived with her father, mother, and brother, all on the eighteen dollars she earned each week. It was a weird contrast for the twenty-five-year-old ingénue and on top of it, she was so exhausted that it was an effort to lift one foot after the other.

It wasn't that Irene was unused to people in the house. As a young girl, curled up in bed, the voices she had heard from the kitchen, the laughter and the sobs, had been Russian, Polish, Ukrainian, Italian. At that time, Black people, Indigenous people, immigrants building the railway, came to talk to Louis Kon, immigration and colonisation officer for the Grand Trunk Pacific Railway in Winnipeg. Now, the people in the kitchen-cum-bedroom-cum-living-room were of all classes. "The Party was underground, and if anybody wanted to find out anything that was going on—meetings, organizations—my father was like the periscope of a submarine. He was visible. He spoke out loudly. He organized public meetings of the Friends of the Soviet Union and, through this, people came to see my dad to see what was happening."

Louis Kon, in the tsar's uniform, had joined the wave of strikes during the 1905 revolution by stopping the presses of the largest printing business in Moscow: his father's. In Europe, where his father then shipped him off to study, Louis saw advertisements for jobs with the Grand Trunk Pacific Railway in Canada—"Come make your fortune"—and had emigrated. He was warm, cultured, well-read, interesting, and interested. He had the ability to make people, in those bitter, frightening times, feel valued and special. "He lent them books, sent them here or there, pointed them in the right direction," his daughter remembered. Doctor Norman

Bethune, poet Dorothy Livesay, economist Eric Adams, and many others who warmed themselves at the hearth of Louis Kon went on to do active political work. But Irene was too busy to notice all the faces. As she rushed to her job, she felt a responsibility beyond her years and a tinge of irritation, the kind she imagined Karl Marx's daughter Eleanor must have felt.

When the market had crashed, Louis Kon had been left without a job, and Irene, feeling like a knight in shining armour, had set forth to become the family's saviour. She had walked the streets of Montreal—St. James, Notre Dame, Ste. Catherine, every side street—into one building, one office after another, saying, "You got a job?" But: "Nobody would even look up at me because they were so embarrassed at having a job themselves. I walked until it was crushing my spirits." When she finally got work, she swallowed insults, wage cuts, arbitrary overtime, knowing that there was always someone who'd be happy to take her place. "I'd come home every night and cry buckets into my supper because I was so exploited. My father would say, 'Bebele, I explained all that to you,' but until you're in it yourself, until you hear it and see it, you don't understand, really you don't." As Irene, in the horrible clutches of depression poverty, watched her youthful dream of stage-lights cut down to the size of a weekly pay-cheque, it seemed that the world around her was exploding. "You'd see these great masses of unemployed demonstrating in Phillips Square," she recalled, "and the police coming on big horses with clubs and crashing them over the head, and everybody dispersing and running and screaming. And, in the meantime, the rise of fascism in Germany and Italy, and the whole war thing looming up and looming up, and the unbelievable, stupid oppression of my father being unable to rent a hall because of police pressure, of my house being raided. And then comes the Spanish Civil War—and many thousands of people suddenly become frightened and more conscious of what is happening."

With the war in Spain, Irene became what she called "truly politically aware." She volunteered to work for the Committee to Aid Spanish Democracy, which "everybody was flocking to, to raise funds and go to meetings and send money and do things." Someone at the committee said, "We have so many people who want to work for Spain, why don't you help the Civil Liberties Union?" The union had just come into being and was carrying on a very active fight against the Padlock Law. There Irene found the cross-section of people she was to meet in all the united-front groups: CCFers, Christians, Jews, Quakers, non-political people—all of whom had vaguely sensed that things were wrong and had been galvanized into action by the war in Spain: "In that whole period there was a terrific amalgamation of all the various shades of political opinion. We would all discuss and we would all talk; we were all united in support of Spain and against the Padlock Law. There were certain things that we could all agree on."

If Irene was exhausted and slightly irritated by the stream of people arriving at her father's door, it was because she herself was swimming hard against the current of events. She had wanted to learn more about why the world was in such a desperate state and, despite her father's warning against functionaries and bureaucracy, had gravitated towards the Communist Party. Two nights a week, after work, she attended a Marxist study group of intellectuals, professionals, artists. Like everyone in the group, she "really, really studied. We had to prepare papers on trade-union history, on Italy, art, England, economics. We stayed home, read, studied, learned, and then got together to drink tea and talk and talk and argue and discuss." After the study group, at 11:00 P.M., Irene would go with friends to the Civil Liberties Union office on the corner of Peel and Ste. Catherine streets, to lick stamps, address envelopes, crank a mimeograph machine. Other nights they would all attend the big public meetings at the YMHA, at Atwater Market, at Prince Arthur Hall, in support of Spain, against the Padlock Law, on behalf of the unemployed. On nights when there was no study group and no public meeting, there would be endless phoning, asking people to join the Civil Liberties Union, explaining what the organization did, talking to lawyers, taking up eviction and labour arrest cases, trying to raise enough money to keep the little office going. In those passionate times, Irene recalled, even the most trivial chores took on a crucial importance. "I remember one night I was exhausted stamping hundreds and hundreds of envelopes, and somebody came in and stood looking at me and said, 'Well, it's not everybody who understands the political significance of licking stamps.' I got a second wind and could have gone on until six in the morning."

It was the love and encouragement she got from those whom she now called her comrades that kept Irene going. "We were comrades and comrades means we were in this thing together, with a vision and a dream of a world where there was going to be justice." She was working on certain issues with CCFers such as Frank and Marion Scott and King Gordon, but they weren't her comrades. At dinner one night King Gordon had said to her, "Irene, if you had been born a hundred years ago, you'd have been burned at the stake." She went too far for them, and they not far enough for her. Her close friends were middle- and upper-class professionals and artists who, like her, were convinced that communism was the only answer to the ugliness around them. She talked endlessly to Raymond Boyer, an academic just back from Europe. She took time to see the paintings of Fred Taylor and encouraged him to use his "facilities, abilities, and talents to help his fellow men." She talked and walked and laughed with Norman Bethune, who had embraced communism with his typical heroic enthusiasm, and she was falling in love with Cam Ballantyne, executive secretary of the Civil Liberties Union. Irene believed, as they all did, that socialism would eliminate economic exploitation; working people would share the wealth and "everyone would be free to develop their full potential."

Irene's was a utopian dream that flew in the face of the evidence around her, a tenacious belief that mankind was potentially warm, cultured, beautiful. Despite the harsh circumstances, or, perhaps, because of them, the realization of the socialist dream seemed possible, even imminent: "Something had to change." Put in simple terms, Irene, like Bethune, believed in universal happiness. "Bethune really thought that life should be a great joy and a great treat," she later said, "and he wanted everybody to be alive. He wanted you to smell the flowers and smell perfume and touch beautiful fabrics and hear beautiful music, and he wanted all your senses to be engaged. He wanted people to fight, laugh, cry, he didn't want them to just sit there like lumps. I think that is when he began reading more about socialism, he understood how our system deadened people, and that part of the reason that people weren't as alive and happy and full of energy as he wished they were, was because they were living under conditions which made it impossible for them to develop their full selves." Irene longed for an egalitarian society so that she could be free from her guilt and concern for human misery; at a certain level she wanted more joy in the world, "not to do good for other people, but to do good for me." The need for social change was so obvious and the conviction that together they could bring it about so strong, that Irene and her comrades pushed themselves to the breaking point. "We believed we could build a better world, a world of cooperation, a world of people who would listen to one another, and it was our love for one another that gave us such energy."

Montreal. 1937
Raymond, now thirty years old, was back in Montreal after three years of studying in Vienna. Nothing much had changed in his family home, except for Raymond himself. As he paced the impeccably clean hardwood floors, he wondered what to do with the stirrings within him. Europe had jolted his political awareness "beyond the woolly Canadian view that you vote every four years and it doesn't make much difference anyway." The level of political argument and political discussion in European newspapers had provoked in him "a curiosity about human beings in the word—why we're here and what to do." After nine years at McGill University, earning a Doctor of Philosophy in organic chemistry, after post-graduate work at Harvard and the Sorbonne, he had, halfway through his studies at the University of Vienna, left the sciences and begun taking courses in the humanities. He did not guess at the ramifications of what he

was observing, yet could not help but notice the political lines being drawn. He wondered at both "the method by which fascism was being prepared in Austria and the techniques of the underground socialist movements that sought to oppose it."

Raymond had grown up, cut off from politics, in a family whose idea of service was rolling bandages at the Red Cross. Now, home again, he desperately wanted to meet groups "concerned with the future of Canada and the future of humanity in general." Knowing his new friend would understand, he dialled an increasingly familiar number. "Hello, Irene," he said. "It's not enough for me to just talk. I want to do something. What should I do?"

Irene suggested that Raymond first had to learn more. He should join a study group and, she added, he should do some political work. Because he was between jobs, Raymond had time "to go around" to the Civil Liberties Union every day where, among others, he met the union's executive secretary, Cam Ballantyne, a journalist fired from the Montreal *Gazette* for trying to organize its employees into a newspaper guild. Raymond later recalled how Ballantyne "had a great way of getting people to work benevolently for the movement," and how "the honesty of the people, their concern for things other than their own personal comfort and advancement, their devotion to their principles," struck a major chord in him. He soon joined the Civil Liberties Union, mimeographing, raising money, organizing meetings, speaking. "He would sit with us in the office and talk!" said Irene. "We would discuss socialism, Chamberlain, Hitler, talk, talk, talk, talk. We were assembling the materials for the foundations of a new society."

At the Civil Liberties Union, Raymond was reunited with an old school friend, Fred Taylor, who, like him, but for the rise of fascism and the Spanish Civil War, might never have entertained a political thought. Fred, too, had just returned from abroad, from England, where he had been pursuing his single-minded study of drawing and painting. Like Raymond, he had graduated from McGill "completely uninterested in and unaware of world affairs." But in England politics were unavoidable and, as he said, "militant people were thrust upon me." A perfectionist, whose attention to detail and quest for excellence would characterize his life and work, Fred "held them at arm's length, not wanting to be deterred from my art." There were a great many political groups and, for Fred, it was "bewildering...I was allergic to these people. I didn't want to make up my mind." Yet, "the effect of politicized people was increasing on me. Some were such charming people and the women were charming, too." At their request, he attended communist rallies in Hyde Park and "a great many evening parties," gradually realizing that he preferred people who supported the Spanish Republican cause to the "repulsive" Mosleyites, a group of pro-Nazi British fascists. When, newly married, he returned to Canada, "everyone was talking about the war in Spain, and anybody that didn't, I didn't find interesting."

Fred and his wife "circulated" in the Committee to Aid Spanish Democracy and the Civil Liberties Union, "fraternizing and associating with the politicized people and the people, like myself, who were becoming politicized through the war in Spain." Irene and others now talked to Fred about the importance of art and the place it would have in the world after the revolution, and he enjoyed both the feeling of belonging to something warm and the concern for himself and his work. It was a welcome relief from the old family constraints: coming down the stairs towards his father on Sunday to be inspected for "church parade," shoes shined, buttons perfect, terrified, as a friend recalled, "that he wouldn't measure up to whatever it was that was expected of a Taylor." He was stimulated by the enthusiasm and talent of those in the Artists' Group, who were committed to producing socially relevant work. He thought of himself not as an effete, isolated romantic, but as "an art-worker" with a definite function and place in society. Along with Raymond, Fred attended a study group led by Stanley Ryerson and made up of six to eight cultured and concerned young men and women. "None of us were Party members or anything else, but we just couldn't conceive of supporting any other group in any other way than the communists were doing." "Norman," a strapping, athletic twenty-three-year-old, was more than happy when he was invited to join the group. He had only just arrived in Canada from England and was finding that, in terms of world affairs, "nobody had the slightest idea of what was going on." His trouble had begun when he had presented himself and his letter of introduction to a titled business associate of his father's in Montreal. In response to a question about how things were in London, Norman had answered that "people were worried about the war." He'd gone on to lament Mussolini's bombing of the "poor bloody Abyssinians," Hitler's barbaric cutting off of heads, and the soup lines of desperate Welsh miners in the streets of London. It was no more than any of his "liberal-minded" London friends might have said, but it was enough to disenchant his father's contact. "I never heard from him again. The Canadian establishment people that I met supported the world fascist movement. To be categorized as a subversive or a Red in Canada, all you had to be, in English terms, was mildly progressive." When Norman found Louis Kon, Raymond, Cam, Irene, and others, he found individuals who would have marched with him in the London parades that took "seven hours to pass any given spot," and he embraced a community incensed, as he was, by the Quebec police and the RCMP, who were "bashing in the heads of any guy who had the temerity to want a union." The process by which he would come to join the Party, as he would later say, "was a chain reaction. You see what's going on. You feel it to be unjust. You can't ignore it. You speak up and speaking leads to common action of some kind." Norman formed attachments, both political and romantic, among his new friends. The group was warm, intense, and inspiring. Under the tutelage of the Communist Party, along with those who "had the particular temperament that sticks its neck out," he studied world events and developed the theoretical base that would inform his and his comrades' future actions.

In the study group, Raymond was introduced to a new science, one which he would continue to research: "the science of socialism." For Raymond, Marxist science was rational, pertinent and, above all, humanitarian. He contemplated its prescriptions for a change in the infrastructure of society—public, rather than private, ownership of the means of production, the abolition of class structure—and as he read and studied, he became more and more convinced of its rightness. The books he was able to read through the Left Book Club were "very important." Banned in Quebec as "subversive" under the Padlock Law, the publications of Victor Gollancz in London and of International Publishers in New York were smuggled from New York to Montreal by Lea and delivered to Raymond's door by Lea's brother Michael. The books in those two big, black suitcases affected Raymond profoundly. The first work he read, *Fallen Bastions*, was a moving account of the fascist takeover of Austria and Czechoslovakia. Written by G. E. R. Gedye, a London *Times* expert on European affairs, it had been published hard on the heels of the Munich Agreement in 1938. Raymond learned how Czechoslovakia, "the armament factory of half the world," had been blackmailed by the agreement the British and French governments had made at Munich with Hitler, and forced to surrender its million and a half trained soldiers and its strategic position. With the Munich Agreement, the way to fuel and oil, to the Balkans and to the Soviet Union, was open to Germany. As Winston Churchill said, "The utmost he [Prime Minister Neville Chamberlain] has been able to gain for Czechoslovakia and in the matters which were in dispute has been that the German dictator, instead of snatching the victuals from the table, has been content to have them served to him course by course."

Although Raymond had been living in Austria, he had been innocent of the evil undercurrent of events there, and now, looking back on his student days, he couldn't think what might have been threatening to him: "maybe a criminal." *Fallen Bastions* opened his eyes to the nature and extent of fascist brutality. It showed him, he said, that "there were good guys and bad guys in the world— something I had never thought of before." It reinforced his anti-imperialist stand and his belief that he and his comrades had no choice but to fight fascism in their own way. Through the study groups Raymond was introduced to more high-calibre political commentary and dramatic fiction about people in political crises. He read Ignazio Silone's 1937 novel, *Bread and Wine*, the story of the Italian underground and the daring young revolutionary who returns to his native village to try and organize the peasants against the fascists; *Hostages*, Stefan Heym's dramatic anti-fascist story; and *Ten Days That Shook the World*, John Reed's vivid rendering of the pristine enthusiasm that infused the Russian Revolution. Throughout was a common message: good men will continue to fight for justice as long as man exists. These books, said Raymond, "showed me that the heroes of capitalism were not the people I admired. The simple people described in Silone's books I admired more than the heroes put forth by the daily papers—members of such and such a club, etcetera. They gave me a contrast, other people I could admire, that I wanted to do something for, associate myself with. It was a tremendous change."

As Raymond became more committed, the Party asked him to speak at mass meetings. Hating every moment of it, he stood up in front of large audiences, slender, straight, always seeming taller than he was, an elegant if shy example of what the Party had attracted to its side. His political activity cut him off from old friends and earned him his family's disapproval, but the Party gave him "relationships that could be honest, based on empathy for each other's belief in justice, in the wide sense." The big break with his family came when he married a Jewish woman; her unforgivable sin was "not so much that she was Jewish, as that she was poor." To some extent, "that was why Raymond had married her," suggested a friend. In communism he had found something more consuming than religion, and through marriage, he paid homage to the working-class nature of the movement. "It always impressed me," he was later to say, "that people who are religious are so for an hour a week, on Sundays. But I didn't find that in the communist movement. It was a totally enveloping way of life. You were a communist twenty-four hours a day, all the time." In the tumultuous thirties the impulse that had once made Raymond want to be a priest was channelled into communism. As Irene was to say, "Raymond wanted to be good."

St. Eustache, Quebec. 1938

"Gilles" sat on the back porch of his family's house, heady, at eighteen, with the feeling that he now understood the forward movement of history and his role in it. Like scenes from a movie, images from his past played through his mind. To the music coming from the player-piano—his childhood companion, the legacy of his mother, a musician, who had died with his birth—he relived his political evolution: alone, in the big empty house in St. Eustache, searching for meaning in philosophy, in summaries of world history; at high school in Montreal, the classical lullabies of childhood mixing with the a cappella singing of young committed voices; the Great Depression; the Spanish Civil War, fascism; joining the Student League, unknown to him, a branch of the Young Communist League; finding first friends, "meaningful relationships," affection; a girl at the Congress of the American Student Union in New York, a Jewish member of the American Communist League, the lullaby cradling her face, his arms, the warmth and the pleasure. All around he had seen unemployment and starvation. The capitalist world was dying. The choice was fascism or communism. In the fascist countries people had work, but their philosophy was racist and repugnant. In the Soviet Union people worked in a humanist environment dedicated to culture, art, music, "everything I liked." The player-piano. Beethoven.

At McGill University, the Players' Club studied Stanislavsky and presented excerpts from the Works Project Administration (WPA) agit-prop play, *One Third of a Nation*, its title a reference to Roosevelt's comment on America: "I see one third of a nation ill-housed, ill-clad and ill-nourished." Communists and socialists, including Frank Scott and Eugene Forsey, took up cudgels against the Padlock Law, speaking at the Social Problems Club and for the Civil Liberties Union. An Old Boys' Mock Parliament, featuring CCFer David Lewis as prime minister, resolved that the democratic countries had betrayed Spain. The student union produced an exhibit of water-colours and photography from the Spanish Civil War to gain sympathy for the Republicans. Lanky, shy Hazen Sise, a graduate of McGill's School of Architecture and a driver for Bethune's mobile blood-bank, spoke haltingly, vehemently about "the need to help the people of Spain who are helping us." Gilles was studying with Charlie Lipton, whose thesis was on Hegel. Hegel's dialectic, the concept of an historical process that developed by a continuous unification of opposites, led Gilles to Marx, and Marx's added materialist dimension revealed the concrete world in a dynamic of unfolding interrelationships. Phoenix-like, an egalitarian society would grow, in all its youthful vigour, out of the crisis. Gilles' father, sinking with the crash, told him to earn a living. His uncle, resplendent in a sixteen-cylinder Cadillac, appeared a crass symbol of what he was supposed to want. "Dialectical materialism was the ideological content that filled the void. All history was the history of class struggle. It was easy to agree with Marx that the working class was getting more numerous and would overcome. We would have peace and social justice. Goddamnit, the 1917 Russian Revolution was a clear vindication of what Marx had said!"

Gilles sat on the back porch of his home in rural Quebec, totally absorbed in Nikolai Ostrovsky's novel, *How the Steel Was Tempered*. The novel's hero had declared that his goal was to live in such a way that, when he died, he could say that every hour of every day had been devoted to the most beautiful thing in the world: the liberation of humanity. The words would stay with Gilles forever. "It was what I wanted to devote my life to. It was a wonderful, happy reason for living. It was my goal."

[CHAPTER SEVEN]

Party Life

ON NOVEMBER 5, 1937, under the new Act to Protect the Province Against Communistic Propaganda, *Clarté*, the Quebec communist newspaper, was padlocked. The ordinance, closing 254 Ste. Catherine Street East, was signed by the attorney general, Maurice Duplessis. The same day three policemen visited Jean Perron, editor of the paper, seized his books, files, and letters, and padlocked his house for one year. The following day the Modern Book Shop, the Artistic Print Ship, and Old Rose Printing were padlocked. The houses of Lea, Louis Kon, Stanley Ryerson, Fred Rose, and other known communists were raided. The Jewish Cultural Centre, established on St. Lawrence near Mount Royal as a fraternal organization for young Jewish immigrants, was raided and its library taken away; the allegedly communist books were destroyed. The organization had a picture of the Yiddish writer I. L. Peretz on the wall. He had a bushy moustache and bore some resemblance to Stalin, and the picture was reproduced in newspaper accounts as a picture of Stalin in order to justify the raid.

In 1938 police raids on all labour and left-wing groups increased, the supposed threat of the numerically small Communist Party used as the excuse for the repressive anti-labour activities. Duplessis, as attorney general, declared the Congress of Industrial Organizations an undemocratic organization. Meetings of the CCF were disrupted or cancelled. Leaflets to organize unions or the unemployed could not be distributed. Anti-fascist literature was seized as "communist propaganda," as were a book on Spinoza, a Gaelic Bible, *The Mill on the Floss*, and copies of *Coronet*, *Pic*, and *Look* magazines. The 1937 film *The Life of Emile Zola*, starring Paul Muni, was banned. People who owned meeting-halls were visited by police threatening to padlock their premises if they rented them to union or left-wing groups. Even cultural events were policed: dances, choirs, and concerts put on by groups such as the United Jewish People's Order. "Bulldogs over two hundred pounds," said a UJPO member. "They didn't have a permit, but what could we do? We made them pay admission. We got used to them." The UJPO meetings were all conducted in Yiddish, but the presence of the police was meant to intimidate; the police came "to look us in the face, scare us that we'd be on the list that they gave to the RCMP and American Immigration. We couldn't go to the States or get our citizenship. That list was their biggest weapon." The city's Red Squad came to every left-wing meeting, first with a notepad, and then with a stenographer. According to Henri Gagnon, the communists knew all the Red Squad spies, especially Boyzcum, "Scarface," from the Montreal anti-subversive squad, "a real sadistic bastard." It was the stoolies that kept the Party members guessing.

When the provincial police came to private homes people would ask them for their warrant. *"Pas besoin, c'est la police,"* they would answer, barging in. They came back to Lea Roback's door many times. "The only thing they knew was that it was a Marx book or a Lenin book if their names were on it. But they would take everything. I remember I had books I had bought in England, Huxley's *Brave New World* and so on, books that had a different context completely, and they would pick everything up." The police stayed for hours and hours, intimidating, going through the books. "They took what they wanted and no one ever saw his books again." People who had been seen at meetings or who had taken a position at meetings were susceptible. Sadie, a Party member active in the trade-union movement and in the Yiddish movement, recalled her experience: "One day I was bathing my child in the kitchen, and bang, bang, bang, they were there, the police. They were there, hollering, 'Padlock Law.' I told them, 'I'm bathing my child, it's winter, it's cold.' There was no reasoning with them at all. It was the law. Just a reign of terror." A time, remembered Raymond Boyer, in which "no library had a book by Marx."

Yet, left-wing culture flourished. Study groups, literary groups, choirs, sing-songs, artists' groups, folkdance, modern dance, and theatre troupes reflected the hope and creative energy of the movement. "Culture for all" was as much a tenet of communist belief as "Jobs for all." Left-wing music, plays and novels confronted the despair and repression of the thirties with a defiant, invigorating shout. As Maxim Gorky, the Soviet spokesman for proletarian humanism, had said, the aim of the workers' and peasants' state was "to create for every one of the 160,000,000 individuals of its multinational population conditions for the free development of his talents and abilities—in other words, to transform the sum-total of potential and passive neural-cerebral energy into active energy, to awaken its creative faculties." This was the vision that had encouraged Stanley to join the Party. Every communist—Irene, Sydney, Gilles, Raymond—lived with the dream of the better time to come, the time when a flowering of culture and education would emancipate the masses from ancient superstitions, from prejudices about race, religion, nation, class. A universal fraternal society would be created, every member of which would work according to his abilities and receive according to his needs.

All the arts were affected by socialist cultural theory. Michael Gold, the American counterpart to Gorky, extolled the new working-class writers who were making democratic the aristocratic art of writing and were helping "to free the proletariat of the whole world from the shameful, bloody, insane yoke of capitalism, to teach them not to consider themselves commodities which were bought and sold." Read in twenty languages, Upton Sinclair's *The Jungle*, "…dedicated to the Workingmen of America," reached its climax with a graphic image of working-class liberation:

The voice of Labour, despised and outraged; a mighty giant, lying prostrate—mountainous, colossal, but blinded, bound, and ignorant of his strength. And now a dream of resistance haunts him, hope battling with fear; until suddenly he stirs, and a fetter snaps—and a thrill shoots through him, to the farthest ends of his huge body, and in a flash the dream becomes an act! He starts, he lifts himself; and the bonds are shattered, the burdens roll off him, he rises—towering, gigantic; he springs to his feet, he shouts in his newborn exultation.

With this as an inspirational image, the working-man became the hero of the proletarian literature of the thirties: Gold's heroes were Jews without money and Langston Hughes's were sharecroppers; there were poems for strikers, lumber workers, and mill-mothers; there were dirges and lullabies for the working class. Canadian poet Dorothy Livesay celebrated her solidarity with the working class, anticipating with joy the revolution:

Now I am alive, having created
My breath one with yours, fighter and toiler
My hands ready, with yours, young worker
To crush the boss, the stifler
To rise over his body with a surge of beauty—
A wave of us, storming the world.

While Livesay created images for the left-wing vision, Kenneth Patchen, in his poem for the murdered labour troubadour Joe Hill, shouted out its defiance:

Let them burn us, hang us, shoot us, Joe Hill,
For at the last we had what it takes to make songs with.

Songs, books, and plays began, too, to speak in a language working people could understand. A vibrant labour theatre spread across North America. Its themes were immediate—the 1931 jailing of the communist leaders of the unemployed were dramatized in the Canadian play *Eight Men Speak*, banned by the government—and its form, developed by American writers such as Clifford Odets and Albert Maltz, was a refinement of agit-prop, theatre designed to provoke people to act. Montreal's New Theatre Group, which operated from 1936 to 1940, produced the Odets classic *Waiting for Lefty* at the Workmen's Circle, in homes, at Camp Nishtgedyget ("Camp leave your troubles behind"), at the millinery union, at the Drama Festival, in Westmount's Victoria Hall, and at the UJPO centre where, among others, Sydney and Annette saw it. The stage for this play is a platform on which actors, playing union leaders, talk to the audience, whom they address as fellow union members. The play ends:

> MAN: Boys, they just found Lefty!
> OTHERS: What? What? What?
> SOME: Shhh…. Shhh….
> MAN: They found Lefty….
> AGATE: Where?
> MAN: Behind the car barns with a bullet in his head!
> AGATE (crying): Hear it, boys, hear it? Hell, listen to
> me! Coast to coast! HELLO AMERICA, HELLO. WE'RE
> STORMBIRDS OF THE WORKING CLASS.
> WORKERS OF THE WORLD…. OUR BONES AND
> BLOOD! And when we die they'll know what we did to
> make a new world! Christ, cut us up to little pieces. We'll
> die for what is right! Put fruit trees where our ashes are!
> (To audience) Well, what's the answer?
> ALL: STRIKE!
> AGATE: LOUDER!
> ALL: STRIKE!
> AGATE AND OTHERS (on stage): AGAIN!
> ALL: STRIKE, STRIKE, STRIKE!!!

Whenever the play was performed, the audience, whether in overalls or formal dress, stood up and joined the actors in their final exhortation. Irving, a thirties theatre director who was initially attracted to left-wing theatre and then to the movement, said, "The strong response to labour theatre reflected a need for something to grab hold of, so people could get up and scream, 'Strike!' instead of just sitting there dully in what was essentially, for most people, a very dull time, and where the only excitement was the actual battle and the fight of left-wing movements and organized labour."

Cultural groups not only attracted, they energized adherents. They served as a creative outlet for often frustrated potential and provided the community with a rich bank of shared images and experience. "One of the beauties of the groups I associated with," Irving remembered, "was that we played everywhere, on the streets, in workers' halls, everywhere we could go." Theatre went out to the people; it didn't wait for them to come to halls of culture.

> When we went to the picket-line, we'd have a few little steps or pieces of wood to give us a level to stand on, a stage. We'd be made up or costumed, with different hats, flags, whatever props we could use, a little table on the side sometimes, and we'd do the performance right there in front of the big line, running about ten minutes. Then that whole section would move and the next one would come, and we'd do the same thing for them. We'd use the union leader's name, or some such thing, as a punch line, and yah, they'd roar.

Willie, another member of the New Theatre Group, remembered the fun they had learning the Stanislavsky method of acting. When Willie was first told to improvise and pretend he was a wounded worker, he limped forward, moaning, "I have a bad wound." "No, no," said the director from New York. "That is not Stanislavsky." After a bit more training Willie got the idea: "Hunched over, clutching my leg, I moved towards the audience and bellowed, 'I am a worker. I have this bloody, disgusting wound because I work long hard hours for a dirty, exploiting capitalist boss. Pchtew! Pchtew! Pchtew!'" For the irreverent young satirists in the New Theatre Group not even Stanislavsky was sacrosanct. Willie recalled the group's short-lived Stanislavsky skit, censored by the Party's cultural commissars. The actors played it with heavy Russian accents:

SINGLE VOICE: Then there is Shakespeare, a famous
    writer. Not a Maxim Gorky, but what do you expect
    —a bourgeois writer. "To be or not to be," he wrote.
    "That is the question." Aha! But what is the answer?
GROUP: STRIKE!

The earthiness and zest of the left-wing expressed itself in community and cultural events. In 1938, in Montreal, Mel Tolkin and Reuben Ship wrote the sassy, burlesque satire *We Beg to Differ*, a collection of eighteen skits which were danced, acted, and sung. In one of the routines, bird trills and cardboard cut-out coconut trees represent the escapist isle of Bula Bula into which everything intrudes: first, a newsboy enters the idyll, calling "Read all about it"; then, centre stage, a man in a roasting pot is, as a troupe member recalled, "being made into mincemeat and he's handing out leaflets." In "Noncombatant," the penultimate skit, a woman, cradling her baby, croons:

The sun is now descending
Over war-torn Spain,
Another day is ending of terror and of pain,
So how can I sing of fairies that dance around you in
    the night,
how can I sing when the air is a hell of terror and of fright,
how can I sing when the airplanes roar,
this, my child, is a lullaby of war.

Sleep my dear noncombatant,
Shut your eyelids tight,
If you're very lucky,
You may sleep right through the night.

Airplanes fly
Through the sky,
Their bombs will make your lullaby,
God is waiting, God is watching, babes in every town.
Does He watch the bombs
That Mussolini's sons drop down.

This plaintive song was the preamble to clenched fists and a full cast marching in the militant finale, "Fist in the Sky." Willie was in the troupe that performed *We Beg to Differ* at left-wing summer camps in New York, as was Irving, and Willie's outstanding recollection of that time was of the size of Irving's genital organ which, "every morning," as his fellow thespians exclaimed, "was pointing straight to Moscow." Willie remembered the ribaldry of the troupe and the fun. They had the best of two worlds: the challenging life of the theatre and the warmth of a supportive community. "Everywhere we went," he said, "it was like family."

Every communist was encouraged to develop his creative and intellectual capacities. Emery Samuel sat for portraits by members of the Artists' Group and was a welcome critic at exhibits. Stanley Ryerson published his books on French Canada with Raymond Boyer's financial assistance and tried his hand at writing an agit-prop play. Sydney became a first-rate square-dancer and caller, whooping it up at fund-raising functions. Annette sang Yiddish songs and from the Russian Revolution in the United Jewish People's Choir. Fred Taylor studied the New Realism of the Mexican muralists Rivera and Orozco, discussed the abundant literature on socialist realism with members of the Artists' Group, and produced and exhibited in that mode, honing his art until he was one of Canada's best social-realist painters. Lea arranged study sessions and lectures at the union, including one led by Leo Huberman, author of the classic Marxist economic primer *Man's Worldly Goods*.

Everyone knew the Spanish Civil War songs and everyone knew Paul Robeson. More than any other people's artist at that time, Robeson was spokesman, legend, bard. Six foot three, strong and powerful, this son of a slave had turned his back on commercial success to dedicate himself, his songs, and his acting to "the people." He was the epitome of "The New Man," a working-class son with the dignity and stature of a king and the dedication of a true communist. He always ended his concerts with his own version of "Old Man River," pledging each time: "I must keep fighting until I'm dying." Sydney had all Robeson's records, as did Raymond, Irene, Fred, and Gilles. When Sydney's children were born, he sang Robeson's "Curly-Headed Baby" to them as their lullaby. Robeson belonged to them; he was them. They all called him Paul.

Ideology blossomed into poetry and art, reflecting and enhancing a romantic left-wing vision. In thought and deed, Party members felt apart from the rest of society. In their own minds they were putting themselves on the line for what they believed and their persecution was a symptom of the establishment's fear of an inevitable social upheaval. They were bound to each other and to the Party through a profound sense of existential responsibility. They would lead history forward. There was a world to win.

Even the publication and distribution of Party literature was a political act. The articles for *Clarté* were written in secret, the copy driven to Ontario or to the Laurentian mountains, then mimeographed in record time and smuggled back into Montreal. As soon as the shipment came in, a trusted Party member, acting as a decoy, would pretend to pick up the paper in one location, while others would in fact distribute it elsewhere in small packets of four or five. Sydney led a crew that took newsprint to the Laurentians, ran off about two thousand papers over the weekend, and brought them back into town. "When we came in with *Clarté* or when the *Clarion* [the English-language communist newspaper] came in from Toronto, it was the fastest distribution ever. The houses were changed every week but the moment it hit the house that it was sent to, the person would load it up and go tearing around. He didn't want to have a couple of thousand newspapers lying around his house."

From 1936 to 1939, *Clarté* published anti-fascist, anti-capitalist material weekly and only two complete issues were seized. With what Sydney called "a certain amount of dedication and guts," members kept alive an alternative, communist point of view. Headlines in the *Clarion* read: "German Italian Planes Ready to Bomb Madrid," "Great Britain Backs Hitler's Anti-Soviet Plan," "Ottawa Says Can't Stop Canadian Aid to Franco." A feature article in *Clarté* signed by E. Roger, Stanley Ryerson's pen-name, analysed the legacy of the 1837 Canadian rebellion against Britain as "a tradition of solidarity between French and English democratic Canadians against all the enemies of democratic liberty." Referring to the Mackenzie-Papineau Battalion, the same issue proclaimed that the names of the Canadian leaders of 1837 "live anew in Spain of 1937."

Raymond Boyer kept a mimeograph machine in his basement and a printing press at his house in the country. Stanley Ryerson addressed the meetings of many organizations, including the St. James Literary Society, of which he said, "We got literary in that way after the Padlock Law." Lea delivered books to Quebec City, to sociologist Father Georges Henri Lévesque, a unique professor at the University of Laval who encouraged a truly catholic education that even embraced banned Marxist classics. Annette walked on picket-lines at five in the morning, with strikers at Dominion Textiles. She distributed leaflets at factory gates, planning her escape route in case the police came, timorously wondering if Rosa Luxemburg had ever been so scared. "We all grew," said Sydney. "We had ideas that were not acceptable, and we had to learn. We had to be good enough to convince people."

Party members had comrades, a community, and a culture. They also had the Party, a force that was to exert its own peculiar psychological reality. Each Party member—Sydney, Annette, Irene, Raymond, Henri, Gilles—was assigned to a small, tightly knit group of six to ten people. Because the Party was often outlawed, each unit was more than ever, as Irene once said, "in it together." Only the members within a club knew for sure who their comrades were, although the same one or two thousand faces appeared at public cultural events and fleshed out the ranks at united-front rallies. But Party business itself was carried out in great secrecy. Since it was illegal to propagate communism, meetings were organized by word of mouth and held randomly in different people's homes. Suspected informers would be unmasked by advising the group of the next rendezvous and then telling all the members but the suspected informer of the real meeting-place. If the set-up was raided, the informer would be denounced. Members lived their commitment without having any formal link to the Party: there were no membership cards because of the danger that a card or membership list could be stolen; dues were paid, but only the treasurer of each club knew the names of those who had paid. "You were a communist if you thought you were," said Sydney, "if you accepted Party discipline, came to meetings regularly, and participated materially and personally in the movement."

The influx of new recruits during the thirties required the formation of additional Party sections. Clubs of clerical and office workers made up one new section in Montreal, clubs of artists and professionals another.[1] Sydney and Annette, along with other newly married recruits, were encouraged to set up their homes in the fast developing, working-class district, Park Extension, at the north end of Park Avenue. For new immigrants, the low-cost housing and open fields held the promise of homes and a future. Here, Sydney and Annette could raise their children in a working-class milieu, and their local Party groups could do community work. All day Sydney serviced clients in his small chartered accountancy firm and Annette, a biochemist, analysed blood samples in a doctor's lab. The rest of their lives—nights, weekends, social time—was taken up with the Party. "We had no friends but those in the Party," said Sydney. "To say it's like soldiers in battle is an exaggeration, but we were in a fight together. We developed an admiration and respect for things people were prepared to do, things they articulated, things they were learning."

Every weekday-evening, after work was over, they met with the other members of their group. Following Robert's Rules of

Order, which they knew like the numbers on a telephone, they first read the minutes of the last meeting and then went through "an incredible follow-up and check-up system" of the decisions made and tasks undertaken. As Sydney recalled, "Directives came down: raise money (no problem); sell *Clarion* subscriptions (difficult but we sold a few); recruit (we hardly ever did)." Quotas of newspaper subscriptions to be sold were set at every meeting, and pledges of money to be given or raised were made. "The careful check took up a good part of the meeting." At the end of the business, the person responsible for the week's reading would lead a discussion on contemporary politics, or "someone who was in before us" would lead a class on Marxism. Believing in democratic centralism, the group thrashed through all policies and ideas in a painstaking attempt to reach a consensus.

Every meeting ended with a session called "Good and Welfare," a regular feature of Party life which reflected the total commitment members had made to the Party. Criticism of others and of directives, and especially self-criticism, were reserved for this time. Party members measured their performance as workers for socialism against their ideals. Trained to think of themselves as labour's most conscious leaders, "the vanguard of the working class," they were tough self-critics. They expected to give themselves wholly to the cause and to find affirmation in service and dedication. Self-criticism, or, as Sydney said, "beating your breast in public," was considered a means to improvement. Confession: "I didn't sell enough newspapers." Self-evaluation: "Because I didn't work hard enough or explain clearly enough." Self-correction: "But, next week, I will correct my mistakes and do even more."

Although the individual was the medium in "Good and Welfare," it was clearly understood that the collective, not personal, good was the goal; each person had to be better, would be helped to be better, as a worker for socialism. "It was considered a low form of conversation to be interested in the personal," said Annette. Communist couples were serious and earnest only about their social responsibilities and even those who hugged and kissed in public were spartan in their attitudes: "Anniversaries were bourgeois," remembered Annette. "Husbands who bought flowers screwed around." Communist youth groups and communist summer camps encouraged egalitarian co-ed socializing but free love was a myth. "The Party was very moral," said Fred Rose. "The free love myth came from the same propaganda as the nationalization of women in the Soviet Union. Actually, they were Victorian up to their ass." Irene identified free love with "a very nasty experience" from high school, "I was going out with a boy to a football game and coming back he drives across the mountain, parks the car, makes a great lunge at me and, absolutely horrified when I repulse him, he says, 'But communists believe in free love and I want some.'" After reading Friedrich Engels' *The Origin of the Family, State and Private Property*, Irene and her group may have agreed intellectually that marriage was unnecessary, "simply a matter of conserving money and passing it on to people" but "everybody recognized that until you had socialism there was no alternative so most people in the movement were married." In fact, comrades were encouraged to marry— "Don't drink out of a dirty glass"— and they usually married each other. "Fooling around" was severely censored. There were leaders who availed themselves of what Gilles called "the principle of sexual freedom"—Tim Buck had a mistress although his wife always sat beside him in public and Fred Rose had lovers—but these indiscretions were kept secret. Party members' sexual mores were mostly puritanical. Anything else, in Annette's words, would have been "a threat to the community."

The community was a network of interlocking lives, of people bound together by the force of history. A Presbyterian minister, a British war-bride, a union organizer, and a painter were part of the community that provided Sydney and Annette with the social and emotional security of a large extended family. May Days, Saturdays, weddings, births, were shared with them. Social events were communally planned. A handwritten list, found in Sydney's copy of *The Jungle*, may be read as a hieroglyph of communal social functioning:

Bob and Marge—record player
Helen—records
Ed—ties
Annette—stockings (nylon)
Glen—electric train, if available
Beryl—set of dishes and small table and chairs
Gert— kiddy bike (pedals, if available)

The community itself was solid and reliable, made up of comrades who were also friends. Marxism, like Freudianism, had opened up an aspect of reality that had been hidden from most people. The difference was that one's emotional life was not invested in personal or domestic concerns, but in the social vision that members embraced with their hearts. "A communist in his daily life cannot live quite like another," said the early communist Reverend Albert E. Smith. "He has the enduring incentive to live in a noble manner." "Good and Welfare" was a ritual in keeping with the concept of religious nobility. It was a seemingly innocuous but insidious process of self-prostration, obscured in members' minds by their hope, fervour, and actual youth. Like sing-songs, social functions, study groups, padlocks, persecution, and their almost palpable dream, "Good and Welfare" was part of Party life. It was a small part of what Sydney remembered when he concluded, "We had great times, wonderful times. We were truly, fully alive. We had ideals."

Bethune, Irene Kon, Fred Taylor, Raymond Boyer and other middle-class teachers, scientists, and professionals were separated from Sydney and Annette and grouped into the closed clubs of the newly formed Section 13. Fred Rose, as Party Organizer and teacher, met with members of Section 13, as did Stanley, who was their mentor. As Party members, they attended regular Party meetings and informal study sessions, but they were never openly communists. Unlike the Park Extension club, unlike Emery Samuel's French Section or Henri Gagnon's YCL groups, the members of Section 13 did not hand out leaflets, did not go to demonstrations, did not march on picket-lines, did not, therefore, risk being photographed

Irene Kon and Raymond Boyer, Montreal, 1939.

or arrested by the police. And they seldom received mention, let alone publicity, at conventions or in the Party press. Section 13 was a closed section. Few Party members knew and no one outside the Party was supposed to know that these one hundred or so "darlings of the movement" were Party members.

Given the middle-class backgrounds of those in the special section, along with their often-romanticized intellectual attraction to communism, it is debatable whether they would all have joined the Party without the protection offered by a closed club. Stanley's rationale for their special treatment was that "members of the closed section could continue working in their given fields." More important for the movement, they retained the respectability necessary to lead the anti-fascist, civil libertarian, cultural and scientific groups organized by the communists in the latter half of the thirties and the first half of the forties.

The members of Section 13 worked tirelessly as fund-raisers and as committed leaders of the broad-based, united-front organizations, such as the Committee to Aid Spanish Democracy, the Civil Liberties Union, and the League Against Fascism and War. Specific interest groups organized by Section 13 reached further into the community: the Artists' Group; the New Theatre Group; and Bethune's Group for the Security of the People's Health—an organization of doctors, nurses, and social workers of various political leanings who addressed the problem of health-care for the poor and the unemployed, studied health-care systems in other countries, and made concrete proposals to the government and professional associations for a more equal distribution of medical services. Fred Taylor would become an officer in the Federation of Canadian Artists, and Raymond Boyer would become president of the Canadian Association of Scientific Workers. If their co-workers in these organizations knew the leaders were communists, they lived with it. As Wendell MacLeod, a socialist co-worker of Bethune's in the health group, explained, "The mood in our circle in those 'Spanish years' was to look at a person's attitude towards the critical issues, rather than at his political affiliations."[2]

Like Raymond and Irene, new recruits to Section 13 were soon immersed in the ongoing activity of the movement. Before television and talk shows, public meetings were the best way to reach people, and Bethune, as well as John Strachey, the brightest star among English-speaking Marxist intellectuals, spoke in Montreal. Strachey's book, *The Coming Struggle for Power*, on the nature of the capitalist crisis and the danger of war, was a seminal book for many in this period, as was R. Palme Dutt's early study of fascism, *Fascism and Social Revolution*. From New York came "subversive" literature such as *New Masses*, cut up and camouflaged in the *New York Times*. Members welcomed the political commentary, enjoyed the cartoons, and passed copies on to friends. At the New Theatre Group's public performances in Victoria Hall, Party members and sympathizers saw left-wing theatre, such as Irwin Shaw's anti-war play, *Bury the Dead*, in which dead soldiers, refusing to be buried, have things to say "to the people who pick up guns to fight in somebody else's war—big things, important things." Sometimes, Stanley Ryerson, Fred Rose, or Emery Samuel, "whoever we got hold of," would lead a study group on the fundamentals of capital and labour relations. Yet, few of the members of Section 13 had time to devote themselves to the study of the exacting work of Marx or Lenin. Once they joined the Party they were caught up in the momentum of the movement. As Raymond said, "We never had a weekend or an evening to ourselves. It was an enveloping way of life."

With the Western world in crisis, with the warmth and excitement generated by the left-wing as their salve, middle-class professionals accepted new values. Harry: "When I graduated no one wanted me as an architect. No one wanted me at all. I could have been dead in the streets for all anybody cared. They only place I felt worthwhile was in the communist movement, where people accepted me wholly and as a valuable person." Donna, who had gone to college before the Depression, found herself working as a salesgirl for thirteen dollars a week. Her husband, who had graduated with her and wanted to write, worked for an insurance company. "None of us were Marxists when we got into the Party," she said. "We were idealists, humanitarians, mainly naïve. We were on the march for a better world, a beautiful world made up of good people working for each other, a world where everyone would get a chance to express themselves."

At the outset some new recruits found that the Communist Party demanded action, discipline, and allegiance beyond the call of duty. When Norman joined Raymond's and Fred's study group in 1938, he was attracted by the anti-fascist, socialist nature of the group, but he resisted the Party because he found it doctrinaire. "I was against the Party because I thought you should be free to believe what you want." In the study group he was introduced to stirring socialist literature and insightful political commentary, as well as to the concept that communists bear the responsibility for the fate of the working class, of the labour movement, of their own nation, of all humanity. It was suggested to him that in the face of repression and class war, there must be iron-clad unity within the Party. In response to his reservations about the loss of intellectual freedom, he was directed to the writings of Maxim Gorky, which assured him that after rejecting "the brutish individualism of the bourgeoisie, the new man is fully aware how highly integral is the individual who is fully united within the collective." A collective, disciplined, highly centralized structure seemed to be necessary to the work Norman found himself doing—producing and printing material—which, under the Padlock Law and then under the War Measures Act, was made illegal. His reservations soon took second place to what he saw as the means necessitated by the struggle, and his old insistence on intellectual freedom was left in abeyance, having been dismissed by the Party as "a class attitude from an intellectual point of view." When Norman joined the Party, he "had to chuck all that out the door. It was like going into a monastery."

Those who chose to be communists eschewed their intellectual and material legacies in favour of a total commitment to social change. Moderate socialists—CCFers, Frank Scott, a McGill University law professor, Eugene Forsey, now a senator and an Independent, T. C. Douglas, and Frank Underhill—worked with communists in organizations such as the Civil Liberties Union and the League against Fascism and War, which represented 250,000 Canadians in 1937. Communists and members of the League for Social Reconstruction, the brain trust of the CCF, discussed issues and found common causes. But there was a difference. The Communist Party was distinguished not only by its adamant anti-fascist policy, but by its methods. Communists took to the streets, demonstrated in public, pasted posters on city billboards—all of these tactics that "liberals," in communist jargon, condemned for inciting violence. As Georgi Dimitroff had said at the close of the 1935 Congress of the Communist International, in the same breath as he called for a people's front against fascism, "We communists employ methods of struggle which differ from those of other parties."

Policy, methods, and, particularly, the Party's insistence on its role as "the vanguard," separated Party members from other progressive forces. "We either disdained other movements or thought of them as something to be used, taken over, or infiltrated, a process we called 'boring from within,'" said a Party member regretfully. "If genuine cooperative efforts were made and friendships formed, we were taken to task for frittering away our time in 'bourgeois' occupations." Raymond Boyer felt that the moderates were "scared of going further because of their careers." Irene thought that they were "scared of the masses, scared of being equal." Although communists were working with other progressive groups, they were, in reality, as cut off from them as they had always been. Their Party lived underground, and its members had developed a militant, sectarian state of mind. For Raymond Boyer, Fred Rose had put it tellingly when he'd told him, "You've got to be able to hate because you can't love people unless you hate those who are doing things to them. That's what makes it possible for a communist to do things that a liberal can't do."

Party members, even those who described themselves as "reform-minded people," had, in joining the Party, taken a leap of commitment that only later involved "self-discipline." They kept their Party going despite repression and in a true Judaeo-Christian tradition, showed the "courage of their convictions." As Fred Rose noted, "The Padlock Law made work so much harder that the membership became steeled to the struggle against this reactionary measure and added members became more determined in their fight."

The endless public and secret "Moscow trials" were being played out from 1936 to 1938, at a time when Canadian Party members were fervent in their hopes for Spain and strong in their trust and faith in communism. Stalin had masterminded the purges of all the members of Lenin's Politbureau, including Trotsky, who, although absent, was the chief defendant. Victims were an ex-premier, several vice-premiers, two ex-chiefs of the Communist International, the chief of the trade unions, the chief of the General Staff, the supreme commanders of all important military districts, and most Soviet ambassadors in Europe and Asia. All were accused of trying to assassinate Stalin and destroy the Soviet Union.

Most Party members in Canada believed the trials were legitimate. The descriptions they read and the eye-witness reports brought back by their leaders declared that the confessions had the tone and appearance of truth. Lion Feuchtwanger's *Moscow*, published in 1937, assured readers that "the whole thing was less like a criminal trial than a debate carried on in a conversational tone by educated men.… Indeed, the impression one received is that the accused, prosecution and judges had the same, I might almost say sporting, interest in arriving at a satisfactory explanation." British MP D. N. Pritt wrote, "Most, if not all the accused…did make their confessions with an almost abject and exuberant completeness." Party organizer Sam Carr, who was at the trials, "didn't realize the degree of terror" and "believed that the trials were right." It is possible that Arthur Koestler's *Darkness at Noon*, a profound analysis of the phenomenon of the trial confessions, might have swayed Party members, but it was proscribed by the Party and few read "the reactionary book." For communists, there was ample historical precedent of sabotage against the Soviet state and little in their lexicon to alert them to the perversion of their ideal represented by the purges.

The few who realized that not fascist spies but the cream of Russian revolutionary society had been liquidated left the Party. So did the few who knew and rejected the annihilation of anarchists by Stalinists in Spain. There was no other way. As Raymond Boyer said, "At the time the Party was monolithic. There was very little freedom to deviate from the Party line. If you felt that way, you quit." For the remaining Party members, the illustrious record of the Party in labour organizing and in its fight against fascism was answer enough. Their purpose was to create international solidarity against fascism and war, and against the imperialism that was spawning both. The Party was an amorphous idea, an allegiance, a responsibility. It spoke with outrage and the poetry of Marx; it promised flowers.

In actuality, the Party was the pragmatic and ruthless survivor of internecine and international wars, and its centre, preoccupied with its own difficult survival, had little use for romanticism. While seasoned apparatchiks developed acute peripheral vision, learning to jump over, backtrack from, and slide out of the way of trouble, most North American Party members were open and trusting with each other, remote even from the reality of *Inprecor*, the newspaper of the Communist International, which was read by only about one hundred people in Canada. Their world view was positive and hopeful, reinforced by a willing suspension of disbelief. Mistakes would be made but they would be corrected by criticism and self-criticism, by discipline and dedicated work. To those who knew him, Norman Bethune provided a shining example of just this kind of absolute commitment. "You can't underestimate the charisma of Beth," said an organizer of Section 13. "He was of a heroic mould, not a plaster saint. He was out there exposing himself to death, braving it with guts and courage." Above all, there was the promise that the Communist Party would lead the world to socialism. A better world would be born after the anti-fascist battle was won. Reading the final pages of *Fallen Bastions*, the second contingent must have identified with the industrialist's wife, who concluded:

> I should feel that we are being compelled to choose be-
> tween perishing in the drought of Fascism and the flood
> of Socialism—perhaps of Communism. Both, drought
> and flood, destroy, and either way, our sort of life would
> come to an end. But when the drought has passed, it leaves
> behind it an arid desert where nothing new can live. After
> the flood subsides, new forms of life spring up, some
> monstrous, some young, vigorous and healthy—we see it
> in this world of ours today. I think that you and I could
> never choose the drought.[3]

CHAPTER EIGHT

The Phoney War

THE LEADERS OF THE WEST had acquiesced to Mussolini's plundering of Ethiopia; they had closed their eyes to Italian troops and German war planes fighting for the insurgents in Spain; they had accepted Hitler's accession of Austria, recognized Franco's regime in Spain; and, finally, in Munich, they had reneged on previous pacts and given Czechoslovakia to Germany. While refugees from German-occupied countries began to arrive in Britain and the United States, the British who would appease the Nazis shouted, "Save Our Sons," and the Americans who advocated isolationism—the "American Firsters"—lobbied against entering a "foreign" war. Jews in Germany were being driven from their homes, stripped, and beaten in the streets, as Italian soldiers and German tanks and warplanes overwhelmed the last stronghold of the Spanish Republic at Barcelona. Communists repeatedly insisted that only a coalition among states, working through the League of Nations, could resist fascist aggression. "Peace is indivisible," they said, echoing Dimitroff. But Western governments, with business and even blood ties to the German aristocracy, time and again rejected the idea of joining with the Soviet Union for collective security.

"So, in 1939, the Soviet nation took a big gulp and swallowed the pact with Germany. Without much liking it either, but the will of the Kremlin was law," wrote Walter Duranty. "Yet they knew that the respite was only temporary, as Alexander's officers knew that sooner or later Napoleon's greed for domination over

Europe—if not, like Hitler's, for world domination—would bring him into conflict with their country."[1] With the Nazi-Soviet pact, the U.S.S.R. agreed to deliver great quantities of oil, grain, manganese, cotton, and other raw materials to Germany; in exchange, they received German machines and spare parts, machine tools, precision instruments, chemicals, and drugs. The Kremlin played its hand, showing a complete and utter disregard for public opinion abroad. As U.S.S.R. Foreign Minister Vyacheslav Molotov explained, the Nazi-Soviet Pact was "in full accord with the basic interests of the Soviet Union." The West was stunned by a pact between countries whose political ideologies were bolstered by hatred of each other, and frightened by this violent upset in the balance of military power between Germany and the democracies. Hitler, secure in the knowledge that Russia wouldn't stop him, deployed bombs and tanks and smashed Poland. The days of appeasement were over. On September 3, 1939, France and England declared war. Seven days later Canada followed suit.

The media in the West decried Stalin's pact with the Nazis as the culmination of a betrayal that had begun with the purges; the partition of Poland by Russia and Germany was the stabbing of a wounded man in the back; the seizures of Little Finland, Bessarabia, and the Baltic states by Russia, were acts of ruthless greed. But the Soviet leader justified the pact, maintaining that the British, with help from the French, had tried to turn Hitler against his country alone. "The enemy," he warned, "is marching East." For the Soviet Union, gearing up for a battle to the death, this *realpolitik* made perfect sense. But national Communist parties failed to distinguish between the validity of the pact in terms of Soviet interests and their own responsibility to have an independent policy on the war; there was no tradition on which to base such a distinction. When the Central Committee of the Communist Party of Canada debated its position on the war, only two people argued for war against Hitler. Fred Rose defended the war as a just war from the beginning, and he was backed by J. B. Salsberg, who was not much support because he was already suspect for his Jewish "nationalist" sentiments. The rest of the Central Committee did not think twice about taking the same position as the Soviet Union. They defined the war in Soviet terms, as "an inter-imperialist war," an in-fight to retain empires and spheres of influence, and in so doing they subverted the anti-fascist commitment of their constituency. Pressured and outnumbered, Rose and Salsberg acquiesced; for those who wanted to stay in the Party, there was, as Raymond Boyer had pointed out, "no other choice." The Soviet position on the war became that of the Canadian Communist Party. Provincial Party leaders were informed and, like Emery Samuel, they adopted the perspective of the Central Committee. "We reversed our stand against Hitler and the appeasers and worked for the line 'Down with the Imperialist War.'"

Some Party members were at first unaware of the new line, such as Sydney's comrade Ed. Seventeen years old, unemployed, and full of anti-fascist fire, he immediately went to join the army. He found himself in a lineup with old vets, unemployed men, and "a whole bunch of bloody communists." That same day the Communist Party called meetings of all its branches, and Ed was told, "We are betrayed. The West will not agree to collective security. Stalin has made a pact with Hitler to save the Soviet Union's neck." For the young men who had just volunteered to fight Hitler, the thought that the Soviet Union would make a pact with Nazi Germany was almost "too hard to take." Ed went to meeting after meeting, as he would again in 1956 when the Khrushchev Report was made public. He was reminded that the British, French, and Americans were trying to turn Germany against Russia; "the Western powers wanted Russia to pull the West's chestnuts out of a Russian fire." Ed's initial revulsion was set against a litany of instances where the West had capitulated to fascism. He listened and argued, studied, debated, analysed, and discussed, all of which gave him a sense of involvement and the illusion of choice. But the bottom line was the Party line, decided by the Central Committee, in consultation with Moscow. Despite meetings far into the night, the line was in fact coming down from the top, not, as was theoretically supposed, being developed through reciprocal discussion. As Sydney was later to say, "The line on the Nazi-Soviet Pact came down through democratic centralism." Finally, Ed agreed that the motherland of socialism was endangered and had to make a pact with the Germans in order to buy time before the inevitable confrontation with the Nazis. "I was confused but eventually I was convinced," Ed explained. "Not a single person in my club felt good about it, but we went along with it. There seemed to be sufficient argument."

The endorsement of a communist-Nazi alliance was to have a shattering effect on Communist parties outside the Soviet Union. For Party members the two years from 1939 until the Nazi invasion of the Soviet Union in June 1941 were to be a trial of faith and loyalty— "a nightmare season," in the words of a leading American progressive. "That's why many of us kept very quiet," Ed remembered. On the one hand, communists didn't believe that the British prime minister, Neville Chamberlain, and Anthony Eden, Britain's foreign secretary, would do battle with Hitler, but, on the other hand, many, like Ed, wanted to fight. The majority of them had joined the Communist Party because of its opposition to fascism, and the Party's about-face went so much against the grain that it was bound to do violence to their ideals. Annette, who never forgot the moment when her club was told by the Central Committee that it would have to reverse its decision to support the war, said, "I can still feel how painful it was." Sydney remembered that he accepted the pact "as a ploy to give the Soviet Union time to defend itself." Raymond Boyer, by then, had "faith in the leaders of the left-wing movement and their explanations of the world.... I had gone beyond the liberal stage of questioning everything."

Pressed to say why he stayed in the Party even though he hated fascism, Ed answered with a single sentence: "I was a very convinced communist." The moral discomfort he felt was eased by the fact that very little was asked of him during this period. "I didn't give out leaflets or actively oppose the war; I worked in the union. Never in my life in the Party did I have so much free time." Remembering the Western imperialist nature of the First World

War, noting the West's anti-Soviet sentiments in the early years of this war and its acceptance of Hitler's aggression before France was attacked, Ed and other Party members were intellectually ready to define this first phase of the war as a phoney war and accept the pact as a necessary evil. But the salt in their wounded ideals was, according to Annette, "the pictures, newsreels, speeches, champagne, and toasts of Stalin looking so chummy with Hitler. It was just too sick. Before we had considered ourselves good, clean people, working in united-front movements against fascism. Then we became cynical politicians, like everybody else."

Educated young adults and other Party members, especially Jews, horrified by the Nazi's antisemitism, left the Party in droves. Indeed, for many left-wing intellectuals around the world, the Comintern line on the war signalled a final and irrevocable break with communism: Victor Gollancz, known and respected as the publisher of the influential Left Book Club editions, and John Strachey, whose books and public appearances had influenced many people to join the Communist Party, were among those who now quit. Yet, although attrition was great, the majority of Party members in North America and some groups in particular were unaffected. Many in the Ukrainian sections, for examples, were not outraged by the destruction of the Polish state, for which they had a historical hatred. For some of them, the entry of the Red Army into Lvov was satisfying, retributive justice. Neither did the French Section in Quebec object to staying out of yet another "English War." "Some of our boys looked at it like a movie from the United States," Emery recalled. "Hurrah, the guys with the black hats are losing."

With the united-front days over, the communist propensity for innovative name-calling reached new heights. Those who disagreed with the Party line were "fellow-travellers who fell off the train at the last bend," "weak sisters," and "partial virgins." And communists themselves became isolated targets once again. As Hitler's conquests increased, so did government pressure against communist activities. Distributors of communist publications were arrested and imprisoned. It was once again difficult to rent halls for meetings. In the autumn of 1939, *The Clarion* and *Clarté* were banned. On the eve of the entry of German troops into Paris in June 1940, the federal government issued under the War Measures Act an order-in-council which banned, not only all pro-Nazi organizations, but also the CPC, the YCL and several mass organizations. Those who were caught by the police were sent to internment camps.[2] "The difference was," recalled Sydney, "that after 1939 we had to watch out for the RCMP as well as for the provincial police."

Communists may have felt that they had temporarily accepted a noxious position on the war so that they could eventually recreate the world. They may have believed that their scientific and rational philosophical system was a totally modern way of looking at the world which, by its very nature, opposed the fanatical superstition of the fascists. They may even have known that they and the fascists would inevitably fight to wipe each other out. But the government considered the Party's anti-war stand treasonous, and in the public mind they were lumped with the fascists they abhorred. From 1939 to 1941, 110 communists would be arrested and interned, along with German and Italian fascists, people of Japanese origin, and some French Canadians who opposed Canada's participation in the war. Faced with the uncompromising federal ban and the imminent threat of arrest and internment, the Party marshalled all its resources to survive. In a move that would have a tremendous effect on the conduct and the minds of Party members, the Canadian Party went completely underground.

CHAPTER NINE

Underground

FRED ROSE SAID GOODBYE to his wife, Fanny, and his daughter, Laura. Laura was happy, lively, four years old. She didn't know that it was illegal to be a communist and that for over a year and a half her father would be in hiding. Only by the way her mother and father were saying goodbye, by the long time her father held her in his arms, did she suspect that this parting was significant. Laura didn't know that, from then on, she would see very little of her father, nor could she foresee the sort of life she and her mother would live, moving from room to room, staying in the houses of people who, as she later said, "went along with" the Party, but weren't well known.

Laura Rose would move six times between kindergarten and grade three, from the "home of the fat woman who ate *mamaliga* and wouldn't let me talk during the soap operas," to the room behind the Lears's living room—always in a room, never in the living room, learning to give another name, not her own, so that the police could not find her father through her. As the years passed, her father would become "sort of an image, an image that I learned to love and respect through other people's eyes." She would hear him spoken of with love and caring "because he cared so much about people and everything he was doing was for the good of the people." But, as she grew from childhood to girlhood, the strength she developed would come from the warmth of her mother and the group that was always around them. Her father came out of hiding every now and then and she would see him for a few hours, and then he went back. "I can still remember the cotton bathrobe and patent-leather slippers I got for one occasion," she smiled. "It was such a happy occasion because he had come to visit." Still, she would say to him once, "Take me with you." And he would say, "I can't." And she, young and angry, answered, "Go to hell, then." And the hurt look on his face when she said that mingles in her memory with a cotton bathrobe and pair of patent-leather slippers.

Sydney and Annette were asked to hide Fred Rose. They were trusted, low-profile Party members, not yet raided, unknown to the police. The young couple considered the matter carefully. Fred Rose was "The Leader," respected, important to the movement. On the other hand, as Emery Samuel remembered, Ernest Lapointe, the federal minister of justice, "was on a rampage, threatening to hang every communist in Quebec." They weighed the danger against the importance of the cause, and said "Yes." Their contact with the Party was stopped; they no longer attended meetings; they didn't see their friends; and they accepted the principle that "the less you know, the less you can tell." As far as other Party members knew, they were "traitors."

Their two-bedroom apartment was in the undeveloped north end of Montreal, on Park Avenue, minutes from the CPR train station. Sydney watched from his kitchen window as his brother, Nat, nicknamed "Slug" took over his shift, driving the old Buick into the lane behind the house. Slug checked to see that the light, signalling "All Clear," was on in Fred's room. He stretched, lit a cigarette, rehearsed the meetings he had set up for the day, and went over the procedure for escape from the apartment to the train station in case of a raid. Then he waited, looking forward to seeing Fred Rose. To Nat, a seasoned veteran of Jewish gang-fights, the tough-talking little guy was like home. He liked Fred's songs, his love of women, the gleam in his eye. The guy was as smart as they come, but, as Lea said, "a *haimesha mensch*...you never had to put on kid gloves to see him." Still, he was the leader— "*der kliner*," "the little one," they called him, but the leader nonetheless. Nat was proud to be his driver. He was proud, too, to have his kid brother Sydney in the underground apparatus. They had made a pact of silence, in case of interrogation, and taken the precaution of putting a farm they owned in their mother's name.

Slug shifted his weight and slouched more comfortably against the car seat. Yesterday, his mother had discovered Fred Rose in the apartment and had chided her sons for doing "dangerous work." Yet it was she, who had fought in the 1905 Russian Revolution, who had formed them. As the morning light gathered about the waiting car, Slug's face softened with a rare, luxurious moment of remembering....It was a long time ago. He must have been very young at the time, maybe six years old, when he first heard the "International." It was sung by his mother, in Yiddish, and it was when they were picking blackberries in Ste. Sophie. He would always hear the echo of that day, her strong voice, in the song:

Arise, ye prisoners of starvation
Arise, ye wretched of the earth,
For justice thunders condemnation,
A better world's in birth.
No more tradition's chains shall bind us,
Arise, ye slaves; no more in thrall!
The earth shall rise on new foundations,
We have been naught, we shall be all.

She had told him that this was the song she had sung in Russia; it was her song and his, the song of all working people who wanted to live without bosses.... "Don't worry, Mama," Slug acknowledged, "your sons, Sydney and I, are in this together. For safety's sake we didn't tell you, and for the sake of the underground we don't tell each other what we do, but we do it for your dream. In memory of the 'International' you nourished us with, for you."

In the room beside Sydney, the radio went off. It was 8:30 A.M. Fred Rose had remade his bed into the living-room couch and was at his desk writing, fully and immaculately dressed. Caught in a reality

Katie, Nat/Slug, Sydney, Sarah, 1936.

that was his by default, he scoured all available resources for news of the outside world. The cheap Spartan radio he had bought with Sydney and Annette was strung all over the apartment with electrical wires. He woke to the news, and listened to every shortwave broadcast from Moscow. He dissected the columns of Captain Liddell Hart, one of Britain's foremost military experts, and he studied arcane military strategy books, such as Max Werner's *The Military Strength of the Powers*. The Soviet Union was as strong as Germany, he read: three hundred divisions supported by eight thousand airplanes and ten thousand tanks, all intended for use on the Eastern Front. The Soviet Union was the only country with the force to stop Hitler's totalitarian war-machine. Totalitarian victory would mean "the utter destruction of the vanquished nation, and its complete and final disappearance from the historical arena. The victor will not negotiate with the vanquished concerning the conditions for peace, because there will be no party capable of negotiations. He will impose whatever conditions he thinks fit. In reality totalitarian warfare is nothing but a gigantic struggle of elimination whose upshot will be terrible and irrevocable in its finality."[1]

The political animal that was Fred Rose paced in frustration. Day after day newspapers devoted entire pages, under black headlines, to the international fever chart: the massing of troops and naval forces, the frenetic movement of diplomatic agents, the emergency meetings of cabinets. The world was teetering on the rim of a volcano. North Africa, Austria, Czechoslovakia, Poland, Denmark, Norway, the Netherlands, Belgium, and northern France—fell. The Jews of Central Europe were condemned to extinction. Roosevelt wanted to help Britain fight the Nazi submarines and German fleets, which were taking a heavy toll on British shipping, but was frustrated by the scare-tactics of the isolationists and by the decline in his own political power. It seemed that Hitler went unchallenged and was unconquerable. With the self-discipline expected of a communist, Fred Rose controlled his instinct to fight. He followed a strict, solitary regime, as he had done in jail. The one compensation was that he was now free, nominally. And the Party was still functioning. He had work to do.

At 9:10 he turned off the news, marked his page, put on his fedora, his full-length dark wool coat, and turned off the light, to alert Slug that he was coming out. Slug started the car. Rose saw only the key people necessary to keep the Party running and these he saw mostly on a one-to-one basis. Today, he was meeting with Bob Haddow, the fiery Scots organizer in charge of the trade-union groups with whom he had coordinated the 1940 unemployed relief strike in Verdun. Other days he met with Emery Samuel, in charge of the French Section; Sydney Zarkin, in charge of Jewish groups; Stanley Ryerson, responsible for closed groups; Joe Salsberg, through whom he reported to the Central Committee;

and Major Sokolov, from the Soviet Trade Commission, who must have been as interested in Canada's policies towards Europe as Fred was in Soviet policy. The safe houses were changed, but the people he saw were always the same. "I moved around, met people at different places, attended to what I had to," he was later to say. "There was a good apparatus, good machinery."

Relying on the dedication of rank-and-file Party members, the Communist Party of Canada succeeded in weathering the Nazi-Soviet Pact. The members in Quebec, initiated into the underground by the Padlock Law, protected not only their own provincial leaders, but a group from the Toronto-based Central Committee. Eda and her husband, a young couple who were taken out of the Party by the leadership in order to keep a safe house, remembered: "We didn't see anybody, moved apartments four times, left the house when Joshua Gershman, Sam Carr, Tim Buck, Stanley Ryerson, and Fred Rose came there to meet, which happened quite a bit." Like Sydney and Annette, they, too, were in the underground because, as Eda said, "We were asked." For a while executive members Joe Salsberg and Stewart Smith lived in a tiny flat in the centre of Montreal, but members of the executive more often lived out of suitcases, stayed at hotels, moved constantly, always one step ahead of the police. Often people from the closed groups were asked, "Can we keep a mimeograph machine in your basement? Can someone stay with you?" In a pinch, members made use of their apolitical relatives, who took in someone, not asking too many questions, because he was a child's college friend or the husband of their child's friend. As Stanley Ryerson figured out, "People from the professional groups played a large role in the underground.... A disproportionately large number of professional houses were used."

These Party members were frequently caught up in demanding, clandestine activity with a meagre theoretical background in Marxism, having had only enough time in the Party to embrace whole-heartedly the romantic vision. A case in point was Scott Benning, who was introduced to socialism by his sister, Paulette.

"You should see what they're doing in Mexico," she told him, when she returned in 1935, full of enthusiasm for the Mexican government's socialist reforms: the expropriation of oil companies, the beginnings of large cooperative farms on a profit-sharing basis. She talked excitedly about the Mexican experiment to the high-school class she taught in Westmount. "The Party heard about this teacher talking communism in the classroom," recalled Donna. "She didn't have a clue that she would lose her job. I invited her to tea, gave her pamphlets. Finally, the time was ripe and I invited her to a teachers' meeting." In the teachers' group, Paulette was introduced to the same social and political literature as Raymond, Irene and Fred Taylor were reading and she passed the reading on to Scott. She joined the Party, and Scott read what she read. "Scott became very anti-war," remembered Paulette, "and when Chamberlain came back from Munich, Scott too joined the Party." In Section 13 Scott found friends who shared his hatred of war and fascism. In the study sessions he was moved more by the socialist novels and Left Book Club commentary than by the more "cumbersome" Marxist texts. After nine months of reading, talking, and defying Duplessis, the Party he had just joined was banned federally and Scott was in an underground organization, travelling from Montreal to Toronto, taking Party leaders to and from meetings, so busy he didn't even have time to get married.

Norman, another relatively recent recruit, was in a group that produced and printed political pamphlets. There was a mimeograph machine in Raymond's house in the country and others in the city, one of which Norman had made from scratch. Like everybody else in the underground, Norman, Raymond, and Scott knew that under the War Measures Act they could be arrested. The threat was different only in degree from their experience of working under the Padlock Law. It seemed that one test of courage and dedication led to another. Whether it was mimeographing leaflets under the Padlock Law or hiding a Party leader under the War Measures Act, communists were becoming accustomed to thinking, in Scott's terms, of "political acts."

The underground directives were severe, and made life underground harder for those with families than for single people. Party members known to the police were told to move once a week; avoid public places; have contact with only one person; and send proxies to public meetings to report back. For every young person arrested, the police found ten older men. One Party member was arrested during his marriage ceremony, another at bingo, and another, who was told by the Party to move but delayed doing so, was picked up and sent to prison for three years. "But," laughed Henri Gagnon, "to be underground does not mean to be dead. They got those who were heads of families, who were known, but the Young Communist League continued to work. We'd give out thousands of pamphlets at a St. Jean Baptiste celebration, put up forty big Red flags, with a maple leaf and a hammer and sickle, on important public buildings. We would work fast and then disappear like lightning. It is easy to hide in a big city if you restrict yourself to the directives."

Henri Gagnon lived close to Emery Samuel, his contact with the Central Committee. They discussed the weekly directives from Stewart Smith and the new leadership group, in which they were advised to stop their flamboyant activities so that state repression would be obvious—so that, as Emery remembered, "we wouldn't be sowing bourgeois democratic illusions among the masses." The message "made Fred mad enough to spit and break glasses," and Emery, who had heard about "Tim [Buck] in the Kingston Jail, about different guys who really risked a lot," couldn't understand why the Party leaders wanted to hide.

The Party directed French-Canadian members to form an anti-conscription front with the Quebec nationalists, and Gilles was chosen to edit *La Voix du Peuple*, the newspaper that resulted from this collaboration. The paper, focusing on the position of Canada in the British Empire, on French Canada in Canada, on conscription, and on Quebec poverty, was published at 254 Ste. Catherine Street East, where Lea had been hit over the head by Quebec nationalists in 1935. In Quebec, where in 1941 seventy-two per cent of the population would vote "no" to conscription, the Party's anti-war policy was acceptable, while elsewhere it placed Party members in increasing danger. Willie, who worked underground within the Canadian army, had a clear indication of that danger on the morning when his anti-war pamphlet was delivered to his contingent. The colonel lined everybody up to tell them that he would find the communists responsible for the pamphlet and "hang them right away." Still, rank-and-file communists continued to keep the Party functioning. The golden, classless future, for which they lived, remained in view, if farther away. In members' minds this was a crisis. After the anti-fascist battle had begun, after the war was won, there would be time to talk. Now, it was a question of endurance, of "staying on the train of history" around this difficult bend.

Routine Party discipline was intensified by the new and stringent rules of life underground, especially the dictum that "the less you know, the less you can tell." Assuming everything was "Party work," a resident of a safe house didn't ask the business of the Russian-speaking gentlemen she passed coming out of her apartment, nor did Raymond, relieved that he no longer had to hobnob with the Quebec nationalists, stop to wonder why he was being directed into weapons research at the same time as Gilles was directed to work against the war. The rank-and-file faced the possibility of arrest and those in the army risked court martial, while the Party cynically hedged its bets, putting people, like pawns on a chessboard, in strategic positions. Unknown to the small group of amateurs in the underground, preparations for an even more dangerous game were being made, one that would result in information being supplied to the Soviet Union. Many of those selected for this activity would have a common history: conversion during the Spanish Civil War; membership in a closed group; experience underground. Those at the top level, who were setting them up, may have believed that the end justified the means, that the end would be a more just world. They dealt fast and loose with Party members such as Eda, who trusted the Party and would, therefore, "never question that there was something I couldn't do." She and others like her, who put their freedom on the line, were far removed from the machinations that would eventually thwart their hopes. Yet, it was their belief that kept the Party going. It was because, in Eda's words, "of the love we had for each other. We could move mountains."

[CHAPTER TEN]

Total War

AT 5:00 A.M., JUNE 22, 1941, "Lilly," Gilles's girlfriend, heard the radio blaring news of the German invasion of the Soviet Union. She looked at Gilles sleeping beside her and listened very carefully. She and Gilles were Party members. They wanted to get married, but Fred Rose had advised Gilles not to marry a Jewish girl because it would alienate the French-Canadian nationalists with whom he was working. This was one of the couple's secret, infrequent meetings. That June morning, as she listened to the radio, Lilly had "the most astute, independent political opinion of my life." She prodded Gilles awake and announced, "Now we can get married." Gilles, half-asleep, said that he would have to discuss it with Fred. "Fuck Fred," Lilly answered.

Without declaration, without the usual protocol, Hitler had broken the notorious Nazi-Soviet Pact. "Help the Soviet Union was not a great theoretical analysis for us," said Emery Samuel. "The war on the Eastern Front threatened another Paris Commune with no Left again for a century." The Party responded immediately to the abrupt reversal in the Comintern's line, changing its leaflets once more, so fast that Emery's wife, who was in charge of *Le Sentinel*, the newspaper at the Angus shop of the CPR, "had to take her newspapers away from one house, put them in the car, and dump them somewhere." The frenetic zig-zag in Party policy which, Emery suggested, "was not the most honourable part of our work," had straightened out for the duration of the "just" war. "For the first time," said Fred Rose, "it seemed that the war was of a completely anti-fascist, anti-Nazi character, and there would be a chance for a different world, not the status quo of capitalist control in countries outside the Soviet Union." Communists, free to answer the anti-fascist call, literally came out of the closets. They did so gladly, convinced by their sympathies and their select reading that, in Ed's words, "Germany didn't have a chance. The war had begun."

The opening of the Eastern Front radically changed the balance of world power and the thrust of international politics. Even if Western leaders were sceptical of Soviet military capabilities, they could not doubt the pivotal importance of the war in Russia. Hitler had won in Europe, and was on the offensive in North Africa. There was, in fact, no other front but the Eastern Front. Soon after the invasion of Russia, the United States and Great Britain, with Canada participating although not as yet a signatory, signed the First Protocol with the Soviet Union, establishing the procedures whereby vast quantities of military supplies, raw materials, equipment, and food could be sent to the Eastern Front. And with the Western Allies and the Soviets on the same fighting side, the Communist Party of Canada could hardly, for the government's purposes, remain illegal and underground. Not only was this now diplomatically untenable, it was a waste of the communist capacity to organize labour for the war effort.

Fred Rose, Slug, and Lester B. Pearson, assistant undersecretary of state for External Affairs, took a boat trip down the Ottawa River. A deal was struck in order, in Henri Gagnon's words, "to normalize the situation." Lawyers representing the communist leaders arranged with the federal police and the authorities that the communists give themselves up and, as Fred Rose described it, "go through the formality of spending a few days in jail." Fred Rose, Emery Samuel, Evariste Dubé, and Henri Gagnon, from Quebec, along with thirteen other prominent communists, came out of hiding and were interned on September 25, 1942. They were accused of being members of the Communist Party and supporting the subversive aims of that organization. Each detainee appeared in turn before the Advisory

Committee in the Matter of the Defence of Canada Regulation, which recorded their case histories and asked them, rhetorically, where they had been. Although for three years they had eluded arrest, they voluntarily subjected themselves to this questioning and other formalities as part of what Henri called "a political accord." Fred Rose readily admitted to all the charges against him and, to the surprise of the committee, appeared to be "proud" of the progress he had made in the Young Communist League and in the Communist Party of Canada. He explained that former "misunderstandings" had been cleared from his mind when the war became a just war, and that the Party had already begun to acquaint people with its new policy.

In all, the communist leaders spent eleven days in jail, playing checkers, taking their allotted exercise, and waiting to be released. On Saturday afternoon, as Henri Gagnon recalled, they were visited by Mitchell Hepburn, then premier of Ontario, "bringing chocolates,

Executive of the Communist Party of Canada before turning themselves over to the RCMP, September, 1942. (Front left to right) Henri Gagnon, Fred Rose, Tim Buck, Emery Samuel, Sam Lipshitz. (Back left to right) unidentified Ukrainian leader, Bill Kastan, Evariste Dubé, unidentified, Sam Carr, Willie Fortin, Stewart Smith, Stanley Ryerson.

like Santa Claus." Morale in Toronto's Don Jail was high, the prisoners buoyed by the prospect of freedom and of the vital work ahead. They were released in October 1942, with the signing of undertakings not to participate in the Communist Party of Canada, still illegal under Regulation 39C of the Defence of Canada Regulations. This last document accommodated the ambivalence of the Canadian government towards communists without affecting the resolve of the communist leaders, whose goals, as Fred Rose later said, were "to strengthen the ranks of the Party and to unite the country in the fight against the Nazis." To the satisfaction of both the government and the Party, the communists were loosed, to take their part in a total war effort.

Henri Gagnon joined the army, as did Norman, Sydney, Slug, and Ed. *La Voix du Peuple*, the successful Quebec anti-conscription paper, stopped publishing and Gilles, its editor, went overseas. Roland Dinel, who had joined the army with the outbreak of war in 1939 and deserted when the Nazi-Soviet Pact was signed, reapplied and was made a sergeant. At her office in the University Tower Building, Irene organized women's committees to collect war materials. Fred Taylor, unfit for active service, began lobbying for permission to paint workers in the munitions plants. Raymond was doing weapons research for the government and Scott Benning was working in the Department of Munitions and Supply. The Party used its skill in organizing and influence in the labour movement to propagate pro-war sentiment. Pep rallies were held among French Canadians in which fathers and sons, as many as twenty in an evening, would speak about why they had joined the fight against the Nazis, why both had felt compelled to make the same choice. In other halls, rented for mass-recruiting, union leader Bob Haddow, his Glasgow brogue rough and sweet, exhorted English-speaking workers to join the war effort. One communist, comparing the wartime rallies to Billy Graham revival meetings, recalled leaping to his feet, his fist raised, to proclaim. "I enlist! I enlist to fight the fascists!" The government recognized the depth of Red anti-fascism and recruited a high percentage of communists for secret-service training, parachuting them with radios and codes behind enemy lines to work with the resistance. So compulsive was the communist march to battle that Tim Buck, bumping into Sydney at Windsor Station, expressed satisfaction that he, at least, was "boarded out," not going overseas. Sydney, "itching to fight the Nazis," was astounded. "All the good people are enlisting," explained Tim. "We need good people here, too."

Back in his old job as Party organizer in Quebec, Fred Rose worked to establish the Party as a legal organization and to mobilize for the war effort, "which was part and parcel of the spur to unionization." By 1943 over 1,100,000 people, or almost twenty-five per cent of the total labour force, would be working in war industries. The total expenditure of the Canadian government for war materials would be ten times that of 1939. There was a greater number of workers in industry, especially in the war industry, and greater freedom to organize. Duplessis and the Union Nationale had been defeated in Quebec, and the Liberal administration, under Abelard Godbout, did not enforce the Padlock Law. Unions would become more powerful than they had ever been, forcing employers and governments to meet with them, getting agreements signed.

When the possibilities for organization arose in the large Vickers' aircraft plant in Montreal, Bob Haddow was chosen by the machinists to start the campaign for unionization. In Scotland, eighteen-year-old Haddow had been a member of the openly Marxist Independent Labour Party, and "the Clyde was openly in revolt at that time." The workers in the Vickers' plant were mostly shipyard workers from Scotland, brought over by the company to teach boat-building, and convincing them was duck soup: "They were nearly all Scots; you didn't have to talk 'union' to them. Oh, sure, right away. In the old country it was just like your bread and butter, you took it as part of your diet. A Party member gave me the names and I saw them and there was no trouble setting up in the Vickers' plant." Seventy-five per cent of aircraft manufacturing was done in Montreal: "We organized every one of them, every last one of them," said Haddow. "I don't know how many thousands of members we had, but it must have been well into two, three thousand. Fairchild's, Vickers', Nordair, Canadair, United Aircraft, all the plants around in here, and we spread across the country, and finally we had a national organization of aircraft workers."

At first it was tough. The government had to get after the management at Fairchild's and tell them, "You get along with the unions or else." Party policy was: negotiate; no strikes if you can avoid them. Haddow set up joint production committees in nearly every plant, with management and trade-union leaders sitting down and discussing how they could produce more. Optimum production for the war effort was the main objective. "Now we couldn't have accomplished that," Haddow remembered, "without improving the conditions of the workers. That had to be done because the big shots had taken advantage of the Depression, wages were at the lowest level, they just had to come up. And we managed to raise wages and satisfy the workers that they were getting a square deal." If the Party could find a place to put a communist in the union movement, in he went. Many young communists worked in the munitions plants. They handed out leaflets at 6:00 A.M. at the factory gates, sat on committees, visited workers, learned communist-style organizing. Bob Haddow: "I would go down and meet workers in their homes. I met hundreds this way. Every organizer had a list that he had to see within the next period of time. In his own home a guy's not afraid to open up and talk to you. It's private."

Harry and Stan Wingfield were stalwart organizers of the nine-thousand-strong, communist-led Canadian Seamen's Union. Harry, the funny, fast-thinking revolutionary from Montreal's Jewish ghetto, and Stan, the tough, fun-loving kid from the slums of St. Henri, had become Mutt-and-Jeff buddies. Eighteen and seventeen, and full of hope, they liked each other, admired each other; they loved each other, really. Harry, the son of parents who took part in the Russian Revolution, was six when he donned the Red scarf of the Young Pioneers and, in English, Yiddish, French, and Spanish, sang:

One, two, three
Pioneers are we

We're fighting for the working class
Against the bourgeoisie.

Harry attended the International Children's Camp where the fees were $2.50 per week, and where "some people couldn't pay and didn't." Cocky, smart, and sure that exploitation could be changed by a united struggle, he fought on behalf of the Seamen's Union for the same food for officers and crew, linen for the bunks, extra money for dirty work, an eight-hour day. "Throughout," he said, "the fantasy was always that of the conversion of the state into a socialist country in which, probably, I personally would play some extraordinary role." Thirsty for knowledge, Stan learned from Harry: "He had the right answers, with no bullshit or long theoretical lingo."

The two youths worked on the Black Gang. Stan's job was firing the engines. Beginning his shift, drained from the shift before, he'd take a slice bar, pushing it under the clinkers on one side of the furnace to break them up. Chewing a sweat rag to cut the smoke and dust, he hauled the ashes out. The trimmer cooled the ashes with a bucket of water, the steam came down to 200°, the engine slowed, then Stan "put on the blood." Shovelling over the coals from the other side of the furnace, he raked them to make them white-hot, adding fifteen shovels of coal into the furnace, cracking open the coal with a slice-bar so that it burned up to 220° again. Then, he would cool the furnace down, build it up again, stoking continuously for fourteen hours throughout the shift. It was hard work but, thanks to the union, conditions aboard ship were better. Stan: "By the end of the war, there was no longer separate food for the officers and for us, the ships were becoming cleaner, the officers were treating us like human beings."

The Canadian Seamen's Union was the largest affiliate of the sovereign power of Canadian labour, the Trades and Labor Congress (TLC), a strong union that would soon win the unheard-of victory of an eight-hour day. Harry and Stan remembered the remarkable wartime voyage of the *Cliffside*, sailing for China, carrying ammunition, an unassembled machine-gun factory, and some Mosquito bombers to Chiang Kai-shek. The communists on board organized a Party group which, along with the ship's committee, virtually took over the *Cliffside*. A small mimeograph machine published a bi-weekly paper, *The Masthead*, which Stan called "the most democratic paper you could have," because of the range of its contributors. Sparks, the wireless operator made available his broadcast facilities and the ship rang with calypso, "Joshua fought the Battle of Jericho," and political harangues. There were discussions about labour history and formal courses in subjects such as German. Everywhere the ship docked, Harry and Stan visited Party members, alerting them to the nature of the cargo they were carrying to the Chinese Nationalists. In Colombo, Ceylon, the ship was held up by dockers who wouldn't touch it. In Formosa dockers tried to sabotage the cargo by rolling the planes off the deck. A member of the Chinese Communist Party in Hong Kong pointed out that the People's Army was two hundred miles from Shanghai, and that the cargo would be bought immediately by the Red Army, so great was the corruption within the disintegrating Kuomintang. The *New China News* described the crew of the *Cliffside* as following in the tradition of the great Dr. Norman Bethune. In the spirit of equality and to assuage his colonial guilt, Harry took over the job of rickshaw *walla*. "It was a gem of a sight," Stan laughed, "to see Harry's little legs pumping like hell, pulling this rickshaw with the rickshaw driver sitting in the seat, a stunned look of amazement on his face, bearded Harry looking like a young Karl Marx."

In industries where there was no union, militants were assigned to organize one. Lea Roback and her friend Ray were sent to the RCA factory in St. Henri. Ray got work as an inspector and Lea got onto the line. Within a short period of time, they had organized the workers. In the thirties Lea had perfected her activist skills in the textile arena; and wartime organizing was, for her, "a terrific time." In 1942 the government, eager to avoid labour disputes and to keep industrial production high and economic expansion rolling, had introduced collective bargaining. Financially solvent unions reached their most advanced period ever. Artists, poets, and theatre people were brought in to address the newly formed workers' educational associations. It seemed that now that the necessities of survival were under control, the time had finally come to look to the full potential of the working-man.

A people's art seemed within the grasp of artists, such as Fred Taylor, who believed in it. Wanting to contribute to the war effort by using his special skill, aware of the war art produced during the First World War, Fred Taylor was becoming convinced of "the power of painting as a weapon." As he learned that Canada was making a tremendous contribution to the war through industrial production, becoming by 1944 the third greatest industrial nation on the Allied side, he determined to go into the munitions plants and paint the workers on the "Industrial Front." For a year, he wrote to Ottawa and visited influential officials who told him that this was not what art was all about. "It was," he said, "just breaking my heart." But finally he obtained C. D. Howe's permission to paint in the war plants. At the same time, through an historic conference organized by the painter André Biéler and Queen's University, the Federation of Canadian Artists was formed, and for the first time Taylor found a sense of comradeship between artists across the country and others like himself wanting "to integrate the contribution of artists into the war effort." Fred immediately went into the Angus shop of the CPR, where workers were making tanks, and he sent word nation-wide to his contacts in the federation that they, too, could go into the plants. "The first important painting I did was of two men working in the very difficult and highly skilled drilling of the nose-casting of a tank. And I was able to dramatize that they were cooperating." Eschewing elitist art themes, he worked continuously in the factories and the mines, one of the earliest painters to honour workers with all the respect his art could offer. His wartime art provides the definitive record of what he wanted the public to see: "the valuable work on the industrial front." A year after he had started painting, Fred Taylor was at a communist conference where he was approached by one of the workers from the Workers' Educational Association, to which he had once presented his work. Taylor recognized the man, although

For Victory and After—Applying the Tracks, Fred Taylor (oil on canvas)
National Museums of Canada

it was his emotion, not his features, which now caught the painter's attention. "You've changed my life," the man said. "All my married life my wife bought pictures of horses even if there was no money. It made me mad. Seeing the painting of the two men struggling together, I understood that paintings speak. Now I understand why she did it." The realization had dissolved a hard anger between husband and wife. Overcome with gratitude, the man shook Fred Taylor's hand. "I came back from work," he continued, "and my wife sent me to the grocery store. When I returned, the whole kitchen was full of my best friends, a bunch of people she didn't approve of for the most part. Then she kissed me"—he grinned— "right in front of them." Fred Taylor laughed. "It was such a reward for me," he later said. "As well as an appreciation of my work, I was reaching an audience which is what all art-workers want. Why did I join the communists? It was like that."

Wartime. Differences were allowed because there was a common enemy. Even the left-wing theatre was acceptable enough for the New Theatre Group to go to Ottawa to perform *We Beg to Differ* for the troops. Eaton's, the largest department store in Montreal and owned by a long-established English-Canadian dynasty, flew the hammer and sickle. Stalin was on the cover of *Time*. Across Canada, Soviet-Canadian friendship societies were formed, as were many organizations sending aid to the U.S.S.R. Mackenzie King and Cardinal Villeneuve spoke at Russian relief rallies. The National Film Board of Canada made a pro-Russian film called *Our Northern Neighbour*. Paul Robeson, the legendary Black singer, filled the fifteen-thousand-seat Montreal Forum in a benefit performance for medical aid for the beleaguered Soviets.

Although people today know very little about the war on the Eastern Front, the world, then, followed its progress as if its very life depended on the outcome. In the first phase of the war the Russians suffered staggering losses. At the same time German submarines destroyed supply convoys to England, Japanese routed the Allies in the Far East, and a large part of the American Pacific fleet was sunk at Pearl Harbor. Leningrad, placed under siege in September 1941, would not be freed for over nine hundred days, not until January 1944, and the number of dead at the Battle of Leningrad would be ten times that at Hiroshima, a sacrifice without parallel in our times. Germans occupied all the Baltic states, as well as the cities of Kiev, Kharkov, and Odessa. They held entire sections of Russia, while the Western democracies looked on, in terror. When the Russian people began to rise up, the anti-Nazi world took a deep breath. For the first time since Hitler had begun his march across Europe in 1933, Nazi armies were driven back, defeated in open battle. But in late August 1942, as the British retreated from Rommel's tanks in Africa, the Germans broke through to the Russians' beloved Volga River. The Nazi offensive threatened to swallow up Stalingrad, a victory that would have ended the war. For six tense months the world waited on the outcome of the bitterest, most savage, most heroic fighting of the war, in the buildings and streets of Stalingrad. Meanwhile, the Russians readied their Stalingrad offensive. In January 1943 the unprecedented defeat of Hitler's armies by the Red Army shook the world. After Stalingrad all of Russia and all of the democratic world dared to hope that they might win the war. For communists in Canada, "This was a high point, after Stalingrad" as Fred Rose remembered. "The whole spirit changed. There was no time before when the spirit had been like this."

There was strong popular support in the West for the Soviet and Communist Party call for a second front, an invasion of Europe by Britain and America. Not only workers and intellectuals, but people in government and military circles respected the overriding reality that the Soviet Union was halting the fascist advance. After the Soviet's long and valiant defence of Stalingrad, it seemed that Hitler could be overcome. In the spring of 1943 the first formal Russian diplomatic mission arrived in Canada. Britain, the United States, and Canada, as a new signatory, signed a Third Protocol with the U.S.S.R. pledging their cooperation for the twelve-month period from July 1943 to June 1944. Prime Minister Mackenzie King's letter in June 1943 to Feodor Gousev, Soviet ambassador in Ottawa, acknowledged that "the governments of Canada, the United States, and the United Kingdom deeply appreciate the great contribution of the Union of Soviet Socialist Republics to our common cause, and the continuing vital importance of the Soviet front. They realize the extent to which war has already consumed or destroyed Soviet resources, and they appreciate her urgent future needs. They, therefore, desire to continue to provide

Factory poster by Allan Harrison for the Quebec Committee
for Allied Victory, 1943

the Soviet Union with the maximum assistance possible in the
form of military supplies, raw materials, equipment and food."[1]
On the occasion of the twenty-fifth anniversary of the Red Army,
February 23, 1943, Mackenzie King, speaking in the House of
Commons, extolled the virtues of the fighting force that had given
"all the free peoples who have been resisting Nazi aggression so
much cause for encouragement and thanksgiving." He expressed
"the fervent hope of all Canadians" that the established diplomatic

relations between Canada and the Soviet Union were but the prelude to "a long period of mutual understanding between our two peoples, both in the conduct of the war and in the maintenance of a firm and durable peace." In July 1943 the Germans threw fifty army divisions and twenty-seven hundred tanks into their last Eastern offensive, at Kursk. Their defeat in the titanic armoured struggle against the Soviets changed history. After Kursk, no one doubted the final outcome of the war. The Soviets were heroes, vital allies. Ideological differences took second place to the pro-Soviet euphoria, and public sentiment was sympathetic to the Communist Party. Among militants there was a great spirit of belief and enthusiasm: belief that victory seemed assured and enthusiasm for a more just Canada that would, after the war, relate peacefully to all members of the Grand Alliance.

CHAPTER ELEVEN

A Communist Member
of Parliament

IN AUGUST 1943 the Communist Party of Canada was renamed the
Labour Progressive Party, and it began a concerted drive to carve
a place for itself in the mainstream of Canadian politics. In a five-
cornered election race Fred Rose was presented as a candidate in his
home riding of Montreal-Cartier. There was now no application of
the Padlock Law to dampen the idealism and devotion with which
communists undertook to elect their candidate—"The Party was
legal," Fred Rose remembered with pleasure—and by this time
their influence was felt. There were about 2,500 Party members
in Quebec. They included 500 French Canadians, and the highest
proportion of professionals and intellectuals of any provincial
Communist Party. The conviction of all had been tempered like
steel by the virulent anti-communism of the previous epoch. Eda,
Bob Haddow, Henri Gagnon, Lea, Emery, Sydney, Annette, Slug,
along with each and every Party member, threw themselves into the
six-week campaign, and a smooth-running election machine went
into action. "We each took a poll, a couple of hundred names," said
Sydney. "We canvassed four nights a week, door to door. Not a single
house missed an election visit by a Party member or sympathizer."
Fred Rose's campaigners talked with the voters and then left a
pamphlet, *Life in Cartier*, which outlined the Party program:
victory over fascism, a fight against antisemitism, and full rights
for French Canadians. At least 120 meetings were held in houses

and yards. Large rallies were organized in halls and in open areas, such as Fletcher's Field, the park in Sydney's neighbourhood where unemployed men had slept, covered with newspapers, during the Depression. The campaign literature was produced completely by Party members, many of them among Canada's most talented graphic artists, painters, writers, and designers. People worked hard and for no pay. Allan, respected for his striking and evocative posters—against the war in Spain and for Russian relief—turned his hand to election posters. Dead-tired at night, sometimes using the facilities of the ad agency where he was art director, he changed the concept of political posters, designing, for example, a poster in which the elector saw, not only the face of Fred Rose, but also, in the background, the ward outlined in white. "If you lived on any of those streets you could vote for Fred Rose," Allan remembered. "We pasted the posters up on fences, three or four deep and twelve feet wide, very attractive, made a big blast on the streets—St. Lawrence, St. Denis, Roy, Colonial—everywhere there was a fence. This I had learned in Europe."

With the solidarity and strength of the communist movement at the time, the dirty tricks of the opposition were short-circuited. "Our influence was so great that the Liberal party could not organize their telegraphing machine because we had friends who reported their activity," said Fred Rose. A group of seamen broke into the Liberal party office where the cards were kept for planning the false votes and destroyed them. Those who had been door-to-door canvassers for the Party, and so knew the constituents, were scrutineers at the polls. Election day was rough, "an old-fashioned donnybrook in Cartier" was what the *Montreal Star* called it. Four newsmen were beaten up, one by a fist well supplied with brass knuckles. An official in the main committee room of the Liberal candidate, Lazarus Phillips, then assured the tattered newsmen that they would have their confiscated film back the next day and admitted that the gang that had attacked them was "pretty stupid to mix with reporters." One of the reporters snuck unobserved into the back of Phillips's committee room, where he saw lengths of lead

Montreal-Cartier by-election poster designed by Allan Harrison,
August, 1943.

pipe, wooden clubs, and other weapons. Fred Rose: "The roving
gangs of hoodlums working for the Liberal party couldn't function
because the people were in the streets to drive them away. There
were thousands of aircraft workers outside our headquarters, and
the goons couldn't attack. The streets were full of people."

With the results in from fifteen polling stations, it was clear
that the race was between Fred Rose and the nationalist candidate,
Paul Masse. Party members listened to the election results outside
Rose's headquarters, cheering wildly when their candidate was
ahead, booing Masse's victories. At 11:00 P.M., August 9, 1943, the
final results were announced: David Lewis, CCF, 3,313; Lazarus

Phillips, Liberal, 4,180; Paul Masse, Bloc Populaire, 5,639; Fred Rose, LPP, 5,789. Fred Rose had won by a hair. The Communist Party had elected its first member to the Parliament of Canada. Within minutes the street was filled with people in spontaneous, joyful celebration. "Everyone started hugging each other," said Eda, "crying, jumping, cheering, running to other people, hugging them. Fred spoke with shy humility, overwhelmed by the tremendous love people were feeling for him and for each other." Thousands and thousands of people blocked The Main and Fred Rose's car was lifted up, practically carried, by the throng. Elation and hope as thick as the crowd mixed with the August air.

> The earth shall rise on new foundations
> We have been nought, we shall be all.

"It was the kind of joy you can't describe," Eda remembered. "It reaches from the tips of your toes to the roots of your hair. It's something you feel so deeply about that it's like having every part of you vibrate. That final step, winning the election, means that everybody understands, that if you work together life can be beautiful. So few have the kind of pleasure I felt on that one fantastic evening." All things were possible. The Liberals had been ousted from their stronghold. The nationalists, even though running on an anti-conscription platform, had been defeated.

Higher by a head than most of the people pressing against him, Slug spotted Sydney, his arm around Annette, her arm around Eda, her arm around Emery, Emery's arm intertwined with Henri's, a single interwoven form. Slug made his way, moving crossways through the crowd, to lift his brother off the ground, hugging, hugging, kissing his face, his eyes, the centre of his forehead.

> Bandiera rossa la trionferà
> Evviva il communismo e la libertà!

The two men held each other close, listening to the shouts and cheers of the crowd. A communist leader, Fred Rose, had been chosen by the people to represent them in the Canadian House of Commons. It seemed the fulfilment of a dream.

Internationally, communism was being soft-pedalled. Stalin, in his need for a second front, dissolved the Communist International in October 1943, pledging, to Roosevelt and Churchill, "a strengthening of the united front of the Allies." At their first meeting, in November 1943, in Tehran, the Big Three assuaged one another and put a curse on the world, tacitly agreeing that each would have a "sphere of influence." Stalin left the conference with the reacquisition of Poland and a firm commitment that the second front would be opened in May.

Communist parties around the world reacted quickly to news of the dissolution of the Communist International and of the lessening of ideological hatred between the Soviets and their allies. "The concept developed," said David, a Party organizer, "that the alliance against Hitler would continue into a period of peace and new social conditions would make a different transition to the new world order." It was at this point that the Canadian Communist Party, renamed the Labour Progressive Party, had its structure changed from a Leninist one, based on small units, to that of an educational organization. Large clubs, with as many as one hundred members, met weekly in rented halls and held open forums where public figures, including reform-minded liberals, gave lectures. The Political Bureau of the LPP praised the federal cabinet for "projecting policies of international cooperation and social reform along Tehran lines after the war." David, who was serving as an army lieutenant overseas during the war, discussed these new developments with communists in the service and found that "they were generally accepted." The thaw showed in election results: it has been noted that "almost every major city west of Montreal had at least one alderman either belonging to the LPP or closely associated with it"; communists J. B. Salsberg and A. A. MacLeod sat in the Ontario legislature; MP Fred Rose spoke to electors in fifteen-minute radio broadcasts from Ottawa and at mass meetings in Montreal. "Communist representatives regularly appeared in respectable, official surroundings, on platforms with bourgeois politicians," wrote a contemporary historian. They were quoted in the press. Dedicated to an all-out war against Hitler, associated in the minds of many with the prestigious Red Army, influential in the growing labour movement, communists were sometimes even respected for their beliefs.

And if not respected, now communists were at least a force to contend with. Canadian government mandarins, watching the Red Star rising in the East, looked on as local communists rode the wave of popular support. After the Soviet victory at Stalingrad, there was no telling which way the post-war wind would blow. Interested or, more likely, conscious of the shifting tides of political fortune, Norman Robertson, under-secretary of state for External Affairs, met with Fred Rose, as did Mackenzie King, who incited the communist member of Parliament to his office to talk.

"Their interests happened to coincide," said a communist who was in Ottawa at the time. "For a politician like Mackenzie King the more information he could get from all sides, the better." Communists held responsible positions in Ottawa and in the army, working with Liberals and socialists, some of whom, like them, had been stamped by the Depression. One such, Alex Skelton, was the son of Oscar Douglas Skelton, who, until his death in 1941, had been Prime Minister Mackenzie King's closest advisor on all public affairs, domestic as well as external. Like many socially conscious people, Alex Skelton, according to Stanley Ryerson, had "got involved in progressive circles in the thirties." He showed a friendly interest in Communist Party leaders and he knew economist Eric Adams, a Party member, very well. During the war, he and Adams worked closely together in the office of the Foreign Exchange Control Board, Skelton in charge of Research and Adams in charge of Statistics and Research.

The Depression and the Civil War in Spain had given communists and reform Liberals, like Skelton, a common humanitarian reference, and for a decade before and during the Second World War, excepting the two years of the Nazi-Soviet Pact, they made common cause in the fight against fascism. Cooperation—to support the war effort, curtail strikes, even elect Liberal candidates—was a tenet of the unofficial Liberal-Labour coalition. The coalition involved the Liberals in the labour movement, and it gave the communists both a more respectable public image and the opportunity to gain on the CCF. Harry, in the Canadian Seamen's Union, remembered that the conservative Liberal James Sinclair, who was minister of fisheries, appeared unofficially at one of the many second-front rallies organized by the communists. "There was an undercurrent of sarcasm but an acceptance of bedfellows," Harry said. By 1945 Party organizer Sam Carr was coming to Ottawa to meet with prominent Liberals to discuss communist support of Liberal candidates in the upcoming election. The Soviets were now "our northern neighbour," and Canadian communists no longer grotesquely "foreign." In the emotional climate of the war against fascism they were often admired for their willingness to sacrifice their personal comfort and tentatively accepted by some for the values and issues they defended. As Irene Kon so poetically described it, "There were not the terrible splits that occurred after the war when everybody sort of disappeared from some of their ideas."

Yet, although everything was friendly on the surface, those in the know saw that at the top military and diplomatic levels, in the army and in the civil service, the Soviets were not really accepted like the Americans or the British. The opening of the second front in Europe met with a two-year resistance, as did the very idea of an alliance with the Russian communists. Communists from Section 13—in the army, air force, navy, at the National Research Council, on wartime agencies and joint American-British-Canadian planning boards—often saw first-hand the unstated hostile reaction of the Canadian establishment to the Soviet Union. "They called them 'Bolshies,' said Norman, who worked with army personnel. "No

Poster designed by Harry Mayerovitch,
National Film Board of Canada, 1944

good mentioning that we were allies. They'd say 'Aw, Jeez, you don't believe that crap. Allies today, enemies tomorrow.'" Scott Benning, who was a senior civil servant in the Department of Munitions and Supply, said he would hear British and American leaders boast that when they were finished with the Germans, they would take on the Russians. "The fascists, reluctantly, were a short-term enemy." He recalled meetings in which military men, forced by protocols to send fieldpieces to the U.S.R.R., contrived to send along with them the wrong handbooks and ammunition.

For someone like Scott Benning, who had at first believed in the good intentions of the Soviet Union because of its support for the Spanish struggle against fascism, socialist and anti-fascist values were one and the same. "The back-stabbing and double-dealing he saw," recalled his son, "were a real source of anger and pain." It was "staggering to Benning to sit in on meetings with people who equated Nazism with communism, whose preference, at the war's end, was to make peace with the Nazis. Benning believed that if there were hope for the future—full employment, social justice, racial equality—the example was the Soviet Union, and he found it intolerable to watch Allied military men making tactical gains on the Soviets through the war on the Eastern Front. Raymond Boyer, working in the McGill Research Centre among scientists and military personnel, corroborated Benning's impression: "The prevalent feeling was that the British and Americans were friends and allies, but the Russians were not." Drinking with his colleagues, Boyer was shocked to find that "they all admired the German war-machine enormously, much more than they admired our own." Even though the Western Allies had, in international agreements, promised the Soviet Union "the maximum assistance possible in the form of military supplies, raw materials, equipment, and food," that was a paper reality. As Colonel John Henry Jenkins, director of Military Operations and Planning, Department of National Defence, later testified, "Information regarding experiments that were in the laboratory stage or research they were not supposed to have." Raymond was forced to confront the Allies' double standard when he and others discovered a process to make the best existing conventional explosive, RDX, in much larger quantities than had previously been possible.[1] When, in 1942, the Soviets asked the Allies about the important new development, C.D. Howe, Canada's minister of munitions and supply, expressed a willingness to make the information available but was advised against doing so by the Americans. The Soviet request was refused. The decision, for Raymond, was insupportable: fighting for their lives, the Soviet anti-fascists had been denied access to a potentially life-saving discovery.

In 1943 the U.S.S.R. set up an intelligence agency in its Ottawa embassy to collect political and military information from its allies.

Colonel Zabotin was put in charge of military intelligence and Sam Carr, organizer of the LPP and a member of the Russian Communist Party since the twenties, ran the Canadian side of the operation with the help of Fred Rose. It is, unfortunately, not difficult to conjecture about how leading members of the Communist Party became involved with Soviet intelligence. A connection between national Communist parties and the Soviet Union had existed since the formation of the Communist International in 1919. Fred Rose and Sam Carr had grown up in a Party whose loyalty was to the Soviet Union, the geo-political mecca for communists. Ruthless in its endeavours to supply its wartime needs, the Communist Party of the Soviet Union cashed in on this allegiance. Using Communist parties throughout the world, it drew respected communist leaders and even resistance fighters into its military intelligence operations. Leopold Trepper, who headed the Red Orchestra, the Russian wartime intelligence network in Europe, wrote that, in Germany, "what happened was absolutely incredible. Known communist militants became leaders of the Schulz-Boysen and Harnack groups [Russian intelligence networks]—Wilhelm Guddork and John Seig as official representatives of the German Communist Party."[2] With hindsight, even communists can see that the use of national Communist Party leaders for Soviet espionage was "absolutely incredible." As Stanley Ryerson said recently, "If you want a party that will be the government of a country, you don't do that." But during the war, Soviet intelligence did not have to do much convincing. David, a Party organizer, pointed out that "it was a state espionage operation, not a political recruitment; but Communist Party people were susceptible to being recruited."

Fred Rose, for example, had grown up in the Communist Party, having dedicated himself to Party work at the age of seventeen. The electrician's apprentice had sat on the International Executive Committee of the Young Communist League in Moscow. As a Communist Party candidate, he had been elected to the Canadian House of Commons. The Conservative opposition leader put a red rose in the vase on his table, and his secretary, a conscript from the youth movement, ate with him in the cafeteria "because no one else would sit with him." Soon, however, he was on joking terms with Prime Minister Mackenzie King, under-secretary of state Norman Robertson, other members of Parliament, prominent journalists, and Soviet diplomats. He began to develop attributes that prompted his comrades to call him, fondly and not so fondly, "a cocky little bastard." His accent betraying his origins, he prefaced his speeches to his constituency with the phrase "Speaking as a member of Parliament." He made it known to comrades in Ottawa that, "when I was talking to Norman Robertson, I told him…" He allowed himself a relationship with Freda Linton, "a luscious woman with a louche in one eye," who, according to another secretary, was attracted to him because "she was working with him, close to that brain, that sense of humour, that twinkle in his eye." The Party "had a magic about it" and, more than anyone else, Fred Rose was invested with that magic. Yet, even so, Fred Rose was moved more by the disastrous course of world events than by his personal good fortune. He set the Allies' resistance to helping the Soviets against the terrible suffering of the Russian people, and he rebelled against the international community's hostility towards communism. Bella, an early activist, remembered: "The war was a hard time for Fred. He saw millions of Russians dying, and he felt that the Western powers wanted more to die. He felt powerless to help." When the occasion arose to help the Soviet Union, as well as his position in and the cause of what he knew as international communism, it was logical that Fred Rose would rise to the occasion. Perhaps, as his son-in-law said in another context, "He had to be a sport." Or, perhaps it was simply as Bella remembered, that "there was no choice for a communist. It was a situation where the Soviet Union was bleeding to death, and the government was refusing to give them information that would help in the development of their own defences. We just felt that anybody in a position to help, would help and should help. It was as straightforward as that." The motivation was there and the particular militant, sectarian state of mind of the communist, along with its corollary, an egocentric hubris, was fortification sufficient to the task.

Fred Rose approached communists from Section 13, such as Norman, Raymond Boyer, and Scott Benning, who felt the Soviet Union was being denied help in a life-and-death struggle. They, as members of the closed groups, were perfect contacts. They were not known communists, yet they had had experience working underground. Because of the Padlock Law and the War Measures Act, they knew that, in the words of Raymond Boyer, "sometimes a revolutionary has to do illegal things even if he doesn't want to." As Norman recalled, "We accepted the illegal aspect. It's illegal but whose law is it: …the law of the people who double-cross an ally." Even though it was, as Stanley Ryerson said, "a partial non sequitur" to argue that their previous work would lead to their being arrested as spies, it was largely these Party members whom Soviet intelligence would organize and draw upon.

Raymond Boyer was working at McGill University and with the Sub-committee on Explosives of the National Research Council, refusing on patriotic grounds to accept any money for his work. When, in 1943, the Montreal *Gazette* published a government news release, along with a picture of Raymond, announcing the new RDX process, Fred asked Raymond about his work. "We have stumbled upon a process for making RDX in large quantities," Raymond told him. Soon after, Raymond heard that the Soviet Technical Mission visiting Canada was having difficulty getting information about the new process, and it seemed very important to him that the Russians continue pressing the government for it. He told Fred Rose that "there was a pilot plant at Shawinigan. Big plants, production plants would be built. Get the Technical Mission to ask for the graphic formula and the engineering to build a plant." Raymond and Fred spoke twice more after that. Raymond listed the materials that went into the new laboratory process, "so the Technical Mission would know what to ask for," and he described the potential of RDX as an explosive, "so they would ask." As far as Raymond was concerned, talking to Fred Rose about what he was doing was a unique existential choice: "I don't know how many other people he [Fred Rose] spoke to. I had no idea what was going on. No idea. Not even a suspicion that others were doing it. Yet, I knew Norman intimately."

To a great extent Raymond Boyer spoke to Fred Rose because the Soviet Union was not being accepted or treated by the Allies as a full partner. "Therefore, it was not as efficient, as effective an ally as it could have been." The now-forgotten exigency was there. "Today we know we won the war, but the end of 1942 was a low point," Raymond recalled. "We were losing everywhere. German subs were sinking almost all the ships on the way to the front. The Nazi army was on the Volga. The United States hadn't even started to get going. Victory was a long way from assured." Raymond had spoken out many times in support of the British, Americans, and Canadians sending a technical mission to the Soviet Union and of a similar mission being sent by the Russians to Canada. He felt that it was vital that there be a closer scientific liaison between East and West. Twenty million Russians would die on the Eastern Front alone, and possibly another twenty million civilians would be casualties. There was no question in Raymond's mind that the Soviet people deserved all the help they could get. As General Douglas MacArthur said on February 23, 1943, on the twenty-fifth anniversary of the Red Army, "The world situation at the present time indicates that the hope of civilization rest on the worthy banners of the courageous Russian army." Sharing the knowledge of the improved RDX process with the Soviet mission "was not a hard decision." For Raymond it would have been more difficult to stand idly by. Christopher Caldwell's theory, that it is the disunity of theory and practice which is responsible for alienation, was important to him. Helping the Soviet Union in this way "didn't imply any kind of betrayal" and was, for Raymond, what any person of conscience, in similar circumstances, should do. Neither did he think of it as a dangerous decision. The anti-Russian hysteria of the post-war years had not yet begun. The "official secret" stamp was not as comprehensive or as inviolate as it would later appear to be. In the McGill chemistry lab where he worked, "security measures were so childish they were practically non-existent. There was not a locked door anywhere." Even though the research team naturally accumulated many government documents, "dozens of students passed through the lab every day." Mili-

tary District 4 did finally send a young officer to make sure that
security measures were instituted— "He gave us a whole lecture on
security," said Raymond— "but it was the first time we had heard
the word 'officially.'" The date was May 1945, beginning of the end
of Raymond's habitation in his scientific garden of Eden.

Scott Benning was more conscious than Raymond of the risk
he was taking. The government-run Department of Munitions and
Supply where he worked was staffed mainly by military personnel,
and there was some, if a loose, notion of security. "He was aware
of some danger," said his son, "but it was not a crucial factor in his
decision. The choice itself was very clear." Scott Benning's anger at
the back-stabbing he saw in his department meetings was deeply
felt, and he seemed to have been waiting for the opportunity to
act. He was relieved to do what he had to do, what would make
him sleep at night. "I couldn't have lived with myself afterwards if I
hadn't done something," he later told his son.

Norman, along with other communists working in Ottawa,
was riding high, feeling that he was doing something in his
department that would lay the foundation for a strong central
government, a government that would respond to the post-war
need for housing and social-welfare programs. His first conversation with Fred Rose about helping the Soviets had to do with
his skill as a writer, and he was not averse to providing the Soviets
with commentaries on the Canadian way of life. Norman had always
acted with courage and conviction, that is, it wasn't getting caught
that worried him, "because that would have been martyrdom."
Neither did he feel that he would be cheating Canada out of anything;
rather, he would be enhancing the Russians' superficial knowledge
of Canada and "acting as an ally." The problem was that "no matter
how committed a communist you are, it is hard to overcome what
you were brought up to believe before you had the new credo." Yet,
when he raised his moral qualms with Fred, Fred would screw up
his face as if he'd noticed a bad smell and, brushing the intrusion
away with his hand, say, "*Feh. Schmuck.*" It was a classical old-guard
putdown. Norman was left to review his position in the light of

a personal history of "turning my principles into action." He had been a member of a committee that had tried to help Canadians coming back from Spain: "a very unpopular task." But he felt that it had been "a worthwhile thing since nobody could deny that Franco was a fascist tool in Spain and to close one's eyes to those things would only mean war and loss for Canada." He had been a member of the Quebec Committee for Allied Victory, which advocated the necessity of very close cooperation with the Soviet Union "in the interests not only of Canada, but of all people in fighting against the Axis." He felt that he had been "true to my real convictions and feelings in doing this, although because of the branding of this work as communistic I lost my job." He had, he reasoned, been faced with making very difficult decisions that had, in retrospect, been right, and he was proud of the position he had taken. He believed that the political commentaries he would write would help Soviet-Canadian relations in the post-war period, and he expected reciprocity in the form of discussion between the scientists he was working with and Russian scientists. "It was only after a great struggle on my part and as a result of that great struggle that I could bring myself eventually to accept this kind of work as something that would, in the long run—I was conscious that it would be a long run—advance the whole cause of international cooperation."

At any rate, in wartime Ottawa, Soviet diplomats and officials were the toast of the town. They were sought after for their boisterous energy, their entertaining stories, their generosity with unrationed liquor, their mammoth parties. Colonel Letson, from the quartermaster-general's office, described Lieutenant-Colonel Motinov, the assistant military attaché at the Soviet embassy, as "a very cheery chap" and liked him "immensely." In this context, for Norman, the opportunity to meet a Russian was "sort of exotic." Believing in benevolent Soviet internationalism, he filled his first report with "lots of political stuff." He thought at the time that he knew what he was doing but, as he would later realize: "I had no conception of the extent of it." The Party and the network were too well organized to give him a clue, and he was left like Raymond with the comfortable assumption that his contribution was unique, "a small informal thing that was happening because I was in Ottawa at the time."

Rank-and-file Party members knew nothing about "the network." They worked and lived completely in the context of an Allied front within which their Party was finally legitimate. Conditions seemed to be getting better: wages were up; seamen looked forward to keeping the deep-sea fleet promised in recognition of their wartime work; munitions workers bought golden Victory Bonds. On June 6, 1944, the Allies landed in Normandy. There were celebrations in the streets of Moscow, rejoicing in the West. D-Day! Stalin applauded the invasion as "a brilliant success for our Allies.... The history of wars does not know of an undertaking comparable to it for breadth of conception, grandeur of scale and mastery of execution." Without doubt, the war would soon be over.

Lea's heart was full to bursting. With one small part of her mind she noted the details of the scene, for posterity, while every fibre of her being was bathed in the happiness of it. The previous night Paul Robeson had played Othello at His Majesty's Theatre. Now he was at Fred's, talking and singing for friends—for Fred and Fanny, for the munitions-plant workers, for Lea. The presence of the man was overwhelming. It was not so much his physical size—he was six feet three and weighed 240 pounds—but the fire in him. A flaming dignity of spirit made him larger than life itself. As Paul began to sing, his deep, throbbing bass-baritone sounded every chord of love and strength in Lea's wiry frame.

> When Israel was in Egypt land
> Let my people go
> Oppressed so hard they could not stand
> Let my people go.

The spiritual was about Paul's fight against Jim Crow, Lea's battle against exploitation—it was a cry for freedom. Note by note, the refrain soared, in tandem with Lea's spirit.

Go down Moses
Way down in Egypt's land
Tell old Pharaoh to
Let my people go.

Lea was thinking about people fighting to free themselves from fascism as Paul began to speak about the working people of Montreal, "people like you who have a right to think of a better life, a more decent life in a world where we can afford that life." He gestured to Fred, and said, "In going back and forth to Canada for many years I've met with him and talked with him and he's given me often such a fine picture of Canada and has shown such great love of his land and great love of the people of his land." As the room filled with the warmth of conversation, Lea looked and saw the twinkle in Fred's eye. This ambiance—friends, talk, good music, comradeship—was what he loved best. "Anybody could have been a leader in the early days—all it took was guts"—but Lea was glad it was he.

Paul Robeson stood up, cocked his hand over one ear to hear himself better, and began to sing "Native Land," the unofficial Soviet anthem. Lea, poised on the edge of her chair, attended. The room hummed, swayed, and sang.

Everywhere throughout our mighty union
All our people flourish free from strife
Side by side the white, the dark, the yellow
Live in peace to reach a better life.
But that now the foe has tried to smash us
Tried to desolate our land so dear,
Like the thunder, like the sudden lightning
We now give our answer sharp and clear.

Lea could taste the hope in her mouth. Paul Robeson, a Black American, singing the Soviet anti-Nazi anthem to English, Jewish, and French Canadians in Montreal. It was symbolic of the internationalism that was soon to come. "We will do it," thought Lea. "We will win over the enemies of mankind, the fascists, and we will make a better world."

As the Red Army fought its way through Eastern Europe, towards Berlin, the American and British troops battled in the West. The second great Allied summit, Yalta, was held in February 1945, with the Russians on the doorstep of the German stronghold. Roosevelt mediated between the mutually hostile Churchill and Stalin, and the Big Three agreed that Russia would help the Americans with the Japanese and that Poland would be its reward. After Tehran and Yalta, most Communist Party members believed that the links for a civilized world had been forged. As Party organizer David remembered, "We published a pamphlet called *Teheran and After*, anticipating a peaceful transition to a new world order." Then, quite unexpectedly, in April, Moscow changed the Party line. The first sign that something different was expected of North American communists came in an attack of Earl Browder. In an article in *L'Humanité*, Jacques Duclos, a French communist leader well-known for his ties to Moscow, denounced Earl Browder, then head of the American Communist Party, for reducing the American party to an adjunct of Roosevelt's Democratic Party: Browder was guilty of "a notorious revision of Marxism, sowing dangerous, opportunistic illusions." "Browder was as astounded as everybody else," recalled David. "He had been following the complete and unequivocal Moscow line." "Browderism," as the old Party line was now called, was out. David: "One moment Earl Browder was the greatest living Marxist in North America, and the next morning, no more Browder as secretary-general....The line changed because the world was moving into a new international phase."

The Soviet Union wanted to consolidate their Eastern frontier at the line where the Red Army had stopped. They denounced wartime cooperation as "rank opportunism" and collaboration with the "bourgeois" parties as "revisionism." Pre-war Communist parties would be reactivated and would be counted on to support

Soviet foreign policy. As communists buried the memory of the Liberal-Labour coalition and the "No-Strike Pledge," the new American president, Harry Truman, took the opportunity when addressing a New York crowd on Navy Day to announce the post-war American line. He repudiated Roosevelt's policies of international cooperation and noted that, "after past wars, the unity among allies, forged by a common peril, has tended to wear out as the danger passed." In May 1945 the war with Germany was over, and the thin veil of cooperation had already begun to shred.

When Fred Rose ran for re-election in Montreal-Cartier, Paul Robeson sent a recorded endorsement to the electors that contained a curiously prophetic warning:

> Your boys in Canada have fought a brave fight, they have died on many fronts to establish a people's world. We have that kind of world in our grasp but dangerous forces have again arisen, forces which up to this time we thought were struggling for a democratic world. These people must not win. They must not take from the people the fruits of their victory and make the sacrifice of no account.

Fred Rose was re-elected with a large majority that included considerable support from those in the armed services. In his first term as Cartier's member of Parliament, he had backed family allowances, lobbied for decent jobs for the "365,000 men in Europe coming back," and warned that "deplorable" slum-housing should be corrected by means of a long-term plan for post-war reconstruction. He had kept in touch with his constituency: mailing his speeches to them, reporting to them on the radio, speaking at mass rallies. On weekends he had received a steady flow of electors at his home in Montreal. Rose's support for a second term as MP almost doubled. It was a vote of confidence in continuing social progress. People wanted to resume their normal lives: to raise kids, go to the movies

Saturday night, maybe even buy a house and grow something. But full-blown economic and political realities took over.

The third Big Three conference, at Potsdam, in July 1945, was less sanguine than the first two. The shape of the post-war world cast shifting, threatening shadows over the conference. The terms of the agreement on zones of influence had never been clearly defined. All talk about how to divide the world—at Teheran, in the British proposal that followed, and in the meeting in Moscow afterwards—had been hint, suggestion, intimidation, insinuation. The language was subject to diverse interpretation, and the arrangement unnatural enough to provoke regrets and second thoughts. How would the three major powers mould the post-war world? Their approach was characterized by acts of mutual deceit. Clement Attlee, British prime minister, and Truman tried to cover up the fact of the A-bomb test at Los Alamos, and Stalin tried to deceive them about the overtures of peace made to him by the Japanese. Each recognized the subterfuges of the other, even if the world was still unknowing. It would take the fallout from the unholy blast of the first atom bomb to reveal fully the poison in the post-war atmosphere.

CHAPTER TWELVE

The Bomb

ANY RESIDUAL ILLUSIONS communists had about a peaceful transition to a new world order were blown sky-high with the atomic-bomb attacks on Hiroshima and Nagasaki. Ed, in Holland when the war ended, heard on a radio report that the two cities had been destroyed. "Right away I just froze," he said. "I almost threw up. America was making signals to Russia." And for the first time Ed felt that the future for which he and his comrades had gone to war—"the brave new world, socialism in the next five years"—might not be realized. "It was a very sad moment. This was another declaration of war." Norman was in Ottawa, walking along the bridge over the Rideau River, when the significance of the bombings really hit home. He suddenly realized what his involvement with the Soviets had been all about. "I felt terrible," he recalled. "I realized that the whole involvement of us in it was not child's play, that the objective of the whole thing wasn't to see if the CCF would win the election in Canada. It was such a dramatic event. I never made another move after that."

With the bomb, the mantle of capitalist power passed from the sagging shoulders of the British into the powerful hands of the Americans, and Allied foreign ministers now stumbled through their painful peace negotiations under the shadow of a mushroom cloud. Everywhere—at the Foreign Minsters' Conference of the five allied powers in London, in government legislatures, at the sessions held to organize the United Nations—the bomb was a subject of debate. The widespread soul-searching that followed the attacks especially galvanised those scientists who were researching atomic energy and therefore aware of the bomb's destructive potential. In December 1945 delegates from research centres in Los Alamos, New York, Chicago, Washington, Philadelphia, Cambridge, Allegheny, Dayton, and Oak Ridge, as well as observers from the Canadian Association of Scientific Workers, of which Raymond Boyer was the president, met to discuss atomic energy. Sharing private fears, they undertook to urge the United States to help initiate and maintain an effective and workable system of international control of atomic energy, a system based on full cooperation among all nations. The American State Department agreed with this proposal, but the American military, with its advantage of "know-how" and a $2 billion investment in atomic-energy production plants, lobbied on behalf of its own right to international supremacy. Caught between conflicting versions of the post-war world, the Special Senate Committee on Atomic Energy thrashed through an atomic-energy bill. It was faced with the important decision of whether to maintain the development of atomic energy under genuine civilian control or to overrule the traditional constitutional practice of excluding the military from policy-making in the case of atomic power. Henry L. Stinson, secretary of war under Roosevelt and Truman, declared himself on the bomb issue: "A long-range nuclear monopoly was not feasible," he said. "The U.S. had nothing to lose by offering to cooperate with the Soviet Union to control the bomb and to share information concerning nuclear research." People's Commissar of Foreign Affairs, Vyacheslav Molotov, decried the use of atomic energy as an instrument of power politics: "It is not possible at the present time for a technical secret of any great size to remain the exclusive possession of some one country or some narrow circle of countries." And he cautioned that the discovery of atomic energy should not encourage "either a propensity to exploit the discovery and the play of forces in international policy, or an attitude of complacency as regards the future of peace-loving citizens." Thus, in an atmosphere of suspicion, which American

Secretary of State James Byrnes attributed in good part to Russia's distrust of its Western allies, the first post-war council of foreign ministers terminated with no accord on any major issue.

Meanwhile, the Canadian government was sitting on its own modest bomb. A cipher clerk in the Soviet embassy, Igor Gouzenko, had defected to Canada and given the government documents proving that the Soviets had a spy network in their country. From the day of his defection, on September 5, 1945, until the arrests of suspects four months later, Gouzenko's allegations simmered, too hot to handle, in the brew of international politics. At the outset, Mackenzie King hoped to play down the affair, to approach the Russians and deal with the matter in a way that would jeopardize neither the foreign ministers' meetings nor the proposed formation of the United Nations. He was, furthermore, unhappy about the way in which the cipher clerk's admissions would reflect on his administration. Thus, while Gouzenko was being debriefed by the Federal Bureau of Investigation and the RCMP, King visited President Truman and Prime Minister Attlee, suggesting that "if Russia was confronted in a similar way with the known facts… it might help to steady things."[1] The prime minister returned to Canada only to be met with the alarming disclosure that the Russians had got information on the atomic bomb from British physicist Alan Nunn May, who had sent them a sample of Uranium 235 from the atomic plant at Chalk River in Ontario. Throughout September the RCMP investigated the people who had been in contact with the Soviets during the war. Those with establishment connections were sifted out from those who were to be publicly exposed, the known communists. As Mackenzie King said in the House, "Pretty much the whole case, as it has since been developed, had at that time been worked out at least in outline by the Royal Canadian Mounted Police."[1] Still, nothing had been made public, and within the government, only Mackenzie King's top advisors were briefed. Fred Rose knew of Gouzenko's defection the day after it happened but was careful not to induce panic. "Lie low," he told his contacts. "Don't talk. Nothing will happen."

From the Canadian point of view the Gouzenko affair was on hold, but in October, the British, hoping to call Mackenzie King's hand, claimed that they would arrest Alan Nunn May for espionage on the basis of the Gouzenko allegations. The British and the Americans suggested to King that he prepare to arrest suspects immediately. Believing that the Gouzenko disclosures would now be made public, the prime minister adopted PC-6444, a secret order-in-council drafted under the authority of the existing War Measures Act, allowing the RCMP to detain persons suspected of communicating information to a foreign power and to interrogate them under conditions determined by the Minister of Justice. But the British arrest of Alan Nunn May did not materialize and, with relief, the Canadian government again shelved the Gouzenko disclosures. When a question was asked in the House of Commons about whether there were still any secret orders-in-council under the War Measures Act, no mention was made of PC-6444.

While the Gouzenko blast was being surreptitiously primed by British, American, and reluctant Canadian authorities, scientists around the world continued to advocate international cooperation in the application of atomic energy. The Federation of American Scientists held educational seminars for newsmen on the devastating effects of atomic warfare and lobbied for civilian control at hearings on atomic energy. The Canadian Association of Scientific Workers, whose members were mostly professionals in the universities as well as social workers, librarians, and nurses, was well informed about the problems involved in the application of science to society, and kept in contact with the American and British scientific associations. Through Joseph Needham, head of the British Scientific Mission in China, the association heard about the proposed formation of the United Nations Educational, Scientific, and Cultural Organization (UNESCO). "We sent a delegation to Ottawa to urge the Canadian External Affairs Department to get in on it," recalled Raymond. "They didn't even know there was going to be a UNESCO." The Canadian government was busy elsewhere, taking action that would define Canada's military position in relation to the United States. Mackenzie King went to Washington and there, along with President Truman and Prime Minister Attlee, signed the Washington Declaration. Canada, Britain, and the United States thereby assumed custodianship of atomic-energy secrets while Britain and Canada agreed to take second place to the United States, committing themselves to "American leadership in the oncoming struggle." "American leadership," as Gordon Dean, chairman of the United States Atomic Energy Commission, revealed in a public interview in 1950, had a specific meaning:

> MR. DEAN: During the war it was a complete partnership. The British decided to give up on gas-diffusion work and they came over to this country and we had a complete partnership...Since the war we have operated under an understanding with the British and the Canadians in several areas which are not weapon areas. We have exchanged some visits in these areas but that is the extent of it.
> QUESTION: In weapons there is now no real exchange?
> MR. DEAN: No.[2]

The game plan calling for a rational approach to the security of "one world" was no longer on the boards. There were still many who believed that the only hope for survival was for the United Nations to control the application of atomic power, but they would soon be traitors to a partisan concept of "national security." The Washington declaration was the first step to the formation, in 1949, of the North Atlantic Treaty Organization. The free world had made its pact.

In the December debate on atomic energy in the Canadian House of Commons, which led to Canada's ratification of the Washington Declaration, Fred Rose's was the only dissenting voice. He read a letter from a constituent into *Hansard*: "I am afraid of the atomic bomb. Alone I can do nothing about it. I am writing to you in the hope that you will do all in your power to see that this great discovery is not left in the hands of a few countries but is controlled by a world organization. This seems to me the only hope for us and our children." But the public did not hear about the controversy over who would control atomic power. To warm people up for the main act—what the New York *Herald Tribune* would call a show of "diplomatic buffoonery"—they began to hear reports, leaked by pro-military American government officials, about Russian spies and a communist fifth column. On February 3, 1946, the well-connected Washington journalist Drew Pearson fanned the fire, suggesting to his radio public that the discovery of "a situation in Canada which disclosed Russian intrigue" was the reason for King's September 1945 visit to Washington. Mackenzie King was in the hot seat. Recognizing that "my own feeling is that this whole business goes much further than any one of us begins to realize,"[3] he dumbly watched the dream of a world government go down the drain without knowing, quite, what had hit him. Even as King took steps that would lead him beyond the point of no return, he felt that Drew Pearson's statement had "in some way been inspired. I may be wrong but I have the feeling that there is a desire at Washington that this information should get out; that Canada should start the enquiry and that we should have the responsibility for beginning it, and that the way should be paved for it being continued into the U.S. This may be all wrong, but I have that intuition very strongly. It is the way in which a certain kind of politics is played by a certain type of man."[4] Although the Canadian prime minister wasn't sure how the information was leaked to Drew Pearson, he suspected that someone in the State Department was responsible. In fact, it was Sir William Stephenson,[5] now known as Intrepid, who had been at Gouzenko's door even before the Canadian authorities had decided, as Stephenson then urged, to "take him."

Now, to the satisfaction of the British, who preferred to cover up their palace intrigues, and the Americans, who didn't think they could convict either of their suspects, Alger Hiss or Harry Dexter White, given their judicial safeguards, Mackenzie King was the one in the public eye. Pressured to act, he instructed that four ministers, a quorum of council for such purposes, sign another order-in-council, PC-411, authorizing the immediate creation of a Royal Commission to investigate "the communication by public officials and other persons… of secret and confidential information to agents of a foreign power." Soon after, the minister of justice ordered the newly appointed commissioners to interrogate and detain people in the public service who were known to be, or suspected of being, implicated in a Soviet spy network. Baulking at being the only leader forced to display his dirty laundry in public, King repeated to his cabinet his earlier hope of talking privately with the Russian government but added that James Byrnes, U.S. secretary of state, and Ernest Bevin, British foreign secretary, favoured a public inquiry. Drew Pearson's broadcast, he noted, had made the matter public anyway. With Order-in-Council PC-411 authorizing a royal commission investigation, and Order-in-Council PC-6444 allowing the government to make arrests, King, the reluctant point man for executing the new Allied policy, was set up to let loose Canada's own little bomb.

On February 15, 1946, in coordinated pre-dawn raids, under the authority of PC-6444, with the executive powers of the War Measures Act, Raymond Boyer, Scott Benning, and eleven other communist suspects were taken into detention. Raymond was arrested at six o'clock in the morning, brought to the RCMP barracks in Ottawa, and processed for incarceration, "skin search and all." Although Raymond didn't know what it was all about and was worried, Scott Benning was less surprised. His wife packed a bag, insisting on including pyjamas, which proved wise, since for six weeks from that day her husband would be held incommunicado. The only news Benning's wife could get was third hand from the RCMP boyfriend of her landlady who told her, "Don't worry. My boyfriend says he's fine. The worse that can happen is that he will be shot." There is contradictory evidence as to how many others, excluding the communist suspects, were originally detained. Although the February 19, 1946, *New York Times* reported that one of those held for questioning was "a high Canadian official," that reference was later lost. The names of the "old boys" given by Gouzenko, such as Alex Skelton, were withheld from the press, and the suspects themselves never publicly investigated. The main targets were the communists. They were denied *habeas corpus*, the right to be brought before a judge within twenty-four hours of being arrested to hear the charges, and they were isolated from communication with the outside world: no newspapers or radios, no visits from family or lawyers. Four would be held incommunicado for two weeks, four for four weeks, and five for six weeks. As Mackenzie King worried privately about "star chamber methods," John Diefenbaker, future Conservative prime minister of Canada, objected publicly to "the police state methods" employed against those in custody: "What was done had no possible justification on the basis of security," he was later to write. "Supposedly, our purpose in breaking the spy ring was to prevent the spread of Soviet totalitarianism, not to adapt its most vicious practices. Anything that the NKVD [the Soviet political police] might have done, short of individual torture, was legalized by Order-in-Council under provisions of the War Measures Act."[6] Although the suspects could neither hear the short-lived debate nor read the news, their arrest made headlines in every major newspaper in the world. Mackenzie King, seeing a Drew Pearson article featured more prominently in the Montreal *Gazette* than his own milder statement, understood that "what the *Gazette* was interested in was the fight of Capitalism vs. Communism."[7] For one brief moment, the communist trials would place Canada at the centre of world politics. For the Western public, this was the moment when the Cold War began.

CHAPTER THIRTEEN

The Spy Show

ON FEBRUARY 14, 1946, Norman, on loan from the army to Canada House, bent over papers with the Honourable Paul Martin at the conference table in London's Dorchester Hotel. Norman was helping Martin, head of the Canadian delegation to the United Nations, with his speech on Canadian world-food production. The tall, cultured acting-captain made his suggestions respectfully, in the lilting Scots cadence he had brought with him to Canada in 1938. He was in top form, a talented writer, doing something he considered worthwhile, at the first plenary session of the United Nations. In the course of Norman's day, a cable arrived from the Canadian Department of External Affairs. It advised him to return to Canada immediately for some important work. A plane had been booked. On arrival at Dorval airport the evening of the next day, Norman was met by an RCMP officer and escorted into the Customs Office. In the darkened room, three pain-clothes men surrounded him. His arms were gripped, and he was ordered to stand with his hands away from his sides.

"Is this an arrest?"

The sergeant in charge read an order for detention signed by the Honourable Mr. Louis St. Laurent.

"What is the authority of the order?" Norman asked.

"PC-6444," said the sergeant. "Save your questions until you get to Ottawa."

Norman watched the plain-clothes men go through his luggage, his papers, his pockets. Everything except his money, comb, and wallet was confiscated. His request for a receipt was refused.

"I want to see my wife. I have just flown in from Britain, and she is expecting me here."

The sergeant said Norman would not be allowed to see his wife.

"If this is an arrest, I surely have the right to call my lawyer."

The sergeant informed Norman that he had no such right.

"What then is the status of my civil liberties?"

The sergeant replied that he had no authority to answer that question.

At midnight Norman was driven to Rockcliffe Barracks in Ottawa where, in the early morning darkness, he saw bright lights shining from every window. He was again searched and examined, then conducted to a deserted dormitory at the top of the building, where he was directed to one of twenty empty beds. An armed and uniformed guard remained by his side, and the lights, as ordered, burned continuously over his bed. The next day, Sunday, passed without reprieve. On Monday the lower windows were nailed shut, and Norman was told that several suicide attempts had already been made by people similarly detained. Two RCMP officers took him to another building, where he was interviewed by RCMP Inspector C. W. Harvison. Norman asked Harvison for an explanation of his detention and treatment and was briefly shown a portion of a public statement by Prime Minister Mackenzie King on espionage, as well as various newspaper headlines announcing the discovery of a huge fifth-column movement in Canada. Harvison told Norman he would not be permitted to receive any news or hear any radio broadcasts. He said that sixty or seventy foreign agents of the Soviet Union had been arrested— "some of them are held here and others elsewhere"—and he added that the Soviet Union had been sold the secret of the atom bomb. Norman now asked for the third time to see his wife and his lawyer. Harvison answered, "Let me make the position clear. Undoubtedly you are deeply involved in this matter; in fact, the justices of the Supreme Court who are investigating have especially instructed me to interrogate you personally. It will greatly help them, and even yourself, if you answer my questions. If you don't, you are merely making a martyr of yourself."

When Norman refused to comment on the Gouzenko documents, Harvison was angry. "You cannot get out of this," he threatened. "We've tangled with you reds before, but this time, by God, we have got you and we won't let you go. The sooner you answer my questions, the sooner you will get to see your wife." Attempting to clinch the interrogation, he asked, "Are you going to stand by and let people with names like Rosenberg, Kogan, Mazerall, Rabinovitch, and Halperin sell Canada down the river?" Harvison then went on to elaborate the enormous conspiracy masterminded by Fred Rose, member of Parliament for Montreal-Cartier against the security of Canada, and he terminated the interview by giving Norman a notebook in which to write out his part in the plot.

Norman was unnerved and apprehensive. He had not slept for three days. The evidence that Harvison had shown him was startling: hand-written documents, other people's testimony, an RCMP file on him since his arrival in Canada. As the days progressed, he found himself, as another communist suspect said, dealing with, "on the one hand, idiots and fools who tried to wheedle you into talking so they could run to their superiors and, on the other, terrifying types like Corporal Smith, a vicious cruel bastard who was always one step behind the inspectors." In the two weeks that Norman was incommunicado in Rockcliffe Barracks, the thought more than once crossed his mind that because he was in the army, he might be shot. He was cut off and increasingly frightened. He felt "completely powerless." Eventually, "because the evidence they presented to me was so overwhelming, and particularly because of the emphasis that I would not be permitted to communicate with my wife or any counsel until I answered questions," he wrote one page in the notebook Harvison had given him. Norman described meeting some person, unknown to him at the time of the meeting, whom Harvison advised him was Colonel Rogov of the Soviet embassy. It was a breakthrough for Harvison. Now, for the first time, he called in a stenographer and began to conduct a detailed, formal interrogation—the basis for the Royal Commission investigation. Norman, caught in the trap of inexperienced people who utter one word, said more, trying to mitigate, to explain. When the interrogation was finished, Harvison had enough material to hand over Norman, his RCMP dossier, and his damning "confession" to the waiting Royal Commission.

With the arrests of the thirteen communist suspects, the propaganda coup was under way. International headlines shrieked treason, but because the Soviet Union was an ally, the suspects could not be charged with espionage, which required communication with the enemy. Instead, they were charged under the Official Secrets Act: with communicating classified information to a foreign power. Civil libertarians, politicians, and journalists wondered why: "If the RCMP had been watching these persons for four months, were familiar with their habitat and had enough evidence to warrant seizure, why could not the regular process of arrest upon warrant, immediate access to *habeas corpus*, provision of defense counsel, laying of the information, and all the other judicial safeguards, have been allowed?"[1] With startling candour, a cabinet minister explained: "If we had let them see a lawyer, he would have told them not to talk."

Norman, no charge having yet been laid against him, was brought, not by subpoena but by the RCMP officers who had detained him in custody, to the Royal Commission hearing. His RCMP escorts seated themselves behind him, and other RCMP personnel sat in a room adjacent, with the connecting door open. Norman had not yet been permitted to see his wife or communicate with any counsel, and he was "alarmed by the series of implied threats" made against him by the police. In the presence of the commissioners, he took the oath and asked to know the status of his civil and legal rights. The commissioners advised him that the commission was a fact-finding body and that he was compelled under the Inquiries Act to answer all and every question put to him by them and their lawyers; he could then, if he wished, have counsel. He was not told about the rule against self-incrimination, Section 5 of the Canada Evidence Act; if he had testified with this protection, nothing he said could have been used against him later, in court. As the hearings proceeded, Norman realized that they were nothing but a re-hash of the RCMP interrogation in the Rockcliffe Barracks. "The RCMP did ninety per cent of the job. All the commission did was rubber-stamp it," said a communist suspect. "If the commission ran into any problems with a question, they simply asked the RCMP next door. If any answer that was given was not part of the plan, they told the stenographer not to take it down."

After two days of crossfire questioning, Norman was released from detention under PC-6444 and instructed to leave the building. On the steps he was re-arrested, taken by car to the Ottawa Police Court, arraigned on charges under the Official Secrets Act, and remanded without bail for a week. He was then allowed, for the first time, to see his wife. Ten days later, he was released from the county jail on six thousand dollars bail. He spent his brief time of freedom trying to avoid subpoenas for other people's trials and accumulating contempt charges for refusal to testify when he was found: three months in Bordeaux Jail for refusal to testify in the Fred Rose case, a year in all for several other cases in Ontario. Soon afterwards he was tried in Carleton County Court, convicted and sentenced to five years in penitentiary on the basis of his testimony before the Royal Commission.

Half the suspects, realizing the political significance of the Gouzenko affair or, perhaps, warned by Sam Carr, refused to testify at the Royal Commission hearings. The other half, trapped and threatened, without counsel, like Norman, gave full evidence. When Raymond, for example, had been confronted with the documents in the RCMP's possession, he had not attempted to deny the evidence of his eyes. Neither had he known enough to refuse to talk. "I had no knowledge at all of the judicial system," he later said. "My ignorance of the law was total." When he came before the Royal Commission, he continued to speak forthrightly and unashamedly, almost as if he could clear up a gentlemanly misunderstanding. "He didn't have a clue of what was coming," said a close friend. Using the simple analogy of baking a cake, Raymond attempted to explain to the commission that the information about RDX he had given to Fred Rose was not sufficient to help the Soviets build plants. They would need detailed chemical reports on how the large quantities of materials were handled and processed. They would need copious engineering specifications. He wanted to say that RDX, for example, was made of two solids and two liquids. To bring the solids and liquids together was difficult. Eventually, all the materials would have to be converted to liquids so that the industrial process would go through pipes. "Multiply that problem by a hundred thousand and you have what you need to build a big plant," he wanted to explain. But the commission was not interested in hearing what Raymond Boyer had *not* told Fred Rose. "They thought that if you told a person what goes into it, you'd have all the information to make it," said Raymond. "They never gave me a chance to explain that it wasn't what they thought."

Caught in a time-warp that left him back in the days of the second front, Raymond failed to realize that he was up against a terribly shocked, absolutely determined government court. So gung-ho was Commissioner R. L. Kellock that he often had to be restrained by his own staff. Described by a suspect as "so ignorant his own people told him to shut up," Kellock was remembered by a colleague as "suffering in later years from a guilty conscience for letting the legal profession down." Raymond, however, didn't understand either the political reality or the horror at the dastardly behaviour of the communists that was driving Commissioner Kellock. "I didn't realize it was the beginning of the Cold War," he admitted recently. "I was still into the Liberal-Labour mystique." The evidence he freely gave about his own and his friends' support for communist causes would, in the context of the evolving Cold War morality, damn both him and those he named. Raymond himself would be tried twice, each trial lasting a month. The same judge would preside at both of his and, also, Fred Rose's trial. Gouzenko alone would testify for four days straight, reciting the same facts and figures that he had told the Royal Commission and would later tell the Fred Rose jury. Raymond's Jewish wife would be called to the stand so that the Quebec jury would find the defendant even more strange. The crown prosecutor would also be a member of the appeal court. Finally, Raymond would be convicted and sentenced to two years in the penitentiary despite the reservations of some members of the appeal court, who questioned the whole witch-hunting tone of the trial and doubted the admissibility of the Gouzenko documents.

As a rule, those who gave testimony before the Royal Commission were convicted in the courts and those who refused to testify were acquitted. The only one of the suspects who succeeded in getting a lawyer was, of course, acquitted. In 1946 the *Canadian Bar Review* discussed the behaviour of the Royal Commission and its implications for civil liberties. According to the law journal, the commissioners had no mandate to actually try suspects, which is the prerogative of the courts only; and yet

> in making their report on each witness, they tested their conclusions not only with reference to the offence-creating sections of the Official Secrets Act, but also with reference to the sections of the act that create statutory presumptions (*the burden of proof*) in favour of the Crown…. One is left with the unpleasant suspicion that the Commissioners considered they had a duty to ensure that it could be proven in a court that the persons, who in the opinion of the Commissioners, had misconducted themselves, were guilty of offences.[2]

The wording in the Official Secrets Act allowed the accused to be tried, not for what they did, but for who they were. The commission created proof against the suspects, often by showing that they were communists or had associated with communists. Despite the fact that the LPP was a legal political party, establishing the suspects' connection with the Party was as good as establishing their guilt. Agatha Chapman, who had a masters' degree in commerce and was granddaughter of one of the founders of Confederation, was in a closed Party group during the war. She was arrested and questioned by the commission after a suspect named her as the hostess of a group meeting. Her interrogation focused on the study group: Marxist literature discussed and read, names of communists who had attended. At the beginning of her testimony, she assumed the right to support the Aid to Russia fund, the Canadian-Soviet Friendship Society, the Ford strike, and her interest in Marxism. She soon saw that such admissions were deeply incriminating. As the browbeating continued, she began to obfuscate, compromised by her identification with communism. By the time the commissioners demanded to know about "study groups, Communism, at your house..." the most she could do was not deny their suspicions. The only thing the commission could prove was that Agatha Chapman was sympathetic to communism. She would, therefore, be acquitted at her trial, even though the commission quoted Section 3(2) of the Official Secrets Act in their presumption of her guilt: "On a prosecution under this section, it shall not be necessary to show that the accused person was guilty of any particular act tending to show a purpose prejudicial to the safety or interests of the State, and, notwithstanding that no such act is proved against him, he may be convicted if, from the circumstances of the case, *or his conduct or his known character as proved*, it appears that his purpose was a purpose prejudicial to the safety or interests of the State" (italics added by the Royal Commission).

On March 2, 1946, the Royal Commission published a sensational, 350-page progress report. In it was the frightening suggestion that the small Canadian spy network was only the tip of an iceberg. The commission's findings were presented as documentary proof of a worldwide spy network, a communist plot to take over the world. It was a situation of "extreme gravity," affecting the safety and interests of Canada. On the other hand, Sir Alexander Clutterbuck, British high commissioner in Ottawa, in his August 22, 1946 dispatch to Dominion secretary Lord Addison, couldn't avoid the impression that "the attempt to give dramatic effect has led at times to unjustifiable extravagant language." Indeed, he found it "remarkable that the document should be issued over the signature of two justices of the Supreme Court."[3] In international press coverage of the report the conventional explosive RDX was confused with the atom bomb. The import was that the Canadian spies were giving the Russians military secrets in preparation for a third world war which the Russians would wage against the West. Within the next four months, three more reports by the commission accompanied by dire press speculation would create a climate of great fear focussed on the communist threat. The full Royal Commission report would be serialized in the Montreal *Gazette* under the heading "The Red Shadow Over Canada" at the same time as that newspaper published the proceedings of the trials, often on the same page. Harold Nicolson, commenting in *The Spectator* on the impact of the disclosures on the Canadian and American public, wrote: "The righteous horror which was expressed appears to me somewhat exaggerated. It is the duty of service attachés to obtain all the information they can, and it has for generations been the practice of some countries to employ means which are neither available nor scrupulous."[4] But, with the bogey-man, the Atomic Spy, cavorting about, histrionic and "righteous horror" overcame reasoned judgement. In the United States, in the later sentencing of Julius and Ethel Rosenberg for espionage, Judge Irving Kaufman could declare, "I consider your crime worse than murder."

After seeing the Royal Commission's report, Prime Minster Mackenzie King knew that the West had fired its first Cold War volley. "The report of the Commissioners will now have been in the hands of the press for over 20 minutes.... I imagine telegraph wires all over the world will be alive with the information it contains as they have not been in days since the beginning of the last war."[5] With the release of the report, British physicist Alan Nunn

May was immediately arrested. Since Nunn Nay had, in fact, given the Soviets a sample of Uranium 235, the Canadian suspects were again identified with the passing on of atomic secrets.

As the public confronted the shocking disclosures, Churchill officially inaugurated the new era with his famous "iron curtain" speech. Not then in power, he was at liberty to use strong words, but his speech, damning Soviet expansionism and calling for a new Western alliance, was in reality a policy statement: it had been vetted by Lester B. Pearson, representing Mackenzie King, and delivered at President Truman's old university in Fulton, Missouri. Then, sharing the platform with General Dwight D. Eisenhower and Field-Marshal Sir Henry Maitland Wilson, Churchill made his position on the necessary union of hearts, conviction, and common ideals among English-speaking peoples even clearer to the Virginia State Assembly: "Peace will not be preserved by pious sentiments expressed in terms of platitudes, or by official grimaces and diplomatic correctitude, or by casting aside in dangerous times our panoply of war-like strength. There must be earnest thought. There must be faithful perseverance and foresight. Great-heart must have his sword and armour to guard the pilgrims on the way." The hard-line position had been voiced by its most eloquent advocate. To speak of peaceful co-existence was, increasingly, tantamount to treason. It was "us" and "them." Patriots and traitors.

News of the *Royal Commission Report* hit the United States in the midst of the Senate committee's hearing on atomic legislation. A week earlier, a new version of the May-Johnson Bill, sponsored by the War Department, had been introduced in the Senate, and scientists and their allies now faced the possibility that the Canadian affair would be used to push through this pro-military bill or to amend drastically the MacMahon Bill, which supported civilian control of atomic energy. The impact of the spy case was heightened by the fragmentary release of information that was laced with rumour and speculation. Headlines referred to "atomic" spies even when the article denied that atomic energy was involved. Those leaders of the American Federation of Scientific Workers who had actively worked to keep the federation non-political regarded the spy scare as a strategy to force passage of the May-Johnson Bill. Their statements underlined the vested interest of the military and industrial lobby in keeping exclusive control over atomic power despite the expressed wishes of atomic-energy scientists such as Dr. Robert J. Oppenheimer, many citizens' groups including the Synagogue Council of America, and the United Nations. All urged U.N. control of atomic energy and many favoured an international conference on the question. The Association of Oak Ridge Scientists sent a letter to its supporters, along with a list of senators on the atomic-energy committee and an exhortation to write to them:

> It is not too much to say that the future course of the world may depend on the action taken in Washington on this subject within the coming days and weeks. If atomic energy is left in the hands of the military, we may expect the continuation of the present situation, in which the War Department and UNO [United Nations Organization] delegates make vain gestures towards the international control of atomic energy. We have, as a result of the War Department's action, initiated an atomic armament race, vitiated the efforts of the UNO and our own State Department, demoralized the Projects and forced the better scientists out of them; we have crippled our atomic energy research and spurred the rest of the world into mistrust and fear of us.[6]

But the spy scare had completely changed the terms of the controversy. By implication, all people urging international control of atomic power were communists, all communists were spies, and scientists with communist sympathies, such as Raymond Boyer, were certainly spies. Further, anyone who supported civilian control of atomic secrets was naïve, as only the military could provide protection from the encroaching enemy. In the early days of March, headlines about the arrest of Alan Nunn May and the Canadian Royal Commission reports dashed hopes that the Senate committee would lose interest in strengthening the military's hand. The Congress's Military Affairs Committee requested that the pro-military May-Johnson Bill be given priority on the House calendar. In the middle of March 1946, coinciding with the arrest of Fred Rose, the Royal Commission published its second sensational report, insisting on the importance of severely increased security measures.

Soon after, the Senate Special Committee on Atomic Energy reached agreement on a revision of the McMahon Bill. The revised bill established an atomic energy commission of five full-time members, appointed by the president with the advice and consent of the Senate. But the committee voted six-to-one to accept the Vandenberg Amendment, which established "a military liaison committee assigned by the Secretaries of War and Navy." The controversial amendment, which allowed for a departure from the traditional practise of excluding the military from policy decisions, determined the direction of the development of the atom. National interest became synonymous with "security," and dominated domestic and foreign policy. The global security policy that scientists claimed was the answer to survival in the atomic age was a dead issue. Raymond Boyer: "I got arrested and the whole atmosphere deteriorated, and while I was in detention, Churchill made his Fulton speech. That was not a good climate for the Canadian Association of Scientific Workers to continue working, especially since I was national president and was accused of conspiracy."

On March 26, the Washington *Post* reported that the chief counsel for the House Committee on Un-American Activities was investigating the scientific community in closed hearings in four research centres. In little over a month, the Red scare would assume massive proportions, totally overpowering what had been a strong popular movement for civilian and international control of atomic power. In the definitive book on the scientists' movement, Alice Kimball Smith writes, "As propaganda against genuine civilian control, the spy hysteria could not have been better timed if it had been planned that way."[7] Raymond Boyer was released from penitentiary into the anti-communist crusade accompanying the outbreak of the Korean War. All traces of the Canadian Association of Scientific Workers had disintegrated. It would be decades before other broad-based lobbies for the international control of atomic power would dare to speak out.

CHAPTER FOURTEEN

The Fred Rose Case

FRED ROSE WAS STUCK LIKE A butterfly on an exhibition mat. He knew someone had taken off from the Soviet embassy and was talking to the police. In September 1945 he had warned Norman, but he hadn't told him what might happen, how to act. In February 1946 he phoned a Party member and told her to tell Scott Benning, "We will be arrested as spies." By the beginning of March he still hadn't been picked up, and he told a reporter, "If I thought I was guilty of anything, do you think I'd be hanging around here in plain sight?"

It was not guilt he now felt, but desperation. There was no mistaking the renewed hostilities implicit in the handling of the Gouzenko disclosures: newspaper headlines, the *Royal Commission Report on Espionage,* politicians' statements, all proclaimed a new and sinister relationship between communism and capitalism, Soviet Russia and the West. But Fred Rose was on his own. Two days after the investigations were made public the Party had decided that any member found guilty would automatically be suspended. Fred Rose was in the public eye, under suspicion, with nowhere to turn. To the press he denied that he gave away information on the last secret session of Parliament. He shrugged his shoulders and quipped, "Anybody who gave information on that session is no more guilty than Winston Churchill, who recently published a speech he made at a secret session in the British house." But these would be practically his last words on the subject. On March 14, 1946, he appeared in his seat in the Commons for the opening of Parliament. Shortly after 11:00 P.M., on his return home, he was arrested. The next day, the newspapers announced Fred Rose's arrest, and that same day, the second report of the Royal Commission, warning of the existence of an organization that was "a threat to the safety and interests of the state," was made public. The March 15 Montreal *Gazette* naturally assumed the arrest was "in connection with the Russian spy plot.... His attitude on sharing the atomic secrets with Soviet Russia was well-known." On March 18, out on bail, Fred Rose returned to the Commons and took his place, as one of the largest crowds ever to pack the galleries waited for something to happen. The *Gazette* could only report that Fred Rose "did not expect to have anything to say about the matter." He was cut loose, floundering. "What can I do?" he said to a close friend. "They haven't given me any instructions."

Not trusting the provincial prosecutor to take the case seriously enough, the government appointed Philippe Brais, KC, as chief prosecutor in the Fred Rose case. "Brais was high up in the echelons of the Liberal Party," said a legal expert. "He was not a crown prosecutor nor even a lawyer who restricted his practice to criminal law. His appointment showed how important the government considered the case." Rose was charged with conspiracy under an undemocratic law left over from the fifteenth- and sixteenth-century political trials in England. Brais established the tone of the prosecution at the first hearing, demanding that the bail be set high because, he alleged, a car with American plates was parked outside the defendant's house, waiting to spirit him away. Bail was duly set at ten thousand dollars. At the next hearing Brais drew the attention of the court to Rose's previous conviction in 1931 for seditious words, adding that the police couldn't locate him during the entire time the Communist Party was banned under the War Measures Act. Bail was raised to the sum of twenty-five thousand dollars.

Defense lawyers called emergency meetings to discuss strategy. Like that of many of the accused, Fred Rose's impulse was to fight.

He knew it would be a political trial and he wanted to make a political statement. "Whatever the consequences," he said, "I mean to go through with it, having enough faith that the good people of Canada will, in the days to come, get a much better insight into the politics behind the spy trials." But the people of Canada never had a chance to hear Fred Rose's side of the story. The Soviet government issued a statement: its ambassador wasn't involved; the secrets supplied were of little interest to the U.S.S.R. given its more advanced technical achievements; Colonel Zabotin had been recalled because of the actions of members of his staff. Colonel Zabotin was indeed recalled, and the *New York Times* reported him dead from heart failure four days after his return to Moscow. Following the Soviet lead, the Canadian Communist Party denied any knowledge of a spy network and publicly rejected any members that were identified with it. An official message came from the Central Committee to all suspects: get your own lawyer, preferably a bourgeois lawyer; no meetings or discussions among suspects; no joint defence… "the future of the Canadian Communist Party is at stake." There would be no political statements, no national Party defense league, no proclamations of ultimate motives, no demonstrations of solidarity. "You are on your own. Don't implicate the Party," was the Party line.

Whether or not Fred Rose personally thought Party members and the public should be made aware of the international ramifications of the trials, he had to accept the directives of the Central Committee. He would behave accordingly or he would be denounced and expelled. He would then lose his place in the national and international communist establishment. If he wanted to remain a communist leader, he had no alternative but to shut up and take it. "The attitude of the Party was to clear their skirts of him," said an organizer of the short-lived Fred Rose Defence League, begun by the Party in Quebec. Representing the Central Committee, David instructed Gilles and the others demonstrating on Fred's behalf to stop and go home. The Central Committee took over the Fred Rose Defence League and, as a member recalled, did nothing, "paralysed it." Tim Buck, justifying the Party's actions, explained to Fred's close friend, "You saw what the British party did with Alan Nunn May. Can we do differently?" Fred Rose was sacrificed to save the credibility of the Party. "The Party didn't give a damn about the fate of the individual," said a suspect in the trials. "The Party came first." The rationale for this attitude is well expressed in Arthur Koestler's *Darkness at Noon*, where Rubashov, a top-ranking Party official, although not guilty of crimes against the state, recants publicly, his last sacrifice to the Party and for his own redemption: "'The Party can never be mistaken,' said Rubashov. 'You and I can make a mistake. Not the Party. The Party is the embodiment of the revolutionary idea in history…. He who has not absolute faith in History does not belong in the Party's ranks.'" Fred Rose had always operated on the principle that the Party came first. He was part of the leadership that, according to Norman, "willfully and knowingly took people that suited their needs and put them where they wanted, destroying marriages, families, careers—for the cause." Now, left out in the cold himself, Fred Rose had to take whatever the Party meted out. "Nobody though Freddie had a chance," said a provincial Party leader. "The boys threw him to the wolves."

With the Party totally on the defensive, Fred Rose's belief that the politics behind the trials would be exposed was proved wrong. From the beginning the ambitious crown prosecutor and the determined judge of the Court of King's Bench made sure his ride to prison would be efficient and direct: the indictment was speedy; the defense counsel's request for the usual particulars of the charge, denied. Jury selection began while the defense still did not know where or when the four or five alleged offences in the conspiracy were presumed to have taken place, only that they occurred sometime between January 1943 and December 1944. Crown Prosecutor Brais rejected the twelve Jewish Canadians who appeared for service as jurors. Defense lawyer Joseph Cohen questioned seventy-three men and women, futilely asking: "Have you read newspaper stories regarding the Fred Rose case?" They had of course all read newspaper reports, and most admitted they

Fred Rose (left) entering court with his counsel, Joseph Cohen, to face charges of conspiracy to commit offences under the Official Secrets Act. Montreal, March 1946.
Libary and Archives Canada

could not be impartial. One juror said, "I was one of the last ones to be picked. I got up and said that I was prejudiced, but I was picked anyway because the defense had exhausted their challenges. I had been following the whole thing in the newspapers and had formed an opinion. Sure I was prejudiced, so were others. Brais knew me; one of his partners, Campbell, was my lawyer and used to play squash with me." Under the administration of Fred Rose's loyal adversary, Maurice Duplessis, attorney general of Quebec, under the direction of RCMP Inspector Harvison, who sat next to Crown Prosecutor Brais, the trial began.

Revolving, slow-motion, in the steel shaft of justice, Fanny Rose was daily becoming thinner and thinner. Born in the Ukraine, orphaned at age twelve, Fanny had made her way alone across the border to Bessarabia; she was not new to hardship. From the moment she had met Fred in the union at the dress factory where she worked, he— so confident, so Canadian, "so full of life"—had been the centre of her world. For the past few years she had enjoyed the peace of legality and respectability. Now, the voluptuous young woman whose beauty the writer I. L. Peretz had extolled, was becoming gaunt. For sixteen days the trial cut away at her flesh, trying to slice into her mind. She held on tenuously. When rumours that Freddie would be arrested had run rampant, Lilly had called the Roses' daughter Laura, giving her the absolution of the all-knowing adult: "Remember, anything you hear is not true. Don't believe anything you hear." When children at school had taunted the ten-year-old in the playground, calling her father a spy, the child had tried to hold on to Lilly's words. When they had refused to sit near her in class, telling her to go back to Russia, the child had told herself, "It's not true. They don't know the truth. I can hold my head just as high." Laura would be all right, Fanny hoped. It was for Freddie she feared. He sat in a courtroom packed with curious onlookers, reporters, and federal cops, a silenced symbol of communist power. The Party had told his friends to stay away. Lea, Stanley, Annette, Sydney, Slug, Henri, Emery—none of them was there. Freddie, haggard, tense, was alone to witness the histrionics of the prosecution and to hear the words of the defector, Gouzenko, making his bid for a new life.

For five days, Gouzenko, the born-again Canadian, gave testimony irrelevant to the conspiracy charge, but designed to influence the jury: code names or, as he called them, "nicknames," pictures of those on the Soviet embassy staff, lists of long titles and heavy Russian names, charts representing the organization of the embassy, diatribes against the Soviet Union, odes to democracy. Gouzenko was the prosecution's main witness and the documents he had taken from the Soviet embassy were its most impressive evidence: sheets from the notebook of Colonel Zabotin, the military attaché; sheets from the notebook of Zabotin's assistant; documents and files on individuals taken from the embassy safe; telegrams between Canada and Moscow; handwritten reports from Canadian contacts. Some of the documents mentioned "Fred" as a recruiting agent and as a contact who reported through Colonel Zabotin. They indicated that Fred had approached Norman, reported a conversation with "The Professor" about RDX, contacted people in New York and England for the Soviets, and passed on information to the embassy from officers returning from the Western Front. The prosecution had no first-hand evidence from Fred Rose, nothing second-hand, nothing that Rose had told Gouzenko—only the third-hand "hearsay evidence" of the documents. Even under the broad rules of evidence in a conspiracy case, these documents would be admissible only if a direct link between Fred Rose and the Soviets could be proved. Given the Royal Commission testimonies, everyone knew the link would be Raymond Boyer. It was suggested to Fred Rose that if the Soviet Union would invoke the principle of diplomatic immunity with respect to the documents taken from its embassy, it would help his case. As the prosecution presented witness after witness to the jury, the intervention of the Soviet Union seemed more and more to be his only chance: two women admitted that they had pleaded guilty to offences against the Official Secrets Act; one said she knew Fred Rose; four men charged in the investigation, including Norman, were brought out; when they refused to testify, they were placed in contempt of court. On the ninth day Raymond Boyer was called. He testified that he had told Fred Rose the new ingredients needed for producing large quantities of the explosive

RDX. "I told him what materials were involved," he said. "I knew it was to help the Soviet Union...."

Fanny shuddered. "To help the Soviet Union." Nails in the coffin. Why didn't he deny it? Why didn't he say his earlier admissions had been given under duress? Raymond stood there, tall, straight, dignified, his reasonable, light voice unafraid. He was in the hands of his establishment lawyer, sticking with his testimony before the Royal Commission, determined not to grovel in court. Though he, too, would be sentenced as a spy, he contemplated the eventuality with seeming detachment. Fanny's control was almost at its end. Now, after Raymond's admission all Gouzenko's documents could choke Fred. Gouzenko's Cassandra-like warnings had become legal proof: of a dangerous situation, a communist fifth column, a Soviet government preparing secretly for the third world war.

Fred Rose's lawyer didn't have Gouzenko's liberty to editorialize. He tried to show that Russia was Canada's ally during the time when Rose allegedly committed offences and that to give information to an ally could not be thought "prejudicial to the safety or interests of Canada."[1] Brais was up and down like a jack-in-the-box, objecting—and his objections were sustained. The defense subpoenaed documents from the under-secretary of state for External Affairs that would establish the alliance of Canada and the U.S.S.R. Under-Secretary Norman Robertson was in England and the subpoena was refused. Attempting to prove that there was a Canadian intelligence network operating in Moscow, the defense subpoenaed reports made by the Canadian military attaché in Moscow to the departments of Defence and External Affairs. The effort was blocked both by the court and by a certificate from acting-Prime Minister Louis St. Laurent. It was "not in the public interest" to produce the reports. D. N. Pritt, an outstanding British constitutional expert, one of the few to plead before the Privy Council, asked to address the court on behalf of Fred Rose and was emphatically refused. On the last day the defense made as much of a case as they could: Doris Neilsen, a former Independent MP, read excerpts from speeches by Prime Minister Mackenzie King, stressing the need for collaboration with Russia and other countries; Tom Fairley, responsible for battle order in Army Intelligence, testified that information had been given to the Russians before D-Day; Colonel Papineau, a veteran of both world wars, reiterated that the military condition of the Allied armies in 1942 was at a very low ebb, and that while the Allies prepared, the Russians bore the brunt of the Nazi attack. Joseph Cohen asked Colonel Papineau if it were not in the interests of the Russian army to have the latest weapons of war. Colonel Papineau answered, "Of course it is."

This was all small potatoes compared to the prosecution's parade before the jury. Fanny Rose waited in hope that the Soviet Union would invoke the diplomatic immunity of the embassy documents and save Fred. They hadn't said "yes," but they hadn't said "no," either. Now, as she listened to Philippe Brais's four-hour summary, she knew it was too late. Thundering words of warning about the infiltration of a communist fifth column rolled over the awed, silent courtroom. Brais called upon the jurors to return a verdict of guilty "in the name of God and Country," and for over an hour Justice Wilfred Lazure instructed the jury on adducing evidence of conspiracy "from the conduct of the parties." He asked, rhetorically, why Fred Rose had not testified if the documents filed by Gouzenko and the statements therein were lies. Why would the men in contempt of court "not come here to deny them?" Why had two women "pleaded guilty to the charge—why was not Sam Carr here to deny them? Why did they not proclaim their innocence?"

Fanny didn't know that it was illegal for the judge to comment adversely on the failure of the accused to testify, but she could hear the presumption of guilt in everything Lazure said. He warned the jury about finding against the accused on the evidence of an accomplice, but then he said: "You have the right and you are at liberty to convict upon the sole evidence of an accomplice, providing you take my warning into consideration." He told them that they would "have to bring in a verdict of guilty even if only one of the offences is proved." He deliberately confused the timing of a conversation referred to in an item marked "Conversation with Professor. Decision of a Secret Session of Parliament" with Boyer's testimony on the RDX conversations; he then drew the jury's attention to the "strange coincidence." The judge's words reverberated in Fanny's head. "Then, he is guilty of conspiracy.... He is guilty of conspiracy." As the jury foreman told the judge that the jury would return a verdict shortly, Fanny remembered Fred whisking her and Laura away on his magic carpet—in a taxi to Chinatown, into his vision of a world where the workers were as happy as the wealthy. Now, it was over.

Twelve flushed and tired jurors went out to deliberate. During the first two or three days of the trial they had argued about the case, but after fifteen days sequestered, four with nothing to do, they were bored and edgy. Despite regulations a radio played in the common room, liquor was allowed in the jurors' quarters, and newspapers, which the jurors read, were left about the courtroom. The jurors were even given beer at lunchtime until one of them fell asleep during a court session. They played "21" and all twelve men got along "perfect." But it was getting tiresome. On the final day, when they went out of the courtroom to reach their verdict, "it was all cut and dried," explained a juror. "They didn't even have to let us leave the dock. We reached a verdict in sixteen minutes, but we waited for fifteen more to make it look good."

"Guilty as charged." The unanimous verdict was rendered shortly after midnight, June 16, 1946. As the jury pronounced its verdict, Fred Rose smiled. He stood there, looking circumspect, still smiling, as his two lawyers and Pritt crossed over to shake his hand. Asked if he had anything to say, he spoke to the court for the first and last time: I never did anything against the interests of Canada, and no matter what has been said, I still insist that it was so." Held in check by policemen, people from the court audience pressed about the dock to see Montreal-Cartier's member of Parliament kiss his wife goodbye. Women stood on tiptoe as uniformed constables arrived to take him to Police Headquarters. In a short while he was seen leaving the dimly lit corridors of the court, handcuffed, between police guards, smoking a cigarette.

Defense lawyer Joseph Cohen's notice of appeal listed thirty-two errors in law and three errors in fact, asking that the conviction be quashed and annulled. Included in the appeal were claims that the judge had erred by admitting testimony of acts and declarations prior and subsequent to the dates mentioned in the indictment, even prior to the passing of the Official Secrets Act; by admitting evidence of matters extraneous to the issue which created an atmosphere of hostility and prejudice to the appellant; and by his misleading charge to the jury. "On the whole," said Joseph Cohen, "everything in this case is so bad that it should go back for retrial."

The lawyers for His Majesty the King, in their brief in favour of the conviction, first quoted Gouzenko: "Russian people, instead of being grateful, organized in Canada fifth column in preparation of making stab in the back of Canadian people." The brief went on: "Evidence shows that Rose was an active speaker in the 'Study Groups' which were organized for no other purpose than to prepare Communistic Cells, and which at a given moment on instructions from Moscow, became spy groups.... Rose would prepare the ground, and when one of the communistic impregnated members of the Study Group was ready to be seduced, and brought into the espionage ring, the 'Contact Man' was notified, and the direct and illegal approaches were made."

One of the most contentious points in the trial and in the appeal was the admissibility of the Soviet embassy documents which, in effect, convicted Fred Rose. The defense claimed the documents were immune by virtue of diplomatic privilege, which had not been waived by the Russians. But the trial judge rejected the objection, saying that the privileges of diplomatic immunity could only be claimed by the foreign government in the matter. The *University of Chicago Law Review*, the only law journal to analyse the question, concluded: "If diplomatic immunity is to have anything more than a mere verbal existence, the courts must exercise the only effective deterrent to executive violation of international law, i.e., in the instant case, refusal to permit the introduction of evidence of admittedly diplomatic documents and declining jurisdiction unless renunciation of the privilege can be shown."[2] The article went on to say that diplomatic immunity had been recognized as one of the most important elements in the preservation of peace among nations, especially in times of international tension. "Rose v. The King is a disturbing precedent in that 'as among men, as among nations, the opinions and usages of the leading members of the community tend to form an authoritative example for the whole.'"

On December 20, 1946, the Quebec Court of Appeal ruled unanimously to reject Fred Rose's appeal. The Supreme Court of Canada, whose justices included R. L. Kellock and Robert Taschereau, two of the commissioners on the Royal Commission, refused to hear the appeal. There was, in their considered opinion, no reason for a higher court to hear this most controversial case.

Fred Rose knew that the state was his enemy, but did he suspect that the Soviet Union and the Canadian Communist Party would cut him loose? How did he feel during this appeal when Joseph Cohen, in reply to a question from the Bench, admitted that the Soviet embassy in Ottawa had not claimed the diplomatic immunity of the embassy documents? "Otherwise," Cohen told the court, "my position would be stronger." How did he feel when he saw the headline "Party Will Expel Rose If Appeal Fails—Buck"? No one will ever know. Fred Rose was thirty-eight years old. He had been a communist for twenty-one years. It was important to his self-respect that he not complain, but appear dignified and proud. Smile—even when he heard his sentence. It would be years before anyone would hear him question his fate.

Fred Rose served his first six and a half months in the damp cold of Bordeaux Jail. "That's when his health deteriorated," Laura recalled, "that's where the arthritis began." He did the rest of his time, five years and two months of a six-year sentence, in the St. Vincent de Paul Penitentiary, described in the 1938 Archambault Commission report as "Canada's toughest prison." Marcel Lavallé, a prisoner there at the same time, described the inescapable sounds that invaded his cell: "Someone is sick and chokes on his vomit; someone else grunts in his dream, a pig in his sty, radiators knock, windows shudder, bed springs creak, and my heart has almost stopped beating."[3] Laura had a very different image of where her father was. In response to her letters he drew his daughter a jolly picture of his "cosy room." But prison was hard for Fred Rose. He was used to living on the edge, feeling that he could control his own destiny. Now, he was at the mercy of implacable authority, in limbo.

Soon after his imprisonment, Rose made a concerted effort to keep his seat in the House of Commons. He applied for and got special permission to see his lawyer and to have his wife Fanny bring him *Beauchesne's Parliamentary Rules and Forms.* In his nine-page letter to the Speaker of the House, he for the first time publicly stated his position. On January 31, 1947, the Ottawa *Journal,* under the headline "House of Commons Makes Vacant Seat of Fred Rose, Communist MP," reported that "no mention was made of his views as the House quickly disposed of the subject, although Rose is understood to have sent a lengthy memorandum to Speaker Gaspard Fauteaux for submission to the House of Commons." The Speaker told a reporter that the letter was returned "because it was not in the proper form." Still trying to make the letter public, Fred Rose wrote to the superintendent of penitentiaries, saying that because the letter was returned to his cell, "the contents of this document remain secret to the members of the House of Commons and to the public." He noted that one member of Parliament had asked that the letter be tabled in the House and was informed that no copy was available. He asked, therefore, for permission to mail the letter either to any member of the House or to his wife. This request went the route of all other potentially controversial Fred Rose requests: from the warden, to the superintendent, to the commissioner, to the deputy minister of justice's office where F. R. Varcoe, the man in charge of the Fred Rose case, answered it unequivocally: "No."[4]

This incident seemed to take the steam out of Rose. Increasingly, he suffered from pains in his legs and back. He had trouble sleeping.

Asking Fanny to help him get proper medical care, he wrote: "I was robbed of the present; I don't intend to lose the future through ill health." In September 1948 he was hauled unexpectedly into court on a substantive charge, one of several held over from the 1946 trial. With the permission of the court to speak, he burst out dramatically: "I have now been in prison for two years. I have spent 6 ½ months in solitary confinement. My health is undermined, my family tortured. Then today I am suddenly surprised to hear that I am again going to be brought to trial. Is this going to be part of a general procedure or is it going to be a 'Rose special'?" Four months later, without explanation, the federal government withdrew the accusation. But his troubles were not over. In November 1948 a convicted murderer, John Boyko, killed his prison-mate, Nick Tedesco, in St. Vincent de Paul. The Montreal *Gazette* headline read: "Slayer Says Rose Made Effort to Convert Him to Communism." The article quoted provincial police, who revealed that Boyko had killed Tedesco "because Tedesco and Fred Rose, imprisoned ex-MP for Montreal-Cartier, were trying to convert him to communism." In December 1949 Deputy Commissioner L. P. Genreau's "Report re: 4857—Rose, Fred" noted that the convict had lost possibly ten pounds, seemed to be "tense and nervous," and appeared to be "losing some of his grip." At his own request, he had been transferred from the library to the yard. He didn't want, he told Genreau, to be "just a sitting duck for anyone who wanted to attack me."

When Rose was released in 1951, balder and thinner, the most startling change was in his eyes. The shine had gone; the bright, engaging gaze, recorded on election posters, had turned inward. Money was collected from Party members and sympathizers to buy him a place in an electrical business, and for a time he worked at his old trade of electrician. He was glad to be out of prison, but the constant police surveillance, the telephone that rang night after night at two, three, four in the morning, the pain of seeing people who'd been friends and comrades cross the street rather than talk to him took its toll. "People who knew I was seeing Fred and Fanny

PRISON TERM ENDED: Fred Rose, former Labor - Progressive M.P. for Montreal-Cartier, convicted of having conspired to communicate wartime secrets to Russia, returned to his Clark street home yesterday after being imprisoned five years, two months. Above, he relaxes with his wife and 16-year-old daughter, Laura.

Fanny Rose, Fred Rose, and Laura Rose after Fred Rose's release from prison, Montreal, August 10, 1951.
Montreal Gazette

wouldn't greet me on the street," said Lea. "It was fear. They just shied away." Finally, the business failed, and Fred found it impossible to find another steady position. "The Party had no place for him," said a friend. "He was becoming a liability. They pressured him to go." A week before he sailed off to Eastern Europe, Fred Rose went to the house of a comrade to say goodbye; he sat and cried. "I don't want to go." Bitter, hurt, he criticized the Party for shunning him, for making him the only one responsible. It was the only time anyone ever heard him speak against the Party. In 1953 he left his home—friends, wife, daughter, father, brothers—in Montreal. Fanny and Laura joined him in 1954, and the next year in the House of Commons, Immigration Minister Pickersgill hinted that the government would take action to keep Fred Rose out of Canada. On April 11, 1957, by Order-in-Council PC-537, on the grounds that he had been living in his native Poland for two years and had "not maintained substantial connection with Canada," his citizenship was revoked. In 1958 the Canadian Citizenship Act was again amended and the section which had been used against Fred Rose was, as a lawyer neatly put it, "completely washed out." When Laura married in Canada in 1958, her father wrote Prime Minister Diefenbaker asking that he be allowed to visit. The request was refused. In 1966, New Democratic Party MP David Lewis, on a trip to Poland, told Fred that he would ask then Immigration Minister Jean Marchand about visiting privileges. According to Lewis, Marchand said, "Yes, sure," but the next day it had become "impossible." "They're determined to perpetuate a lie about me. They'll never let me back. But I'd match my political past with any one of them," Fred Rose wrote from Poland three weeks before he died.

CHAPTER FIFTEEN

Evidence

WHAT WAS GIVEN, and by whom, through the Canadian spy network? By far the most important Soviet contact named by Igor Gouzenko was not a Canadian, but the British physicist Alan Nunn May, who came to Canada to work on wartime research projects in Montreal and Chalk River. From him, within days of the American bombings of Hiroshima, Colonel Zabotin obtained samples of Uranium 235, an essential element in the manufacture of the atomic bomb. As journalist Blair Fraser pointed out, "By far the biggest fish to be caught in the Gouzenko net was Dr. Alan Nunn May. So far as is known to the public, the other information transmitted to Moscow was trivial."[1]

In the post-war press coverage of the spy trials, the information Raymond Boyer gave Fred Rose on RDX was represented as a damning and sensational "secret." But RDX had nothing to do with the atomic bomb, as the press implied; it was a military explosive. In testimony before the Royal Commission, at his trial, and at the Rose trial, Boyer admitted that he'd given Rose some preliminary information about RDX—including the ways it could be used in wartime—so that the Russians would press their request for further information. He denied, and there is no proof whatsoever to the contrary, that he'd told Rose the actual process for making RDX or given him the plans necessary for building the plants—discoveries that had taken Allied chemists and engineers several years to figure out.

The spy-trial propaganda touted RDX as a top-secret weapon and implied that Boyer had passed on to the Russians everything they needed to begin its production. In fact, the original discovery had been made by Woolwich Arsenal, in England, and published in its chemistry journal prior to the Second World War. The information that a new process had been discovered was publicized in the Montreal *Gazette* on November 6, 1943, along with proud headlines and pictures of Dr. Boyer in his lab. It is generally accepted that the new ingredients used in the improved process were not secret after 1942, when production began at the pilot plant in Shawinigan Falls; hundreds of workmen knew what went into the process, as did interested villagers who watched freight cars of materials unload. Although C. D. Howe, minister of munitions and supply, could not at first grant the Russian request for information on RDX, in 1944 his department authorized two representatives of the Soviet Technical Mission to tour the Shawinigan plant. Kenneth Howe Cheetham, a thirty-five-year-old chemist, assistant to the director of research in explosives and chemical production, was instructed to show the Russians the operation. Subpoenaed by the defense in the Boyer trial, he testified that for two hours the Russians studied the complete manufacturing process, including the building where the materials were classified; the room where the mix was made; and the form of the special new reactor, resembling the slide of a trombone, from which they could deduce the method and order in which the ingredients were added. Throughout, the Russian explosive experts asked pertinent questions which Cheetham answered, since his instructions had been "to tell them everything they wanted to know without reserve."[2] On the train from Three Rivers to Montreal, after dinner, the two Russian scientists took out the notes they had made in the plant and Cheetham helped them fill in the gaps and oversights in their documentation of the process and manufacture of RDX. Of course, whether or not the Russians had officially been told more than Raymond Boyer had volunteered, he could still be accused and convicted of conspiracy to commit offences under the Official Secrets Act. An official secret is simply that which the government designates as such. Indeed, the absurd mandate of the Official Secrets Act was made clear by the trial judge in the Boyer case, who charged the jury, "Whether the information was important or not, known or not, secret or not, partial or complete, that has no importance once the law has been broken."

In the scare-crazed hysteria of the post-war period, patriotic critics such as Rebecca West believed that traitors had given Russia the weapons with which it would immediately attack the West. Judge Irving Kaufman, in his sentencing of Julius and Ethel Rosenberg, surrendered himself to the paranoid xenophobia of the time. He referred to "this diabolical conspiracy to destroy a God-fearing nation," and went so far as to insist that the Rosenbergs "had put the atomic bomb in the hands of Russia and had thus caused the Communist aggression in Korea, with its cost to America of 50,000 casualties."[3] In their 1951 pamphlet on the only atomic spies of any significance—Klaus Fuchs, Pontecorvo, David Greenglass and Nunn May—the United States Joint Congressional Committee on Atomic Energy assessed the spies' combined activities as having advanced the Soviet energy program by eighteen months at the minimum. "This is not to imply that Russia could never have broken the American atomic monopoly through her own unaided labours," the committee added.[4] It seems a safe guess that, without the help of the atomic spies, none of whom were Canadian, the 1949 Soviet bomb would have, at most, been delayed a year or two. The manufacture of the bomb depended entirely on the existence of great industrial and technical resources and a body of trained scientists and technicians. These the Russians possessed. The most valuable single piece of knowledge they got from Americans was that the bomb could be made and exploded, that fission was possible, and this knowledge they got without the help of the atomic spies. As Lord Addison, the Dominion secretary had pointed out to Prime Minister Mackenzie King before the Canadian spy trials began, "scientists once they were working on a matter which had been successful elsewhere were pretty certain to discover the process which led to their final result." Addison told King that all the scientists and their equipment from the former great German research centres that were now in Russian-occupied parts of Germany had been removed to Russia. Addison believed that "we must count on Russia getting that secret."[5] Actually, the most significant military information the Soviets got from Canadians was on radar. The damage done by the spy trials is not to be found in the "secrets" given or in the augmented power of the Soviets, but in the way the trials were used: to inaugurate the Cold War, to justify the arms race, to strengthen the secret service, to smash the militant unions, to repress dissent, and to leave the world teetering dangerously on the edge of brinkmanship.

Ultimately, twenty Canadian communists were accused of offences under the Official Secrets Act and publicly named as spies. Fred Rose was sentenced to six years, Raymond to two, Norman to six (five for conspiracy, one for contempt), and Scott Benning was acquitted. In all, nine were convicted, nine acquitted, one fined, and one charge dropped. The Official Secrets Act was not used against all those who contravened its broad mandate. The commission did not publicly investigate members of the political and military establishments, such as Alex Skelton, who, given the same treatment as the communists, might have suffered their fate. Instead, when such a name reached the public, the commission excused it. Others, whose real names were never publicly exposed, were demoted, moved quietly to less important positions. For the spy show, it would have weakened the caricature of the communist spy to taint establishment leaders with treachery.

Only a very select few, those who have seen all the secret files on the period, know how many others reported or spoke inadvertently, once, twice, or four times, to Canadian or Russian agents during the war. A significant number of people in the civil service supported international cooperation, and estimates of the number whom the Soviets considered sympathetic to them range from thirty to three hundred. Not many Canadians made regular and direct contact with the Russians, probably fewer than ten in all. Slightly more made routine contact with Canadian communist agents between 1943 and 1945. On an informal basis, others, communists and non-communists, gave information to the Party during this time because their political sympathies were involved with the fate of the Soviet Union and the battle against fascism. Contacts such as Norman, Raymond, and Scott Benning were conscious of the choice they, personally, had made, but they had no idea of the nature or extent of the intelligence network. They did not know that a file was kept on each of them in the Russian embassy in Ottawa and in Moscow, and that the file included their cover-name, length of time in the network, a photo, and even their ethnic designation: "Anglo Saxon," "French-man," "Jew." As a close friend of Scott Benning said, "They did one thing after another. They didn't understand what was coming." The initial information requested from contacts was often innocuous: biographies of Canadian statesmen, a manuscript on Canadian-British relations, reports on sessions in Parliament— all of it public knowledge and a normal part of the intelligence information collected by embassies abroad. "Jack" exemplified the attitude of many who were approached in wartime. In uniform at a party in Montreal, he was greeted by Colonel Zabotin as a "comrade in arms," then asked for a handbook on the "twenty-five pounder," a simple artillery field-gun. Jack would have given it to him if he had been able: "The guy was a colonel in the heroic Red Army. He was fighting back Hitler at Stalingrad while we were buggering around in Africa." A respected journalist, a non-communist who was in the Soviet Friendship League, said matter-of-factly, "If someone had asked, 'How many training schools are there?' I would have said, 'I'll get you that.'" At the height of the war against Hitler, the Soviet Union was a vital Western ally. It was possible to feel that helping the Soviet cause was, in Scott Benning's words, "an anti-fascist act."

The truth about the spy trials remains clouded not only because of the reticence of those implicated, but also because of the unavailability of original documents: Mackenzie King's diary entries for November and December 1945, when the decision to proceed publicly against the communists was made; documents taken by Gouzenko from the Soviet embassy and later entered as court exhibits; Fred Rose's letter from prison to the House of Commons; and, of course, nothing as complete as the RCMP, FBI and MI5 report of Gouzenko's September 1945 debriefing. Today, for example, it is impossible to find a complete transcript of the Fred Rose trial anywhere; it has disappeared from lawyers' files, the Quebec provincial archives, the federal archives, and the Justice Department, and if it does exist in the still classified material in the Gouzenko file, it is not available to the public. With the conviction of the communists, the Canadian government obviously considered the case and the files closed.

[CHAPTER SIXTEEN]

The Denouement

THE CANADIAN COMMUNIST Party's tie to the Soviet Union had begun to strangle the baby. The fact that Fred Rose, the most visible Canadian communist, was collaborating with Soviet agents proved the dual allegiance of the Communist Party of Canada and served as a focus in the ideological war for the hearts and minds of English-speaking peoples. Despite the small number of Canadian communists who had given information to the Soviet Union, the trials were used not only to reveal the worst, but also to smear the best in the movement. They proved so effective as propaganda that even today political discourse in North America has not recovered its freedom. Actual victims of the trials were so badly traumatized that most will still not talk personally, if at all, about their experiences. The only one who did recalled that he read a psychiatric journal in prison characterizing the communists involved in offences against the Official Secrets Act as insane. So great was his dissociation at that point that he himself had "a sneaking suspicion that to have accepted all that dogma *was* insane." Yet, he believed that the Soviets had collected information "to devise their own military programme," not, as Gouzenko would have it, "for the purposes of making war." He was spared that guilt, but, he wondered, "What separated me from my peers? What made me so strange?" Prison removed him from the immediate Cold War hysteria and, he felt, "purged me. It was better to do time than not. The guys who got off suffered more." One such, a brilliant physicist, although acquitted at his preliminary hearing, was blacklisted in North America. In order to work, he, his wife, and child had to leave home, family, friends. "For them," said a friend "the tragedy goes on; it has hurt them in every part of their lives. They carry it for life." Another suspect who was acquitted went to Poland where his wife, cut off from her past, suffered a nervous breakdown. Scott Benning stayed in Canada. Every time he found a job the RCMP was there to warn his employers that they had hired a spy. "They had a vendetta against Scott," said a friend. "They pursued him to the end of his life." Agatha Chapman went to England; her arthritis, quiescent until the time of the trials, flared up wildly, totally crippling her, and she committed suicide.

For rank-and-file Party members, the most cogent effect of the trials was their own fear. "To have the Padlock Law was one thing," said Lea. "But to be associated with a spy was worse. You couldn't do or say anything." The atmosphere was again warlike, but communists were the new enemy. As Gilles's wife, Lilly, said, "The espionage case made things very heavy. We were looking over our shoulders and seeing the enemy around, and they *were* around, that was a fact." Headlines in the *Canadian Tribune* at the time read: "Cry Havoc and Let Loose the Dogs of War" and "Peace in Danger." Given his experience with RDX during the war, as demolitions instructor at Camp Petawawa, Henri Gagnon, for one, was incredulous. "I was exploding fifty pounds of RDX every hour. I was told that any of the Allied officers who came and wanted samples, or wanted to know what it was made up of, or how it worked, was to be given it." Henri was sure that "these trials must be a plot of the bourgeoisie against Fred Rose." Many others gave the suspects the benefit of the doubt. "At the time we were surprised," said a Party member. "We were sure the trials were a fraud because we were used to Red-baiting." Even if members suspected that the charges were grounded in fact, they knew that, as many people said, "any one of us would have helped the Soviet Union." For most, Fred Rose's action wasn't treacherous but, quite simply, "stupid." His betrayal, if they judged it as such, was not of Canada but of his constituency. As a supporter from that period said, "When an entire generation elects a member to Parliament, he should keep his hands clean."

The spy trials came after a major wave of disillusionment following the Nazi-Soviet Pact. "The major ideological problem," said David, "was not spies on behalf of the Russians, but why did the Russians take our one MP, our one Party organizer. Whose interests were we serving?" But the Party members' suspicion of the leadership took second place to their almost impervious loyalty. "I had worked like a son of a bitch to get Fred elected," said Eda, who had known him since the thirties and worked with him in the underground. "Night after night, I went out with my children under my arms. Then, to see the whole thing go down the drain was very hard. But my loyalty was to Fred. I had to say that it was the system that did it, not the Party." Fred went to see Lea before the trials began to warn her that the Party was entering a very difficult phase and that he would have to go "into the clink again. It's something I have to go through." She wasn't scared, but she remembered, "It was as if my stomach tipped over." She watched as Fred Rose covered for "the Old Man," Tim Buck. She saw that "Laura was only a little tyke and Fanny was having to be the mainstay," and she drew her own conclusions: "Freddie didn't get a square deal. He shouldn't have had to carry the whole bag." So thinking, she dug in for the long haul and continued her work with the unions. The Party was on the defensive, but most members' basic allegiance to it remained intact. "There was not a mass desertion," said David, "but a dwindling of forces over time and an inability to gain any serious adherents."

The full import of the trials and, more particularly, of their party's intricate relationship with the Soviet Union would not really be understood by the members until the break within the ranks in 1956. Most did not yet realize that the rigid Party hierarchy bred disrespect from the Comintern down, that the self-serving Communist Party of the Soviet Union took liberties with Communist parties the world over, that, in the words of Stanley Ryerson, "there was a pathological relationship between the Canadian Communist Party and the Communist Party of the Soviet Union, a submissive pattern of political organization." But until 1956 the nature of this relationship would remain obscured by an almost mythological belief in Soviet communism. As a Party leader said, "Until then, anything we could do to help the Soviet Union was okay." In the decade following the trials, Party members, isolated from effective organizing and worn down by repression, would be increasingly locked into a rigid concept of the discipline and sacrifice necessary to save the world. The trials in Canada, the first of the ideological trials staged in North America in the late forties and fifties, had set the stage for a rabid anti-communism that soon engulfed both them and all other forms of dissent.

John Grierson was one of those who got hit by the compulsive sweep of all progressive forces that followed the trials. During the war Grierson was Canada's most powerful propagandist, head of the Wartime Information Board and director of one of the country's best propaganda agencies, the National Film Board of Canada (NFB). Grierson was not a communist, but a strongly independent civil servant with the aggressive style of a Calvinist Scottish clan chieftain. He had hired communists as well as non-communists, knowing that they would use their creative talents unstintingly for the war effort. "Are they Reds?" he had asked. Then, "Are they known?" If the answer to the second question was negative, "Hire them" was his attitude. As head of the Wartime Information Board he had produced a poster pushing for a second front. As director of the NFB he supervised films such as *Our Northern Neighbour*, a sympathetic look at Russia, "one of the great nations of the earth," which ended hoping that "together with our Russian neighbours" and the cooperation of all nations, we would "eliminate tyranny and slavery, oppression and intolerance."

It might have been because of films like this that the Federal Bureau of Investigation opened a file on Grierson in 1942, which was not closed until 1954. Nevertheless, in 1945 he was actively advising the Canadian, British, and American governments on

National Film Board of Canada Commissioner John Grierson (right), and Harry Mayerovitch, director of the Graphic Arts Division of the Wartime Information Board, 1944.
Canadian War Museum

their post-war propaganda needs. When FBI Director J. Edgar Hoover heard that Grierson might take over an American State Department film unit, he wrote the American Embassy in London for information on Grierson, adding, "from information appearing in Bureau files, it is indicated that John Grierson is communistically inclined and that several of the films he has produced in Canada appear to be written and directed from a pro-Soviet viewpoint." All it would take to help Hoover destroy Grierson's influence and prestige was Igor Gouzenko's passing mention that Grierson had employed one of the trial suspects. Gouzenko had testified that Grierson was not an agent, but the post-war trials were an ideal place for those in power to grind and sharpen any axes blunted by the democratic anti-Nazi alliance. Those who might be powerful opponents of the new Cold War philosophy could be selected, isolated, and named. Grierson was "questioned in the Russian spy case," as the Washington *Times-Herald* put it, and by the time his name made the New York *World Telegram*, he had become the "Canadian Atom Spy Case Figure." Grierson was kicked out of the United States and cut off from producing propaganda for social progress or international cooperation—his now tarnished vision for the post-war world.

In Quebec the Communist Party pulled itself up by the boot-straps, retrenching along pre-war, Leninist lines. Henri Gagnon was asked to leave the army to become provincial organizer. "There was no more Party after the Fred Rose affair, just some old-age clubs. His prison sentence had done a lot of damage. We had to start over." He called together militants with enough experience to reconstruct cells, cell committees, sections, political committees, youth groups, and committees of organizers. Gilles, college-trained, bilingual, an intellectual with a flair for public speaking and writing, was appointed Party leader, to work with Henri. David, English-speaking, a tough union organizer, was sent to Quebec as the Party's man-on-the-scene. Stanley Ryerson, education director of the National Committee, remained in Toronto, the National Executive's resident expert on Quebec. The Party geared up again, holding meetings, making house-to-house visits, and demonstrating in support of the communist candidate Mike Buhay, who got 7,000 votes in the 1947 by-election in Montreal-Cartier, more votes than Fred Rose had received in 1943. It seemed that although "the Party had lost its trousers in Canada," true-blue Canadian patriotism had not overrun Quebec.

What seemed most pressing was the terrible shortage of housing for returning veterans and their families. "None of us had homes," said Ed, who had just returned from overseas with Beryl, his British bride. "Eventually someone took us in, but many, like Henri, his wife, and child, didn't have a place to live." Basic materials for building were unavailable. There were no apartments advertised in the newspaper. The practice developed of paying "key money"— forty dollars rent and two hundred dollars for the key. Still, there was nothing. War brides with kids and no place to live went to the Red Cross. Some went back to England. "Housing was a major problem. It broke up families and caused much grief," said Ed. He and other veterans who had heard about squatters in England and Germany put an advertisement in the paper, calling for a meeting of veterans with no home. "The place was jammed. Hundreds of people came, everyone prepared to do something drastic."

Party members on the veterans' committee in Montreal invited a reporter from the Montreal *Herald* to see the conditions in which veterans were forced to live: in a hovel where frost seeped through the cracks, sick kids lay two to a bed and a woman sobbed, "This is all we could get." While the reporter asked where the husband had fought in the war, a photographer recorded bleak images of the crowded, squalid room. By the next day the story was front-page news, and the Squatters' Movement was born. "That's when Henri came in," said Ed. Henri squatted with six other families in a vacant house on McGill College Street, and he and the Veterans' League led two hundred families into eighty abandoned buildings, among them two empty gambling halls, an unused military barracks on St. Helen's Island, and an abandoned military hospital. The city called in the RCMP, who arrived and pointed their automatic machine-guns into the pleading faces of mothers and children. It was a heyday for press photographers and reporters, a major organizing victory which forced C. D. Howe, now the minister of reconstruction and supply, to make some provisions for veterans. For the Quebec Communist Party, it would be a last show of strength, rekindling, briefly, the fighting spirit and making headlines across Canada.

It was at this time that the French Section of the Party in Quebec began its fatal confrontation with the Central Committee in Toronto, whose executive wanted Henri Gagnon to end the Squatters' Movement and concentrate on the great communist takeover of the Canadian veterans' association, the Canadian Legion. The Legion, whose founders were English-Canadian, meant nothing to French Canadians, and when Gagnon went to the Party's Provincial Committee he fought for and won the right to continue with the Squatters' Movement. Meanwhile, the Central Committee was making plans to support Mackenzie King's plan to recast the British North America Act. Henri declared that this would require discussion about the relationship between the two founding nations of Canada. "I remember saying, 'Listen, I'm not ready to give a blank cheque to the Liberal party.'" The French Section formed "schools" to study the constitution so that its members could make an intelligent contribution to the Party's position on dominion-provincial agreements. They demanded that Comrade Buck translate and publish his 1946 report on the constitution so they could debate the question of Quebec nationalism. Henri: "In Quebec the national question was being discussed, and the Central Committee more or less categorically refused to discuss it."

The official "ministerial" line of the Party was that the national struggle came after the class struggle. Stanley Ryerson, in his introduction to the science of socialism, *A World to Win*, stressed that "Communism should be internationalist in character." He quoted Lenin, who had said that for policies to be correct, they must be based on "a sober and strictly objective estimation of *all* the class forces in a given state (and in neighbouring states, and in all states the world over), as well as the experience of revolutionary movements." The

Henri Gagnon, President of the Veterans League, with members of three families housed after being evicted from the army barracks on St. Helen's Island, Montreal.

Quebec leadership agreed but at the same time felt that the national question would not go away. It supported the National Executive's campaign against Canada's participation in NATO and collected signatures for the Stockholm Peace Appeal, a world-wide petition urging peace with the Soviet Union but, they argued, neither of these was a lively issue in Quebec. "We believed," said Gilles, "that it was necessary to merge working-class concerns for betterment with the cultural concerns of the French-Canadian nation for autonomy and self-determination." Emery Samuel: "We wanted to bring socialism to the national movement. Join societies that English Canada couldn't get near, get inside, make yourself a friend, fight for their needs and convince them that the working class was the future, socialism was the future." The very idea of working with Quebec nationalists set off alarms in the National Executive. The executive identified Quebec nationalism with Duplessis, corporatism, and the Catholic Church; further, for the first time it was presented with a strongly led, autonomous national movement outside its own control. Henri Gagnon was a formidable leader. He lived for the struggle and was in constant personal contact with other militants, his home the centre of political activity. "He had no personal life," said Gilles, "nor did he want one." His availability was his strength, and he was loved for it. Through the Squatters' Movement he had offered hope to the flotsam from the war. From coast to coast, headlines and pictures reported the squatters' progress, and the National Committee watched uneasily as an ideologically impure, grassroots Marxist movement developed strength in Quebec.

In the summer of 1947 Gilles was sent by the National Executive to its National Party School in Sudbury. Henri gave way briefly to the fierce pressure on him and also went to Sudbury, but he soon returned to the squatters' fight. Gilles, however, stayed for the entire three-month session and, in later life, would confront his experience there, slowly and painfully unravelling how it was he could have gone to the school supporting his French comrades, but returned from it convinced to stand behind the Central Committee's position....

Summer, 1947
National Party School. Sudbury.
His head aching from late-night reading—Lenin, on learning communism; Dimitrov, on leadership forces—Gilles walked through the fields on his way to the criticism and self-criticism session. Ahead, he saw someone flat-footedly hurrying into the

meeting hall. Recognizing the familiar, Chaplinesque gait as that of Stanley Ryerson, Gilles experienced a wave of feeling for the Party's school that had to do with "a contact in depth with other people not achieved in normal existence." These evaluation sessions started, he said, "from the viewpoint that a communist was a person who had chosen to devote his whole life to the liberation of humanity. He had to put away pride, individual interests, anything that would stand in the way of the cause." A communist could not live as others did. The man with a mission could not run down any old lane, chasing after butterflies for his own pleasure, but had an enduring incentive to live in a noble manner. In the session "your strengths and especially your weaknesses in the service of the cause, that is, the Party, were laid bare by your comrades. With full frankness, you accepted what they thought of your work as a fighter for socialism. It was quite an exhilarating experience. You bared your thoughts, shared them."

Normally, it was a good experience, but Gilles was starting to feel a concerted pressure on him from Stanley Ryerson and Tim Buck to change his position on the issue of Quebec nationalism. In a session the month before, Tim Buck had pointed out that Gilles and Henri Gagnon had different styles of organizing: Gilles was more democratic, while Henri had a tremendous will and determination that was individualistic. Henri "was lacking in depth in seeing the other side." Gilles had to agree that Henri didn't always consult the local executive, and he himself knew Lenin's writings on the necessity of Party discipline in "gathering, organizing and mobilizing permanent troops." Several weeks ago, in another session, Stanley Ryerson and Tim Buck had reminded Gilles that his own "origins were bourgeois." Lenin, he knew, had warned against the intensely individualistic bourgeois intellectual, who feared the Party as a factory designed to produce a product labelled "working-class power." No doubt, they suggested, Gilles was being influenced by petty bourgeois forces and habits of mind in his support of French-Canadian nationalism. As a Party leader he had to rise above his conditioning and lead Quebeckers into the worldwide class struggle for socialism. "A Party is the vanguard of a class," Lenin had said, "and its duty is to lead the masses, not to reflect the average state of mind of the masses."

Stanley Ryerson and Tim Buck were sure that Gilles would agree that his opposition to the federal government's Rowell-Sirois Report on Dominion-Provincial Relations, which proposed the centralization of social services, would in fact lend support to the demagogy of the Duplessis government. Gilles must remember that national struggles serve bourgeois interests, and that the Party must seek to unite workers across national lines. They were sure that Gilles would accept the iron discipline necessary to the Party's survival, and split with Gagnon and the French Canadians, who were taking on the proportions of a dreaded "faction." Because the Party represented a unity of will, it could not afford to be "liberal" nor to accommodate factions—hence Lenin's demand for the "complete elimination of all factionalism" and the "immediate dissolution of all groups, without exception, that have been formed on the basis of various platforms," on pain of "unconditional and immediate expulsion from the Party." The nationalists in Quebec jeopardized the very nature of the Party as a single system with higher and lower leading bodies, with subordination of the minority to the majority, with practical decisions binding on all members of the Party. If Gilles were to reread Stalin's *Foundations of Leninism*, he might be cautioned by a key sentence, set in italics, "*The Party becomes strong by purging itself of opportunistic elements.*" The National Executive had no doubt that Gilles, respecting its decision on the class nature of the struggle, would consciously and voluntarily submit. As all Party members knew, only conscious discipline can truly be iron discipline.

Every verse of the litany had been chanted and Gilles had no doubt what was expected of him. "The negative side of a criticism and self-criticism session was that when the leading group in the collective had an axe to grind, they could do it in this way. Ryerson and Buck had a special ideological axe to grind, and the purpose was to create disunity between Henri and me so they wouldn't have a bloc of French Canadians against them." Perhaps because of the theoretical chapter and verse he had been cited, perhaps because he wanted to stay in the Party "and play a prominent role in leading a certain portion of humanity," when the time came to take a position, Gilles didn't do, he said "what I should have done."

Fall 1947, Toronto
Communist Party National Convention.
Communist delegates from across Canada met to discuss their policy on French-Canadian nationalism. Henri: "Everything was supposed to be discussed. Put all the cards on the table, discuss them, and then take decisions." But the decisions had already been made. On the train from Montreal to Toronto, Stanley Ryerson, member of the National Executive and the National Committee, wrote, in neat, classical script, the surprise resolution that would open the convention. He and Henri were on opposite sides of the fence. Diametrically opposed. Henri, from the point of view of a National Executive, was a trouble-maker; Stanley, a reliable Party functionary. "The Party leaders had decided that they were the trustees of Marxism," said Henri, "and Stanley did the job for them." They showed it to Henri the day before the convention, the sheet of paper with a resolution that included a list of accusations against members. He wasn't among those named. He told them, "Look, I've been in the Communist Party for a long time. If you have accusations to make, prepare a trial, a Red trial, then you can find them guilty or not guilty. As long as I'm provincial organizer," he added, "you can't get away with this kind of thing." The next day his name, with three others, was on the list. "The Central Committee had decided to take organizational measures," Henri said. "The part had to be subordinated to the whole, even if it meant sacrificing the Party in French Canada."

The convention began with the surprise resolution. Gilles, "knocked into line at the Party school," stood up and read: "This Fifth Provincial Congress of the Labour Progressive Party notes the existence in the Party of a tendency, hostile to Marxism, and crystallized in a group having the characteristics of a faction. The tendency in question, which constitutes an anti-Marxist, nationalistic deviation, is characterized by...." Henri recalled the accusations against Emery Samuel, Gérard Pellerin, and Marcel Lapalme that he had read the day before—"contemptuous attitude towards internationalism; ... hostile attitude towards the central leadership of the Party." And there was the charge of antisemitism, a grave and divisive charge given that many Montreal Party members were Jews. Gilles continued: "... these comrades must cease holding any responsible positions with the Party.... Comrade Gagnon must immediately correct his attitude and undertake a struggle to improve the quality of his work." As David, then on the National Executive, said, "The Party couldn't have a bunch of east-end upstarts in Quebec telling the Central Committee what to do. The French comrades had to acknowledge the supremacy of policies made by the Political Bureau of the Central Committee." Disgusted when he heard the resolution, Evariste Dubé stood up and said, "Go to hell. I'm leaving." One hundred French Quebeckers followed him out of the room. Over 150 others, most of the original working-class cadre, would leave the Party soon after. Emery Samuel, out of respect, left the room with Dubé, conscious that "the Communist Party floundered when Dubé stood up." Gilles summarized what happened after that: "They left. The vote on the resolution for them to toe the line was carried. That was that."

For Henri and Emery, it was merely the beginning of the end. In the wake of the convention there was more name-calling, more resignations and expulsions, then rejections by the Party of repeated appeals for readmission. Without having been given a hearing, Gérard Pellerin and Emery Samuel had been accused of being anti-Marxist, anti-internationalist, antisemitic, and had been expelled. Henri: "Emery was a Party official, and Nancy, his wife, was a member of the Party, too. At one point Nancy was approached and told that if she wanted to stay in the Party she couldn't stay with her husband. Even people's love affairs—that's how bad it was. She stayed with him. They were both expelled. Two years later Samuel went to B.C. to earn a living. Heartbroken. You know, when somebody puts so much into the Party, and then…It hurts."

Later, it would be Henri Gagnon's turn. The denunciation of him came down from the Central Committee, to the Provincial Committee, to the council, and then to each club. Because the Party was retrenching along Leninist lines, there was little communication among its groups: on the one hand, infiltration could be curtailed; on the other, Emery Samuel and Henri Gagnon could be denounced and expelled while most members of the Party would have no way of knowing them or what had happened. "The [Party] centre wouldn't let the French group have a say in the elaboration of policy," said a provincial leader. "Stanley and Tim would lead the Party from Toronto." As David recalled, "We did quite a good job on Henri. We were good at that. A year later we wanted to talk to him and get him and his group back, but in the minds of the English-speaking members he was the enemy. He was done for." Lilly, who was in the French Section, knew Henri Gagnon well, having both worked and socialized with him for years. He had been best man at her wedding. "It was traumatic to end a friendship that had been so close," she said, "but that's how breaks took place in the Party. You were either a friend and a member and loyal or, if you persisted with your differences, then you were suspect as an enemy type." Or, as Ed put it, "You were a non-person when you left the Party."

The threatened split between the French Section and the Central Committee became fact. It coincided with Stalin's break with Marshal Tito, who, contrary to Soviet policy, was developing heavy industry in Yugoslavia in order to guarantee his country's political independence. Tito, too, was branded a "nationalist deviationist." Henri:

> In 1946, '47, we had launched a movement—the Squatters' Movement—that left the Fred Rose affair far behind. If that had been followed by a fairer stand on the national

issue, the two together might have led to something else. But that's problematic. We'll never know. The fact was that once socialism crossed the border into more than one country, the Third International was finished. It was a new ball game. The vision developed after the 1917 revolution and the concepts for the struggle developed on that basis were outdated. But they weren't changed within the Party.

In 1948 members of the Communist Party of Yugoslavia came to see Henri. He sent them away, saying, "I have enough miseries of my own. I don't need yours."

The expulsion of the militant, experienced French-Canadian leaders and cadre greatly weakened the Party in Quebec. Largely working class, this group had proved themselves in the unemployed movement, in the union movement, and in the underground. It was an unprecedented loss. Their expulsion foreshadowed the dogmatic, hard-line approach that, combined with government repression, would make life increasingly unrewarding for communists in the coming decade.

CHAPTER SEVENTEEN

The Post-War Labour Putsch

CAPITALIST GOVERNMENTS could not roll back socialism in Eastern and Central Europe, but they had compromised it adroitly on the home front. As the Party closed its ranks, to become an even more disciplined, centralized organization, the Canadian government quietly continued its witch hunt—of leftists, internationalists, pacifists, and of other "subversives" in the civil service, the Canadian Broadcasting Corporation, and the National Film Board. Finally, the attack on the left-wing unions went into high gear.

For employers, the government and American unions trying to take control in Canada, militant unions were the most troublesome, dissident lobby left. After the war, when employers laid off workers and reduced wages in the attempt to get back to pre-war conditions, class-conscious trade unions organized successful strikes across Canada—among loggers in B.C., seamen on the Great Lakes, rubber and electrical workers in Ontario, textile workers in Montreal and Valleyfield, steel workers in Hamilton, and lumber workers in the Ontario north woods. During 1946, 139,474 workers would walk out for a record number of working days. The strikes were under attack from scabs, goons, and labour legislation—but the militant unions fought back. Harry, as organizer in the Canadian Seamen's Union (CSU), headed the Flying Squad, a crew of thirty young but seasoned sailors, including his friend Big Stan. The Flying Squad protected strikers, shaking trucks that carried scabs, marching alongside young dressmakers, pouring sugar into gas tanks. As

Harry recalled, "We went barrelling along the middle of the night for a new appointment with destiny." Militant labour had been a necessary evil during the war years, but it was now an anathema to post-war capitalism. Mackenzie King articulated the problem: "I rather think that... there is a determination to bring about a complete change whereby Labour will have control of Government, that the strikes today are symptomatic of the determination to force the issue. I really think that Labour throughout the world has come to believe as Communists have stated, that its interests are one against all other classes in society and that in large part they are to hold to Marxian doctrines."[1] It would take five years for the continuous Red-baiting to purge completely the left-wing unions, but the move began almost immediately after the war's end. On January 26, 1946, Bob Haddow was expelled from the International Association of Machinists on trumped-up charges, but really because, in his own words, "I was a Commie, openly one. They were waiting to do a job on the communists and they did it everywhere they could." Coinciding with Fred Rose's arrest, Pat Sullivan quit the Canadian Seamen's Union. As president of the union and secretary-treasurer of the Trades and Labour Congress, he had been one of the most powerful union officers in Canada; he left, therefore, with a fanfare, accusing the union of being under communist control. He then formed a rival, or dual, "union" and proceeded to raid the CSU for members. From then on, the battle between the Canadian Trades and Labor Congress and the American Federation of Labor for autonomous control of the Canadian trade-union movement would be coloured Red.

The positions held by Party members and sympathizers in the two bodies that governed Canadian labour—the AFL-TLC and the CIO-CCL—gave the communists power in the labour movement. Communist-led unions—the Canadian Seamen's, Mine Mill, International Woodworkers, United Auto Workers, United Electrical, and Fur and Leather Workers—saw the workers' struggle not only in economic terms, but in ideological terms, as a struggle for the emancipation of labour. They were militantly anti-capitalist, as well as outspoken critics of the Canadian government's participation in NATO and the American government's Marshall Plan. As the new head of the 7,000-member Fur and Leather Workers' Union, which he helped build, Bob Haddow publicly denounced the Marshall Plan for its effect on Canada's development of foreign trade and for taking jobs away from Canadians. He called NATO a threat to world peace and suggested Canada develop its own policies towards industrial development, foreign trade, and external affairs.

The answer of the leaders of the Canadian Congress of Labour was that unions "should free themselves from Communist leadership, realizing that Communists are loyal in the first instance to Russia, rather than their own countries, and that in the case of war they will form centres of treason and sabotage."[2] Coming in the aftermath of the spy trials, this would prove a potent argument. Within five years all the large communist-influenced unions would be purged from the TLC and the CCL. In 1948 the Mine Mill Union was suspended from the CCL "as an example to others," and in the same year the British Columbia District of International Woodworkers was suspended. In 1950, invoking the technicality of non-payment of dues, United Electrical was suspended. Its appeal reached the CCL convention in the frenzied wake of the Korean War and the anti-communist crusade of Senator Joseph McCarthy. The Executive Committee of the CCL bolstered the suspension of United Electrical with a ten-page declaration that described communism and democracy as engaged in a life-and-death struggle. Communism was "the greatest tyranny the world [had] ever known" and was "everywhere on the march." The document concluded that the communists had "set up a Fifth Column in every Western nation, consisting of devoted fanatics." The executive recommended a constitutional amendment giving the council power to expel any union "which was following the principles and policies of the Communist Party." United Electrical lost its appeal; the amendment was passed. The Canadian Seamen's Union remained, posing a special threat to the government, but by 1950 the union, with 12,500 members, would be finished, leaving only the left-wing Fur and Leather Workers' Union to be expelled in 1951. "The reasons given for the expulsion of left-wing unions," concluded labour historian, Irving Abella, "were spurious and almost fatuous. At any other period and against any other unions they would have been dismissed out of hand."[3]

The Canadian Seamen's Union was the largest affiliate of the Trades and Labor Congress. Because it was a left-wing union with the power to tie up shipping on the Great Lakes and the Atlantic, it was not a popular union with the government. Because it had struck for, and won, improved wages and living conditions, and the eight-hour day, it was not in favour with ship owners. It did enjoy the unequivocal support of its members, as proved by a government-adjudicated vote in 1946, as well as considerable esteem among the other unions and the public. It would, therefore, take the concerted effort of ship owners, government, and the American Seamen's International Union (SIU) to destroy it. Helped by the Red scare, the CSU would be expelled and discredited just three years after Pat Sullivan had formed his illegal dual union.

In 1948 the three largest shipping companies—Colonial, Sarnia, and Canadian Steamship Lines—declared the CSU a communist union and refused to negotiate with it. Despite the fact that Sullivan's rival union had few members and was not affiliated with the TLC, the ship owners broke their agreement with the law, the government, and the chosen bargaining agent of the seamen and signed with Sullivan's union. It was a gross violation of collective-bargaining procedures, but the government took no action. Following the companies' refusal to negotiate, which was illegal, the CSU struck the Great Lakes. Sullivan, arrested for pulling a gun on a seaman in Montreal, challenged the union to "fight it out." Enough non-union crews were sailing to threaten the livelihood of CSU sailors, and the situation was ripe for violence. Union men, whose average age was twenty-two, tried to stop the strike-breaking ships.

Fights erupted. Strike-breakers were protected by the police, and union members were arrested and charged with criminal offences. Harry Davis, president of the CSU, described the situation: "The ship-owners, after building a terrific red-baiting smear campaign, have broken the country's labour laws and are attempting to force their stooge, the traitor J. A. (Pat) Sullivan upon the backs of the seamen. To the lawlessness of the companies, the King government has answered by sending RCMP to fight the union...At the same time, Sullivan's hoodlums are brought in to beat up our organizers and to intimidate seamen."[4]

The CSU Lake Strike had the formal support of a conference of seven hundred delegates from the TLC and the CCL, representing half a million members. Trades and Labor Congress president Percy Bengough called the strike situation one of "lawlessness with-out parallel...national emergency." Fighting continued. Stan Wingfield: "At that time there was a hell of a lot of Red-baiting going on. In the States, it was really built up to a hysteria. On the East Coast of the States we had no support. The International Longshoremen's Association would have marched into Montreal if they had their way. The CSU was classified as Red, communists, a bunch of radicals. We were the agents of Moscow, every ship was really a communist agent, it was a hot thing going. And they played it up in the newspapers." As the strike wore on, the American SIU moved into Canada, merging with Sullivan's union and thereby inheriting its illegitimate agreements with the three large shipping companies. Although it was an illegal manoeuvre, again there was no government intervention. The takeover effectively ousted the CSU as bargaining agent for its members working inland on the Great Lakes. In the thickening Cold War atmosphere, the strike and much of the CSU's original base on the Great Lakes were lost.

Less than a year later, twenty-three private companies operating ocean-going vessels announced a cutback in wages and, more importantly for those with a political past, the abolishment of the CSU hiring-hall. The report of the conciliation board made the companies' attempt to eliminate militants explicit, excluding "from the personnel employed by the companies and from the union all subversive elements." Discussions were begun in Ottawa with the minister of labour to head off a strike of seamen working on these ships, but the talks were doomed to fail. The government's chief concern was how best to dispose of the Canadian Merchant Marine, operated by private companies but government-owned. Every time it sold a ship it was confronted by "Save the Canadian Fleet" pickets from the CSU. The government didn't like the union's insistence on preserving a merchant fleet, and "perhaps as well," suggested Harry, "it didn't like the idea of a merchant navy outside its control." To settle their problem, Hal Banks, a convicted gangster, was allowed into Canada through a deal between the American State Department and Canadian Immigration Department authorities. He immediately announced that the East Coast shipping companies had signed a new contract with his union, the SIU. Despite the fact that the American union had no legal status in Canada and that shipping, like broadcasting, is a regulated industry, all further meetings between the government and the CSU to head off a strike were discontinued. The Canadian union seemed to have no alternative but to prepare for its march to the end. As a former CSU member said, "They'll get us anyway, so let's give the bastards a run for their money and go down fighting."

Back dues and contributions were collected for the deep-sea strike. Stan: "Most of us went to union headquarters on St. François-Xavier, which was also a kitchen for those doing picket duty. Our other hall, on Inspector Street, had bunk beds so those who were broke would have a place to sleep." Stan was on the Education Committee. He handed out leaflets explaining the strike to seamen and dockers, and patrolled the waterfront. "Any scabs we happened to see we tried to educate." He was also on the Food Committee. "We'd go around collecting from small shops in the Cartier district. They'd give us a lot of handouts, but by the end, the handouts were getting smaller." A lot of seamen started going over to the American union. With the backing of the ship owners and, indirectly, the federal government, Hal Banks was winning. "Any place where the ship was tied up," Stan recalled, "scabs were almost literally escorted aboard by the RCMP. In Quebec the company goons were even worse. Ourselves, we would try to fight for our rights and try to stop scabs going aboard. We'd get our heads beaten in." The violence that erupted during the CSU strikes or because of jurisdictional disputes with the SIU cost sixty CSU members a total of sixty-seven years in jail sentences.

The support of the Trades and Labor Congress for their union affiliate went beyond traditional duty but was approaching the limits possible for liberals in the Cold War. In 1949, at their annual convention, the TLC expelled the Canadian Seamen's Union and accepted the SIU, under Hal Banks, in its place. Canadian Seamen's Union president Harry Davis called a meeting on the Montreal waterfront and told his men to join the SIU because the strike had to be called off. Stan: "Some signed up but most couldn't get in. I was blacklisted, classified as a Red; no way they would have taken me." The 1962 inquiry conducted by Mr. Justice Norris into the corruption and disaster wrought by Hal Banks and his organization in Canada concluded that "one of the most cruel and oppressive instruments of control by Banks was the 'Do Not Ship' list," Bank's term for a blacklist. Stan Wingfield was one of the 2,042 seamen blacklisted, and he left Montreal to join a group of seamen staying in the CSU hall in Toronto. "I had no job so I figured what have I got to lose. Once in Toronto, it wasn't long before I realized it was just as bad there as in Montreal. Christmas-time, we managed to raise enough money to give a bunch of deep-seamen a turkey dinner. I'm sure most seamen that day had the same feeling I did, which was one of bitterness against the ship owners and the federal government, and one of sadness that the CSU was no more."

Soon after, the Canadian Merchant Marine, owned by the people of Canada and the third largest deep-sea fleet in the world, was sold to private interests at twenty-nine per cent of its original cost. It is not clear whether the government acted out of fear of a militant civilian naval service or whether, because of its fumbling post-war economic policy, it shied away from a merchant marine that might later require subsidy. Whichever, ship-building, along with other valuable industries that had grown up in wartime, was allowed to die. The government's promise that Canada would reward their seamen's valiant wartime work with a merchant fleet was as empty as the seamen's future. Seamen watched as ships, sold to other countries or registered under foreign flags, were sailed away by underpaid, non-union crews. Stan said he could not be a deep-sea sailor in Canada now and he doesn't want to be "a sweetwater boy." As for shipping out on a Yank ship: "The possibility would be very small for me." Even though he was not a member of any political party, he still retained his position, "like many of us here," on the blacklist.

In 1950 the Canadian Labour Relations Board revoked the CSU's certification because of communist domination of the union. By then the union was powerless anyway; a symbol of the intensified post-war battle between Canadian and American unions, and between the Left and Right. Years later, when his activities were investigated, Hal Banks escaped to the United States. Efforts to extradite him failed when Dean Rusk, then secretary of state, refused to cooperate.

Stan Wingfield and "Kidney," aboard the *SS Cliffside* to China, mid-Atlantic, November, 1947.

Budding wartime labour relations everywhere suffered the post-war frost. In 1950 the Progressive Conservative leader George Drew proposed in the House of Commons that legislation be introduced making communist activities an offence punishable under the criminal code. J. W. Pickersgill described the reply given by Prime Minister St. Laurent:

> He agreed with Drew that ideological warfare had been going on for a number of years between Communism and what he called "Christian civilization," but there was no agreement in free countries as to the most effective way to deal with Communist propaganda. He recalled that when the government had been urged to legislate to purge the trade unions of Communism, it had relied instead on the unions themselves to get rid of "these obnoxious influences." He was quite confident that the unions "did a much better job than could have been done by the police attempting to enforce any laws adopted in his parliament." He thought Canadians generally had been satisfied "with the autonomous purges" that the labour movement had carried out.[5]

Duplessis, back in power in Quebec, didn't rely on autonomous purges; he revived the Padlock Law and instituted anti-communist, anti-labour legislation. Bill Number 5 empowered a government-appointed board both to certify unions and to deny certification to any union whose officer was a member, supporter, advocate, follower, or sympathizer of any Marxist or communist organization, movement or philosopher. From 1947 to 1950 the Quebec Labour Relations Board revoked the certification of 12 per cent of its trade unions, refused certification to another 17 per cent, and knowingly certified 114 employer-initiated and financed associations.

By 1949, 67,000 Quebeckers were unemployed. Harry, as head of the Montreal Unemployed Council, went to Ottawa to see various federal party leaders. His experience reflects the success of the movement at that time. The demonstrators showered the members of Parliament with leaflets. "We were picked up very gently and heaved out on the outside steps of Parliament," Harry recalled. "I remember coming home that night and I went to see my mother. She looked at me, she was so proud, and she had pinned up over the sink a picture of me from the Montreal *Herald*, and underneath it said my name and 'Out He Went.' She was so happy, and then I went to Horn's Restaurant, where my father used to hang out, and he was so happy too."

The second wave of Duplessis repression knocked the smile right off the Party's face. Strikes occurring in the Province of Quebec were denounced by Antonio Barrette, minister of labour, as the work of communists bent on "revolution." Anti-labour laws and violence were used with renewed vigour.

Ste. Anne River
Summer. 1951
Gérard Fortin was on a marathon, going from logging camp to logging camp, hiding by day in barns, in the bush, holding meetings at night. He was trying to set up union committees, to sign up the 100,000 non-unionized bush workers and lumber and sawmill workers to the Union des Bucherons de la Province de Québec Independant (UBI). As he slumped, dead tired, onto the floor of an old abandoned blacksmith's hut, he thought what an uphill battle it was, organizing men from big families, from small villages where the priest was still king. He remembered the pain of his first break with religion…He was sixteen. It was Christmas. He had just run away from home to work in the bush. The priests and the company were preparing a midnight mass in the largest camp. His friends, two old-timers, anti-clerical and pro-communist, were urging him not to go. That first midnight mass away from home made Gérard feel lonely. "Midnight mass, it meant so much the midnight mass at home and the big meal after. They were leaving with the horses and sleighs, and I almost went after them. Then I decided, I stay. The

258

two old-timers were happy, saying 'We got one at least won't go to that phony show.'" Gérard knew that "to give up the religion is no small thing when you were brought up in the religion." Later, when he was a seaman, he used to make communist recruits throw the rosary away at sea, "overboard, you know, the *chapelet.*" Now, lying on the floor of the old hut, his last thought, as he sank into a deep, exhausted sleep was, even with the religion, 1,400 out of 1,600 men at the last camp had signed up for the UBI. He was stretched out, asleep, when the company goons finally got him:

> I woke up just in time; a goon was stepping with his big boots, big you know with nails underneath, stepping in my face, so I was lucky he just caught me in the chin.... But he broke my left hand and then they were really coming in; there were three. Lucky I caught the foot of the main goon and he fell off balance. I still remember his name, it was Pat Claire, an English-speaking guy in Quebec sent to beat up a union organizer. There was steel on the floor of that blacksmith hut so I got a piece about two foot long: I said, "The first bastard that comes in..." but in the meantime my left hand started to feel the pain and what really saved me, saved my life, was the two bush workers who came by. The goons could have dropped my body in the river; it was during the spring drive, floating the lumber, they could have dumped me.

Gérard made it back to Quebec City where he was summoned to court. From evidence at his trial, he learned that Duplessis had authorized the lumber companies to use violence, if necessary, to kick out the union. Twenty witnesses testified against him, but his two witnesses were nowhere to be found. He was convicted of trespassing and assault, and became the subject of anti-UBI propaganda with a Russian theme. The weekly paper of the Farmers' Union of Quebec ran a caricature of Gérard and the secretary of the UBI being led by Stalin like two horses. *L'Action*

Catholique published daily invectives against Gérard, calling him a Moscow agent. Every parish priest in villages where there were bush workers read a pastoral letter warning against joining the communist union. Despite improved living conditions and the increase in the two-dollar cord, members stopped paying their union dues. Abitibi Paper signed a back-door agreement with two AFL unions. Gérard: "we had discussions with the Provincial Committee of the Communist Party and the comrades in the unions, which were helping us with a little bit of money all the time. They were under attack themselves; the United Electrical had lost everything in Montreal and there was only left Bob Haddow, who had been kicked out of the Machinists and was with the International Fur and Leather Workers' Union, so we decided to fold. Publicly. Officially."

Once there was a shepherdess
Who watched over her sheep
But the sheep have no more wool
Fa la la la lal de
They have shorn them all
They have sold them all
They have beaten them up with so many blows
That the sheep have changed themselves into wolves
The better to boggle the bogeymen
Fa la la la lal de.[6]

The poet Gilles Henault, who wrote this poem during the post-war labour putch, had joined the Communist Party in 1946. The communist movement seemed to offer an antidote to the trauma of his desperate Depression childhood, an answer to the drunk ministers and municipal graft he saw as a journalist. Marxism, "one of the great *pensées* of our time," dealt with man and human aspirations. The philosophy made him feel that he was "not just an object that is displaced, put here, put there, pushed and pulled." Seeing the surge of the labour movement right after the war, he felt he could join with other people to change a few things, and in that way, the human being would develop. The impulse that drove Henault was "like fighting to become a flower when you are just a stem." The "shady" expulsion of the French Canadians in 1947 and the post-war difficulties of militant labour caused the poet to leave the Party. Even though the leader in Quebec was French, Henault explained, "the Party was made up of anglophones and the direction came from the Central Committee in Toronto. That made an anglophone Party in a French province. Also, communist union leaders lost their direction of the unions because Duplessis was engaged against them in a war to the death."

In a session of the Quebec Legislative Assembly, Duplessis solemnly announced discovery of a communist plot to bomb Montreal's City Hall and another plot to bomb the archbishop's palace. His provincial police graduated from intimidating communist-led meetings to beating up anti-NATO demonstrators on the street... Annette tried not to think of the comrades who had been attacked. She walked bravely into Eaton's Department Store, keeping close to her seven-year-old daughter, the child she had conceived when the Soviet Union entered the war, when she had dared to hope that the world would be free of fascism. She was now carrying a another child, and she was afraid of the proposed North Atlantic Treaty Organization, the Western anti-communist alliance with a nuclear arsenal as its base. Doing her duty in the anti-NATO campaign, Annette went resolutely up to Eaton's ninth-floor bathroom, holding her daughter tightly by the hand. She told the little girl to go to the toilet and stay there for two minutes. Opening the bathroom window, she seated herself on the window-ledge facing the stall. Frightened, her heart beating hard against her pregnant belly, she called out, "Are you okay? Do you need anything?" while all the time her hands were moving quickly behind her back, showering thousands of anti-NATO leaflets down on Ste. Catherine Street. Done, she hurried the child out of the bathroom, holding tight to the little hand, feeling the new life inside her, torn between her duty to the movement and her fear she would be arrested with the child.

Annette's' leaflets announced a mass anti-NATO demonstration on The Main, in the block between Sherbrooke and Prince Arthur. "We knew we would be attacked," said Ed, "so we stood in doorways, apartment buildings, waiting for the signal to come out." When the communists appeared, so did the waiting police force, "out of their doorways with their guns and clubs." Gilles was standing courageously in the middle of the street, making a revolutionary speech to no one, gesticulating, exhorting. "It was comical," said a participant. "No one was listening, no one except us." Mounted police charged down the street and then back again, followed by the Red Squad. "They ran us down, and then they beat the hell out of us," said Ed. "They chased me into a quiet little alley. Three or four cops came at me with clubs, one guy held my hand behind my back, and they just hit me and hit me. Then they threw me in jail with about twenty other guys. It was overkill."

Communists had been smeared and isolated by the Red Scare, but the North American establishment's determination to stomp communism out was to become yet more brutal. Raids and surveillance intensified. Montreal's Red Squad infiltrated the United Jewish People's Order and coordinated raids on members' houses. Provincial police raids increased. One day David was on the phone to CSU organizer Dan Daniels. Unexpectedly, David yelled that he was being raided and hung up. Dan quickly started sorting the books that Harry had hidden at his house, deciding what had to go. As he was packing, the doorbell rang. Another raid. The police took books, manuscripts, private letters. Most of the books and all the manuscripts were burned. That night Harry was raided as well. Across Canada a special division of the RCMP compiled twice as many dossiers as in previous years, and its personnel was increased accordingly. The RCMP trailed Reverend James G. Endicott, who addressed groups on the Stockholm Peace Appeal. They photographed people attending Canadian Peace Congress meetings. In Quebec communists going from door to door to have the Ban-the-Bomb petition signed had to place a lookout at the end of the street to warn the one ringing the bell when the police arrived. Duplessis's obsessive denunciation continued: communist saboteurs were responsible for the destruction of his bridge at Three Rivers, for the crash of a jet place at Canadair, and for the burning of nineteen floats in the St. Jean Baptiste Parade. Quoted in *La Presse*, from his speech at the Cap de la Madeleine, Premier Duplessis concluded that, "the principles of liberty, equality and fraternity of the French Revolution appear to us false and futile."

In August 1950 Ethel and Julius Rosenberg, a working-class couple from New York's Lower East Side, were arrested and charged with conspiracy to commit espionage. Their execution three years later, at the time of the bloodiest fighting in the Korean War and at the peak of Senator Joseph McCarthy's anti-communist campaign, would remain, forever, a most horrifying touchstone for these times. In March 1951 the Rosenbergs were brought to trial. They were convicted and sentenced to death by Judge Irving Kaufman in April. An appeal to the Supreme Court was lodged, but the Court refused to review the case. An appeal for clemency was sent to President Eisenhower, supported by Albert Einstein, the Pope, thousands of clergymen, public personalities, and Save-the-Rosenbergs committees around the world. In March 1953 a stay-of-execution was granted pending a new appeal to the Supreme Court, but again the court refused to review the case. The execution date was reset for June 18. On June 17 one Supreme Court judge agreed to consider new evidence and granted another stay-of-execution. The full Supreme Court was recalled from summer recess and, by a vote of six to three, reversed the decision. On June 19 Sydney, Ed, Beryl, and hundreds of others travelled to Ottawa to stand vigil outside the American embassy. Annette had been greeted by RCMP photographers as she got off the train, but as she walked slowly back and forth, counting the minutes until 8:00 P.M., it was not her own security that concerned her. Hoping against hope for the Rosenbergs' safety, she pictured the faces of Bobby and Michael, their young sons. She had seen the boys in the *Guardian*, the American communist newspaper, and read Ethel's and Julius's letters from prison:

Hello, Julie Dearest,

Since Wednesday and all the good, sweet words that passed between us, I have been walking on air. My dear one, rest easy, I am forever fortified in your love…

As for the many offers of assistance the *Guardian* has received from readers with regard to the children, I feel the closest bond with these "strangers." I am speechless with admiration for my new-found brothers and sisters! I love you,

Ethel

My dearest Ethel,

As I read this week's *Guardian*, the letters to the editor, the superlatives used made me feel humble. I think the thing that stands out is that we are just ordinary people similar in many ways to the writers of the letters, and in our case they see part of themselves, and the thoughts strikes them that they, too, are threatened with a similar catastrophe….

By now it is Monday night—one day closer to seeing you…

Your own,

Julie

Annette was convinced, as was every other person standing vigil, that the Rosenbergs were innocent. "They were very decent people. It was just so cruel, so vengeful. A great big state was taking it out on two little people." In committee headquarters, Harry worked frenetically, putting out press releases every hour, "acting as if what we did so far away could have an influence in Washington." The world was slipping away; he worked instinctively, struggled to hang on. Annette was clinging to shreds of hope from other vigils. A week ago, before the U.S. embassy vigil in Montreal, the Reverend Glend Partridge, her neighbour and comrade, had warned that the

Demonstration demanding clemency for the Rosenbergs,
Ottawa, January, 1953.
Library and Archives Canada

McCarthyism which had condemned the Rosenbergs was spilling over into Canada; his own children had been taunted and beaten because he was chairman of the National Committee to Save the Rosenbergs. "We must protect our cherished democratic rights," was his response. "Save the Rosenbergs! We must go out and fight!" Annette and Sydney and about fifty others had gone to the consulate on Stanley and Ste. Catherine Streets and hoisted "*Sauver les Rosenbergs*, Save the Rosenbergs" banners. As soon as the first team of about twelve had started marching, police bore down and took their banners. Immediately, on another corner, banners were raised and another parade to the consulate moved out. The police moved in again, grabbed the banners and attacked. A seaman was clubbed and kicked, a woman thrown bodily into a patrol car, three members of the second team arrested. New groups kept appearing and those who were not arrested brought new banners. The police became more savage. They grabbed anyone they could lay their hands on, beat them and bundled them into patrol cars. The gathering crowd jeered and booed the violence and a shower of Save the Rosenberg leaflets descended from the window of a nearby office building. Thirteen of Annette's friends were arrested, eleven women and two men, not counting the three U.S. citizens arrested by mistake as they emerged from the consulate. Finally, after an hour, a contingent of police on horseback arrived, rode into the crowd and dispersed it. Still Annette had felt elated. She had the feeling that they would go back tomorrow, the next day, and every day until the Rosenbergs were saved, no matter what.

"Truth can be fought for and won," Glen had said.

"Life is stronger than death."

"Julius and Ethel must not die."

"Julius and Ethel will not die."

Annette shifted her "Clemency" sign to the other side and moved closer to Beryl. Behind them, Ed and Sydney walked together. Ed felt numb and defeated. He knew the Rosenbergs were going to die and there was nothing he could do about it. Since his beating, on The Main, he had reached a low point, a point of no return. He felt completely isolated from the man on the street— when "only seven years ago we had been popular." Before, he might have thought communists were losing the battle, but as he now went robot-like to the car-radio for news, he had an inkling that they were losing the war. As it neared eight o'clock, Annette walked painfully, more slowly, barely controlling a paralysis of desolation. Then she saw Ed, running up and down. "They are dead," he said. "They've killed them." Now, Annette broke. And cried—bewildered, beaten, outraged, angry tears. "The Rosenbergs were scapegoats. The American government was trying to intimidate a whole population. This is what would happen if you had any sympathy for the Soviet Union or took part in any radical movements." Glen spoke of the "crude, barbaric execution" and his conviction that "when the war-fevers of this present time are passed away," Julius and Ethel Rosenberg would be "cleared of the guilt smeared upon them" and he, too, almost broke down. As Annette remembered that night, she cried again. "I'm still crying," she sobbed, "after all those years."

Communists grieved deeply for the brave and dignified couple, for Ethel, the strong woman, whom they felt they knew, for the children, and because, as Sydney said, "It could have been any one of us."

CHAPTER EIGHTEEN

The Final Years

MEMBERS DESCRIBED THE years from the Atlantic Security Pact, signed in 1949, to the Khrushchev revelations about Stalin, in 1956, as a "political treadmill." Because of the Gouzenko affair, the Canadian Communist Party had the dubious honour of being among the first Communist parties in the world to experience isolation and stagnation. Members could feel the Cold War in their bones and see its effect on the previously "favourable" people who now slammed the door in their face. The issues were there and they were dutifully tackled, but the spirit was gone. Party work was carried on against unrelenting odds. "The more people who left, the more responsibility there was for the ones who stayed," said Annette. "We held the whole history of the world in our hands, didn't we—our children's future." Revolutionary *élan* was replaced with dogged stoicism. "We just thought, the smaller the Party got, that everybody had to do a little bit more, like in Orwell's *Animal Farm*, when Boxer says, 'The rest of us will just have to work harder.'"

In the community group of Park Extension, Annette, Sydney, Beryl, and Ed, all with growing children, were trying to influence the quality of education. They ran community nursery schools, and child-rearing seminars, started a library, petitioned for stop-signs, and presented a detailed, carefully researched brief to the Protestant School Board, asking that a high school be built in their underprivileged district. Three hundred people used to attend home-and-school meetings, "before TV," and there, according to Beryl, "we got our adrenalin going." Annette and Beryl attacked the sale of violent comic books, while Christian mothers, to combat communism, stood up to defend war stories. "At one point our friend Gertrude Partridge raised a hand, got up, and said she wanted to make a correction: that February 14 would not be a Wednesday, it was a Thursday. A teacher stood up, who was known as an independent—she was trusted by everybody—and she said, 'Mrs. Partridge is right,' and as she said those words there was a gasp throughout the hall." Beryl also criticized the practice of charging children for books and publicly humiliating those who couldn't pay. Her neighbour, from a poor family in the Maritimes, felt Beryl spoke for her, for what she'd suffered as a child, and thanked her, saying, "I am so proud to think that I know you and you are my neighbour." After that the neighbour started taking an interest in other issues, like the high school. "Then there was a provincial election," recalled Beryl. "She asked me who I was going to vote for, because by this time she had so much confidence in me. I said, 'The LPP candidate,' and she never spoke to me again. She said, 'But you're one of them. You're really an enemy. You fooled me completely,' and she was speechless. She really let me have it about how I had taken her in by pretending to be concerned about the children."

The Cold War, begun in 1946 with the trials of the communists, gathered momentum in the McCarthy era. Radio glorified the communist witch hunts with "I was a Communist for the FBI." Popular magazines such as *Reader's Digest* and the *Saturday Evening Post* featured stories on "the evil potion" of communism. Headlines in Canadian magazines shrieked, "Door-to-Door Spy Hunt in Ottawa," "The Enemy Within—Domestic Communists Require Very Careful Watching—Foreign Languages Groups are Red Hot Beds," and "Canadian Shop Papers are Communist Poison."[1] For the children, instead of hockey cards, there were Red Menace bubble-gum cards. As the gap between truth and idiocy in the anti-communist campaign widened, so did the public's capacity to swallow the idea of another war. Following major features in the *New York Times*, *Look*, *Life* and *Newsweek* on how best to bomb Russia from the air, the October 1951 issue of *Collier's* magazine featured its one unique war spectacular: "Russia's Defeat and Occupation, 1952–60: Preview of a War We Do Not Want." The story, profusely illustrated, mapped, and diagrammed, claimed the cooperation of high Washington officials and coolly promised success—at the end of a three-and-a-half-year war during which thirty-two million Soviets would die.

But despite persecution and ostracism, Party members wouldn't give up. "Nothing was happening," said Sydney, "but the dream of socialism was still a very worthwhile thing. We had lived through the Spanish Civil War, tried to stop the Second World War, enlisted in the army, and we continued after, trying to do whatever was humanly possible to raise a family in a peaceful, decent world." Although communists were increasingly cut off from the rest of the population, their daily lives were reinforced by their alternative community and culture—camps, schools and social gatherings, often given sustenance by the energy and humanism of folk music. Although they were blacklisted, the pioneering folk quartet, The Weavers, and Pete Seeger, on his own, continued to share their love of music with audiences across North America. Singing together, people did not feel alone. They clapped, stomped and belted out—the dream.

> Well I got a hammer and I got a bell
> And I got a song to sing over this land;
> It's the hammer of justice, it's the bell of freedom
> It's the song about love between my brothers and my sisters
> All over this land.[2]

Many who were then children remember, as did Laura Rose, the bond between people, the warmth and goodness. Fred Taylor's son felt "a positive, energetic, joyful spirit. The competition thing was absent. You didn't see people winning over each other. School was the antithesis of the warm family feeling I got from being with left-wing people. There were so many people who knew me, cared about me." Jerry said that he was ten years old before he lost the belief that his world of "nice communists" was the norm. It was in the spring of 1952, when Jerry was in the sixth grade, that the Red

Squad padlocked the United Jewish People's Order. The padlock on the cherished building precipitated the closure of the Morris Winchevsky Jewish School, which Jerry had happily attended since he was four years old. One child of communists remembers her fight with her public-school history teacher in which she hotly defended her parents' point of view; another recalls the embarrassment of being sent home from the 1950 Park Extension Annual Parade, "because I was dressed as an Indian, carrying a sign saying, 'Let's Bury the Tomahawk with the Soviet Union.'" "I always knew there was an 'us' and a 'them,'" said a communist worker's daughter. "As a child I would sometimes watch my grandmother cry at the end of a day in the factory. She taught me that there was no such thing as a nice boss and gave me a certain view of how the world worked."

Although communists were, as Jerry learned, "an embattled minority," the community was sufficiently dynamic to maintain its beliefs. Homes were filled with books, records, pictures—*Spartacus*, the Maccabees, Patrick Henry, Tom Paine—images and talk of "that ancient and unfinished struggle for human freedom and dignity."[3] Marxism was not taught as a lesson but, as Irene said, "it was just part of the way you lived, it was part of the way you thought, part of the way you behaved to other people." Families read the papers and they talked together. Friends came over to discuss. It was considered important to be honest, to treat people with respect, to fight for justice for all, especially for those who were most subject to the inequalities of a system they didn't understand. Understanding was all-important. "Each day, at supper, in the living room, we talked about world events with an urgency that encouraged being informed," recalled the child of communists. "We would take the pulse of the world because it mattered so much what was happening. It mattered because we believed that, with other people, we could change things, we could have a say in how the world would be." Basic to their communist philosophy was the belief that all people were born good, that they were corrupted by poverty, exploitation, and war, the evils of capitalist society. If people could live in a socialist society that took care of their needs and allowed them to develop their full selves, they would be strong, capable, loving. There would be no crime, no problems. As Irene's daughter said, "My mother's and father's view of socialism was like heaven. One day the millennium will come, one day we'll get there and struggle will cease." The Marxist theory of socialism promised that socialism would inevitably triumph, but that, with effort, communists could make it triumph sooner. "If we all pulled together, we could get socialism maybe years before it would come with historical inevitability and make life happier for all much sooner," remembered Annette. "It was a big responsibility." As Jerry recalled, "The sense of purpose in life, of self-transcending purpose, was incredibly strengthening and nourishing." Members were bound together by what Jessica Mitford called "the magnet of socialist reconstruction of society," but even more so by their inextricably close personal ties: friendships, children, love affairs, marriages, often a shared history going back as many as twenty years. Many members echoed Annette: "The best people that we knew, people that we admired the most, got along with best, liked, and just felt the happiest being with, were in the party. That's why we stayed."

During the fifties members didn't question the correctness of the Party line. With grim and serious earnestness they just got behind it. "We didn't have to think," said a provincial organizer, "only work and work and the world would be better." They called for family allowances and fairer labour laws. They condemned the takeover of Canada's natural resources by American interests and demanded a new constitution and a bill of rights. They financed the legal appeal to have the Padlock Law revoked, called for a five-power conference to end the Korean War, put whatever energy they could muster into the peace movement, and tried to bring up their children to live, as Beryl said, "like human beings, on their feet." As the fifties ground on, the dutifulness members felt they owed to the Party, given freely before, became more onerous. Members were older, had growing families, and they could no longer say, as Fred Rose had said, that they worked hard "for the satisfaction of seeing results." Ritualistically, they continued their Party work.

Lilly couldn't escape a nagging guilt about her kids. She wanted to spend more time with them, but the week was filled with "a series of obligations and drudgery that I hoped some year would disappear." Resigned, she considered her schedule: Monday night, a section meeting; Tuesday, a repetition of Monday at a club meeting; Wednesday, a council meeting "with an agenda of more than thirteen items"; Friday night, a meeting to discuss special activities, the elections, and omnipresent financial campaigns. "Meetings often lasted until eleven, with tremendous repetition of the same thing week in, week out. Every organization had to have its meeting even if only five people met." Lilly felt relief one evening when Annette scandalized a women's group by suggesting, "If there are any more 'points' to be raised, I think we should raise them with our husbands, at home." Lilly smiled and figured that Thursday night would be her only night to sell the communist newspapers *Combat* and the *Tribune* door-to-door. Saturday night there would, she knew, be a fundraising event, and Sunday at 1:00 A.M., she suspected she might find herself at a special conference. "If you had a social evening it was to raise money," she explained. On dozens of Saturday nights sixty members of the French Section would get together in Lilly's and Gilles's small, east-end flat to eat a spaghetti dinner: one dollar for dinner and extra for drinks. "If someone had more than his quota of booze and crawled down the stairs, that would be secondary to whether the Party had cleared $100 or $125." Between 1948 and 1949, $75,000 was raised by the Party in Quebec and stashed in different bank accounts in Montreal; the money, representing a great many spaghetti dinners, led the treasurer to comment, "Never has so much money been raised by so few."

Increasingly, the Party became a self-defense organization, turned in on itself and cut off from political realities. Members needed a leave of absence to miss a meeting. Party leaders pushed members to sell copies of the *Tribune* to the non-communist members of every local group they managed to organize; whereupon the members, realizing that the organizers were communists, would leave the group—and, Beryl remembers, "they would really hate us after that." People became more obsessive in criticism sessions, laying blame and taking blame for situations beyond their control. Leaders kept a tight rein on those suspected of any deviation from the Party line and people were called up more often on charges. Gérard Fortin was brought to Montreal from Quebec City to manage *Combat* and to organize the St. Henri district. In Quebec City he left behind eight groups. "Then I came to Montreal and boy, if they had a hundred members in the French Section I'd be surprised." He castigated the leadership for sitting in meeting after meeting instead of going out to recruit. "They said I think a little too much of myself, so I was called on the carpet to analyse my national deviation or something. It was kind of a trial, like we had on the ship, a trial committee. Finally, they gave me time to think of my position on the French Section, and then I had to apologize and say that maybe I thought too much of myself." Harry, who dared to criticize Soviet art, was reported and co-opted; he was made chairman of the Cultural Committee so that, as a loyal communist, he would submerge his own views and perceptions, and push the Party line that "a people's culture is based on social realism," which, to his later embarrassment, he did. "For a couple of years, I just parroted the Party line with no conviction. We had a Cultural Committee which was composed of leading artists from theatre, graphic arts, and I'd be pushing the line and it was ludicrous. But I felt that it was a minor thing to do for the greater good." What Gilles remembers most about the final years were not the issues the Party stood for, but "talking and talking in the St. Louis district until my vocal cords went." Ed recalled, "My time was seventy per cent meetings, thirty per cent collecting money, selling *Tribunes*, and interminable discussions among ourselves on the basics in Stalin's treatise on linguistics."

Members were prisoners of a single language, a system of discourse rigid enough to choke any independent thought. It had always been, as Sydney said, that "if you brought in facts from another newspaper, they would be rationalized within the system, or you still had a bourgeois mentality and had to overcome it." But now, the mental gymnastics boggled the mind. "You'd have a heading," said Harry, which would be called, 'The Fight for the *Turn*'—the 'turn' would be italicized, and there was a ponderous weight about the thing. 'The Fight for the *Turn*,' the turn being the turn upward and forward like at the moment you're going down and you have to turn to go upward. Or you'd have an article, 'From the Particular to the General, and from the General to the Particular.' That's like how many angels danced on the head of the needle. I mean that's jesuitical sophistry, that *pilpul, pilpul*, which was its equivalent in terms of esoteric rabbinical studies. It isn't real and it wasn't real because the reality had to do with Soviet state power. How we related to that, which was shaping where we were as the thing was going, we didn't really talk about."

Communists invented little catch phrases such as "What's freedom?" People would say you're not free if you can't vote, you're not free if you can't disagree, and communists agreed that you couldn't do either of those things in the Soviet Union. "So," said Harry, "we went back to Spinoza, who was a descendant of sorts of Kant, and he had this great phrase, 'Freedom is the recognition of necessity.' So once we had that, we then knew what freedom was; it had no other meaning. If one were to say, 'You won't be free,' we'd say, 'Bullshit. What's freedom? Freedom is....'" Similarly, when someone questioned the single-party system in the Soviet Union, "we reassured them," Jerry recalled. "True there was only one candidate. But the process of selection was vigorously democratic." A complete intellectual construct of catch phrases defined freedom, democracy, class, power, virtue. Communists' entire perception of everything was shaped by communist constructs and communist dreams. With an ear for the ridiculous, Jessica Mitford produced the definitive satire of left-wing usage, the second language of all Party members (which follows on the next page).

QUESTIONS	ANSWERS
7. What must we do soberly?	7. Evaluate, estimate, assess, anticipate (correct answers); go down to nearest bar (incorrect answer).
8. List various kinds of struggle.	8. All out, political class, cultural, principled, many-sided, one-sided, inner Party
9. What-illating petit bourgeoisie?	9. Vac.
...	
11. What does one do with cadres?	11. One develops them, trains them and boldly promotes them, poor things
12. List as many words ending with ism as you can think of. Warning: obvious ones like fasc, social, imperial, etc. don't count.	12. Chauvin; diversion; narrow-sectional; exceptional; liquidation; adventur; revision; sch (got you there); opportun; confusion; Browder tail of Khvost (obs.); Keynes.
13. What is happening to the contradiictions in the situation?	13. They are sharpening, and deepening. Also unfolding. (Sometimes they even gather momentum with locomotive speed.)[4]

As the Party got smaller, the realities of decision-making became more stark. "Anybody that thought a decision of any kind, of any importance, was made on a club level, or a council level, or a sectional level, or a city level, was fooling themselves; and I don't think anyone had such illusions," said Lilly. "Basically, these things were decided in the National Executive, not even in the National Committee, which was a large body of about forty people with regional representation. The executive was a nucleus of full-time staff in Toronto, and that's really where decisions were made, in reaction and confirmation of what was being discussed with the Soviet people." As Ed said, "We never really elected the National Executive. Conventions were run by a small group of people from the National Executive who had prepared for weeks: an agenda of who speaks when, timings of resolutions and motions on the floor, slate of candidates. Rank-and-file delegates couldn't nominate against the slate or discuss potential leaders." Whatever the illusions were before the fifties, it was, as Gilles quaintly said, "very hard to contest a leader." As Party leader in Quebec, Gilles dealt with Tim Buck, Sam Carr, Paul Phillips, and: "If you criticized Tim Buck you wouldn't get away with it." "Gilles tried, but followed [the National Executive's] direction," Lea explained. "David was a tough egg—ba-boom, ba-boom, the Lord has spoken. Stanley took orders from Toronto and Toronto took orders from the Soviet Union. When we had Freddie, you could reason with him, discuss. He wasn't rigid. But after, the Party was just going to pot."

Yet, Party members accepted the centralized leadership, and they blocked out or censored anything that would subvert their faith. Anna Louise Strong, who had changed worlds—from America to the Soviet Union—wrote confidentially to a political compatriot that the people "on whose side I felt myself to be fighting—they wince so if a single weakness in the U.S.S.R. were noticed...So I let my audience pressure me into giving what I knew was a partial picture." Lies and especially lies of omission systematically covered up Soviet "mistakes." Members coming back from the Soviet Union kept quiet about many of their experiences there. The trains full of prisoners Gilles had seen in Moscow after the war, going north, soldiers with machine guns riding guard—he didn't tell anybody about them except his wife. "Janet" had also seen the trains and neither did she speak up. "I thought maybe I was too young to understand." Members focused on the external repressions, and there was talk again of going underground.

In 1938 John Strachey had addressed the question of "the sacrifice of that complete independence in the intellectual and material sphere which those who come from the favoured classes in Britain and America enjoy so fully and prize so much." He had asked, rhetorically, "But is this sacrifice too high a price to pay for the salvation of human society?" By the 1950s Party members had accepted the Party, right or wrong. A Party leader said, "When we became communists, all the lights went on. We read Marx, Lenin,

Engels, and we said, 'Yes.' The problem was that it became the revealed truth and we checked our brains at the door. The content was different but it was like a religious experience. We adopted the secular religion of communism with its dogma, priesthood, hatred of anyone outside the pale." Watchful, careful and, yes, hopeful too, Canadian communists, in their most difficult period, channelled their idealism into dead ends. Harry: "That was a period when the house was raided and there was constant harassment. When you are beleaguered like that, there is a camaraderie, a sense of oneness, a sense of martyrdom is what it is, which can sustain you for quite a while until you suddenly discover that everything written in *Darkness at Noon* is true—what your friends, although you haven't thought of them as friends, have been saying is true, and that's what happened in 1956."

[CHAPTER NINETEEN]

The Revelations

We owed allegiance to an ideal that we held inviolate—no exploitation of man by man, the right to an education, everybody gets
work, no racism, no discrimination, equal opportunity for all.
The ideal was great, but we believed that it was embodied in the
Soviet Union. –*Sydney*

AT THE END OF APRIL 1956, Tim Buck reluctantly reported to the
select National Executive of the Canadian Communist Party on
the denunciation of Stalin, delivered by Nikita S. Khrushchev, first
secretary of the Soviet Union, at a secret session of the Twentieth
Congress of the Communist Party of the Soviet Union in Moscow.
Tim Buck had not been invited to the secret session. British
Communist Party leader Harry Pollitt, cursing, had told him about
it, as they waited in the lineup for the funeral cortège of Polish Party
leader Boleslav Bierut, in Warsaw. Buck had gone back to Moscow,
and in his hotel room, someone from the Canadian desk read him
the speech in its entirety. He made copious notes: "massive arrests,
torture to extract confession, repression against respected political
and cultural leaders." As Tim Buck read these notes to the Canadian
National Executive, Gilles, now a member of the inner circle, listened
in shock. It was "hair-raising." For eighteen years Gilles had devoted
his love, his life, to the Party. Now, he was to begin an agonizing
six-month period of re-evaluation. As the months wore on, he
would wonder increasingly, "How are we going to build socialism
with what we are carrying?" He would argue that the Party should

279

declare: "This has nothing to do with our concept of socialism." He would think out concrete proposals and make motions, hoping that maybe they could cut loose from the Soviet Union, from the stigma of being thought Soviet "stooges" that had haunted them since the spy trials. But "certain comrades were opposed to revealing all the gory details." When the larger National Committee met in May, Tim Buck downplayed Khrushchev's report, pretending he hadn't really heard it: "There were rumours from Moscow, a few things had happened, they would be corrected." Frustrated, Gilles wondered privately if there was any hope, if he should resign. He felt the only solution was for the membership to know the full, tragic story of "the workers' paradise" so that a mass catharsis could take place, so that the monolithic international communist movement could die and a truly democratic Canadian party take its place.

In June 1956 the American State Department released a fairly full and reliable text of Khrushchev's secret speech and arranged for it to have worldwide publicity. The translation, published in the *New York Times*, affected the membership like a volcano, totally blowing away Buck's attempts to cover it up. "I don't think it took twenty-four hours before our club met," said Ed. "The first thing we discussed was whether it was true, and almost everyone considered it true. We were in utter shock. We didn't know what to believe, think." But the four-page denunciation from the Soviet head of state could not be denied. Stalin was not "a dear father, wise teacher, genius," as Khrushchev had written on "the precious date of his seventieth birthday," but a despot, and a murderer. Sixteen million Soviet citizens had, in the words of the Khrushchev Report, been "physically annihilated." Stalin's mass terror was used against dissidents, Party cadre, Central Committee members, and ethnic minorities. As Rosa Luxemburg had prophesied, "The dictatorship of the proletariat will become the dictatorship of the Party, the dictatorship of the Party will become the dictatorship of the Central Committee, the dictatorship of the Central Committee will become the dictatorship of one man." Soviet communism was rotten. The Khrushchev Report cut to the heart of belief. For most Party members, the treadmill stopped.

The mythology of communism had always been inextricably bound up with the Soviet Union, the prime example of a communist state. No one had desired or dared to think it less than perfect. "Our tie to the Soviet Union was because of our hatred of capitalism," said Sydney. "If a marriage broke down it was because people were poor and under pressure. Disturbed children were from poor homes. Whatever was bad was capitalist; whatever was good was socialist. The Soviet Union was all good." Criticism of the Soviet Union came from "enemies of the working class." When two women intellectuals from Section 13 were upset at learning that there were no divorces or abortions in the Soviet Union, they addressed their "problem" to Bella Gauld, a respected early militant. She explained that the Soviet Union, surrounded by hostile forces, had to produce babies because it needed soldiers. "We walked out of there feeling stupid," recalled one woman. "Why couldn't we have figured that out?" The Soviet Union was a planned, rational, cooperative society in which everything, once understood, made perfect sense. Stanley Ryerson, without having ever seen the Soviet Union, passed on the mythology. "There's one thing you have to learn," he told a fresh recruit. "The Soviet Union is not our society. Soviet man is a new man, and we can't grasp what that is." What had been required was not rational scepticism but faith. When members read the Khrushchev Report, many, like Beryl, felt "sick, absolutely sick." Idealism turned into horror because, as an ex-Communist writer said, "Stalin, our beloved leader, was a paranoid maniac." Ed had not been scared when the police beat him, "but this was scary. Losing your faith, your ideals, was scary."

Every week, twice a week, big meetings open to all Party members were held in the Mount Royal Arena, near Park Avenue, where Sydney and Annette had first heard Norman Bethune speak about Spain. Things were rougher in Montreal than elsewhere, and Tim Buck, David, and other National Executive leaders were sent from Toronto to pacify the membership. In the course of the initial meetings, Tim Buck admitted that he had known about the Khrushchev Report as early as March. "He knew and he didn't tell us," said Sydney. "That added to the resentment." People got up and attacked the leadership for hiding things from them. Person after person rose, holding sections of the *New York Times*, reading parts, especially about the liquidation of the Polish Central Committee and the murder of the Jews. "We wanted explanations," said Ed. "We didn't trust the Party, the leadership, or what we had considered sacred." No one spoke up for Russian communism.

The Jewish section, now the largest section of the Party in Montreal, was confronted with the brutal truth of Soviet anti-semitism. Many had joined the Party because it was the champion of religious and racial equality and they believed that there was no antisemitism in the Soviet Union. They now knew that the popular Yiddish writer Itzik Pfeffer, whom they had met in Montreal during the war when he had come to raise money for the Red Army, had been imprisoned, sentenced to death, and executed. Solomon Mik-hoels, the innovative theatre director, had died in a mysterious car accident during the 1948 anti-cosmopolitan purge of Jewish intellectuals. When J. B. Salsberg went to the Soviet Union in 1953, he had asked about the rumours that they had been liquidated. David had told Sydney then that Salsberg was trying to undercut pure socialism: "even to question was a deviation." Salsberg had lost his seat in the Party secretariat and on the National Executive. Now, Jewish members knew that Soviet Jews had lost the right to cultivate their Jewish culture: to send children to state schools, where they received instruction in Yiddish; to publish their own periodicals and newspapers, or to develop their own literature and theatre. They knew that in 1952, after a wave of mass arrests, the majority of Yiddish cultural leaders in the Soviet Union had been shot. Jews lived, stigmatized as aliens, with the terror of Stalin's equivocal attitude to national minorities hanging like a sword over their heads. Party members wondered now at the communist double-think that had had them fighting in the thirties for Spanish refugees while staying silent about Jewish refugees. "Why didn't we speak out? I would assume that enough stuff came out then but that we tended either to disbelieve or to push it aside because for the longest time we were silent," a woman recalled sadly. "It's in that area that I feel guilty. Being Jewish I didn't necessarily have more responsibility than a non-Jew but certainly equal responsibility and I was a person who spoke up for other people. A large percentage of the people in the Party were Jewish and I think we had brainwashed ourselves that internationalism means you don't speak up for the Jews. Especially if you're Jewish. It was a crazy kind of thinking." For many, the sense of self-transcending purpose was gone. The ideals had no more power to strengthen and nourish.

Gilles, Harry, and the other four members of Quebec's Provincial Committee were not yet prepared to give up making Canada socialist. They were not "old-timers" and they eschewed blind allegiance to the U.S.S.R. They discussed among themselves making common cause with others. It was clear to them, as Gilles said, "that it would not be possible to lead people collectively to build a better life within the Canadian Communist Party while it was tied to Soviet communism." For a week following publication of Khrushchev's speech in the *New York Times*, the Party in France issued statements criticizing the Soviet Union, and during this time, Tim Buck allowed Gilles to raise the question of the superficiality of the Soviet Party's analysis of the previous twenty-five years' abuses, all of which it attributed to "the cult of the personality." On June 26, the National Executive even declared publicly that it "didn't consider Nikita Khrushchev's explanations on the violations of Soviet democracy from 1934 to 1953 adequate." It asked what incorrect theories and conceptions led to Stalin's extraordinary powers and went so far as to lay the responsibility for the failure of the system on the entire Communist Party of the Soviet Union. After much debate, the *Canadian Tribune* was empowered to publish the Khrushchev Report, giving it wider circulation among Party members. Gilles, understanding the kind of forces that had expelled Henri Gagnon in 1947, brought up the question of Henri's expulsion in the National Executive. At his insistence, during this self-critical and relatively open few days, Henri and his group were rehabilitated. Soon after, however, the communist leaders in France went to Moscow and were induced to close ranks and reaffirm the solidarity of the working class. Tim Buck, falling in step, decided there had been enough criticism from the Canadian Party. Four days after it had criticized the Soviets, the National Executive repudiated its stance by publishing and distributing the Soviet tract "Decision on the Elimination of the Personality Cult and its Consequences," which was to be the final word. At the July meeting of the National Executive, Tim Buck reasserted that the Canadian executive was part of the world communist movement with ties to the Soviet Union. His article in August's *National Affairs Monthly* directed all serious socialists to forget retrospective preoccupations and get behind a unified fight. The Party centre—Tim Buck, Stanley Ryerson, David, all except Gilles and Salsberg—held tightly to the threadbare dream of the Third International.

But Party members were beginning to hear more and more, even more than was printed. In Poland students demonstrated against the Soviet regime. Eastern Europe stirred. Hungary would be next. People wanted plain talk, not a jargon of dreams. By August, when Tim Buck came to Montreal with what one member called "his whole bullshit line," the people in the meeting hall, according to Ed, "just laughed at what he said. They hooted him." As discussion in the hall became more heated, Buck began denouncing his critics as "revisionists," "liquidators," and "rotten elements." For the first time the epithets failed to have an effect. The membership in Montreal, supported by members in other parts of Canada, insisted that J. B. Salsberg accompany Tim Buck and the Party delegation, on its way to the Soviet Union to seek guidance and report on the extent to which the Soviet Communist Party had abandoned Stalinist practices. Salsberg was trusted to give the membership another point of view. They were to be back in October and would report at a big public meeting. When the meeting came, it destroyed any residual hope.

In the weighted silence of the full hall, Gilles heard Joe Salsberg say that all the things in the report were true, except that it was much worse. Then he watched Tim Buck rise and, with the sincerity that was his trademark, tell the members that they had no right to question fundamental issues; they should carry on as before. Outraged, fed up, people, as Harry recalled, "began to boo, scream, shout, perform." After the meeting, Gilles drove Tim Buck to the airport, saying, "We have no credibility. Where does this take us?" But the old soldier of the International had nothing to say and no questions to ask. Gilles himself had accepted this kind of discipline from 1947 to 1956, but he couldn't any more. He had gone through six harrowing months of meetings with the membership, the Provincial Committee, and the National Executive. There was no way to influence the Central Committee to take a new path. Questioning deeper than "the cult of the personality," even questioning the cult of the personality in respect to the Canadian Party itself, was discouraged. All criticism of the Party remained forbidden. Trotsky's name was unspeakable. When Harry asked Comrade Buck if he would agree to an "analysis of Marxist thought," Buck turned white. "He would not tolerate any questioning of fundamental Marxist theory." At the last National Committee meeting in Toronto, the leader of the Ukrainian communist group in Winnipeg had criticized the Quebec provincial leaders for being concerned about Jews and not about the working class. "We realized," said Harry, "that Tim Buck and those around him were tied to the Soviet Union. They couldn't say shit even though they had a mouthful of it."

There was nothing Gilles could do. After he dropped Tim Buck at the airport, he parked his car and thought for an hour. The pleading of his friends to hold on, not to leave the Party, wrestled with his absolute conviction that "the Party wasn't worth saving." It wasn't a moral principle. "It was the practical impossibility of working within the Communist Party of Canada to build a better life." That evening he told the Provincial Executive that he was quitting, resigning from the executive and Party. The five other members of the Provincial Committee had also been through exhausting and traumatic months of meetings and discussions. They had concluded, according to one, that "the Party was the prisoner of the Soviet Union." Four months after the publication of the Khrushchev Report and after "months of discussion, stone-walled all the way," all six of the paid staff functionaries of the Communist Party in Quebec quit. It was the first time in the history of any communist party in the world that the leadership had abdicated *en masse*; it was unusual, as well, in that no opposition movement was proposed, no committee of reform, no self-promotion to lead anything else.

Still subject to a reflex loyalty to the Party, with the guilt of a traitor giving something to the bourgeois press, Harry arranged for Gilles's resignation statement, subscribed to by all six members of the Quebec Provincial Committee, to be published in the Montreal *Gazette*. The statement, addressed to the National Committee, the Provincial Committee, and the members of the Labour Progressive Party, argued that it was now impossible to build a viable Marxist Party within the framework of the LPP. The Canadian public was averse to the LPP because of its ties to the Soviet Union, a country without freedom and rife with antisemitism, and Tim Buck refused to weaken Canadian Party ties to it. Gilles explained that he had seen in socialism the most complete liberty, the very opposite of fascist terror and oppression. He had foreseen with hope the day new relationships of production would bring to the people of Canada not only a fairer standard of living, but also the elimination of man's inhumanity to man. The article ended with a quote from Gilles: "I feel now the need to seriously examine that truth,...to try to separate what is valid from what is not valid."

The membership was hit again. If there was a pyramid of communism, the top had just fallen off. Several hundred Montreal Party members followed their leaders out of the Party. As Sydney remembered, "The Party just fell apart. There were no more provincial meetings, section meetings, council meetings. There was no sense holding branch meetings. No one was asking for money any more. It was a slow dying away." Party members were left, as Ed said, "empty and sick at heart." Ed felt, he said, that "I sacrificed my life, things for my family, for nothing." Earning a living had been secondary to Party work and he had not questioned his job, but now, "all of us looked around and wondered what we were going to do." Some felt disorientation and a loss of belief so profound that it was like the end of a marriage or the death of a loved one. "I think people were in a state of shock," said Lilly. "It was like a mass funeral was taking place in the family. A large number of people were really dying. There was shock, there was bewilderment, there was a state of insanity."

Gilles was "shattered" and very much alone. The euphoric feeling of understanding the movement of history, and his place in it, had settled like ashes in his mouth. He felt "sick." He had been prepared to give his life for the movement. His belief had ordered his whole purpose and his everyday activity. At age nineteen, his father had kicked him out of the house because he was a communist. His uncle had disinherited him. For ten years he had been Party secretary in Quebec, working every waking moment of his day for thirty-five dollars a week. Now, he didn't know what to say or do. He couldn't answer the telephone. People outside the Party either suspected him or lauded him in terms he couldn't countenance. He wasn't wanting to denounce the Soviet Union and he couldn't rationalize what had happened. He couldn't help anyone else. Remaining Party members accused him and the six leaders of "abdicating their leadership role." The only empathy he could find was with those who had just left the Party and then only until they, too, began their new lives. Gilles felt as badly as it was possible to feel and still live. "Over a few months you realize your whole world view is not true and you have no view to replace it. Your wonderful, happy reason for living is just a dream." By his own estimation, it would take him ten years to feel well again.

Harry had never believed in anything else but communism, and now he, too, was forced to rethink all that which had been given to him by his parents, as a belief. "All of a sudden you try to break the cobwebs, and it was very hard for me because, really, I'd grown up very religious and all of a sudden all these moorings were just floating down-river." In the days following his resignation, Harry's house was full of people. "They loved me on a personal level, but couldn't understand why I had quit." But Harry's gruelling and futile attempt to change the Canadian Party's relationship to Soviet communism had shattered his arrogance as a leader. He no longer wanted the mantle of the New Soviet Man. He explained that he had joined the Party for humanistic not power motives, and there was now no reason to stay. "But we didn't have a give and take in the Party, and people wanted an organization," Harry remembered. "The feeling I got was that I was a quitter. It was very difficult for all of us at the time. Really, it takes years."

Beryl and Ed called their three children together and told them they were leaving the Communist Party. The eldest was happy, looking forward to the time her family would have together. The youngest was worried. "Who is going to stop the bomb being dropped now?" he asked. As time passed, couples like Beryl and Ed and Sydney and Annette slowly developed new habits: reading together at night, listening to music. "We were so tired by then that it was a relief to stop going to those goddamn meetings," said Sydney. "Twenty years is a long time." The truth about the Soviet system would be, for many, an illumination, like the initial impulse to join. One Party member said, "There was a flash going in and a flash going out." Canadian communists refer to the Khrushchev speech as "The Revelations."

The majority of the Quebec Communist Party left with the provincial leaders. Out of nine hundred members, about three hundred remained. More public meetings were held. Gradually, the remaining members began to split into two groups. One group called themselves the New, and the other group called themselves the Marxists. The New wanted to continue the discussion. The Marxists were behind the Party centre. Two members of the National Executive were dispatched from Toronto to organize a convention to elect new provincial leaders. They deliberately issued documents to clubs which were New too late for these clubs to have delegates properly accredited for the convention at Rialto Hall. When the delegates from the New clubs arrived, they were told that they were not eligible. Buck had ensured that the upcoming national executive election would be carried out by delegates who would ratify his victory. The disenfranchised part of the Party was in the majority, but as one of the more tenacious leaders said to a protesting member, "In politics sometimes you have to do very unpleasant things." With Quebec again secured under the Central Committee's wing, Henri Gagnon and his group were once more expelled. Gérard Fortin stayed on. "After the Khrushchev speech, I guess there was no other way after the mass resignations, but I didn't resign, I held the fort. I stayed in the party until '58, but the party became a madhouse. You had people calling others CIA agents and those who were following Tim Buck's line wouldn't budge an inch." In 1958 Gérard was called a CIA agent and kicked off the Provincial Committee.

Of all the people through whom this story has been told, only Stanley Ryerson was still in the Canadian Communist Party; he would leave in 1968, when the U.S.S.R. invaded Czechoslovakia. Fred Rose was stateless, in Poland. Norman, Scott, and Raymond were trying to rebuild their lives after the trials. Lea, Sydney, Annette, Nat, Harry, Ed, Beryl, Gilles, Lilly, and even David had quit. The old Communist Party was finished. The Cold War trials, the arbitrary handling of the French-Canadian nationalist aspirations, and, finally, the response of the Party centre to the Khrushchev revelations had destroyed the movement. The bulk of French Canadians left the Party in 1947, and most Jews left in 1956. On the average, members who remained were over fifty years old. The Canadian Communist Party would never again resurface as a viable movement: it would become as Stanley Ryerson said, "no more than a barely marginal force."

After 1946 a Central Committee member had assured a questioning youth: "History will prove us right." History may never prove anything, but it does help us learn.

Afterword

What I have gone through in the past thirty years or so has had
its effect on my memory...I'd love to see you but, for reasons I
cannot explain in a letter, I could not give you what you expect
from me...

My father was reading the letter from Fred Rose as I entered his
library. He finished, carefully folded the pages, and sat quietly, head
down. When he looked up, I could see that he had been crying. I had
given him the letter expecting him to be interested, not suspecting
it would cause him pain. I had yet to learn that memory caught
unaware is as raw as an exposed nerve, naked as a blush...

Gilles, in his first interview since 1956, talking more than he planned
because I am the first person who knows what he is talking about.

Irene, her eyes in mine, remembering leaving her communist
cocoon; she describes entering a world so suspicious and cold that
every instinct she has to be loving and open with people is "slowly
frozen."

Stanley, gathering up papers in his cluttered university office,
mumbling, "pathological relationship to the Soviet Union...pat-
terns of subservience...," forgetting for a moment his gentleman's
agreement with the Party.

Raymond, pacing the kitchen as I read transcript files. When I wonder where the other principals are, he smiles: "They're all dead but
me."

Fred Taylor, describing a dark room with two bubbling vats, foundry fire the only light. Around him, workers waiting for the crucial moment when molten steel will flow into immense forms, making what only Canadians can: a massive unseamed Victory Ship hull. "Pour!" Fred yells, and the memory resounds through time.

Lea, hitching up her skirt, climbing on the chair, on the counter, to reach the teacups on the top shelf, holding forth on ex-labour leader Jean Marchand, later Speaker of the Senate. "When I think of Marchand in the Asbestos Strike and now—it's to vomit," she proclaims.

After a few meetings in 1956, Lea quit the Party with a curse and no loss of momentum. Revolutionary struggle may have gone awry, but it is not over. For her, there remained "so much work to be done among the people." At eighty, she "cannot sit back." She regrets that she hasn't the energy that she had when she was twenty, but she tries. "I feel that if we don't act, if we don't do something…" Lea rounds up people and marches in anti-nuclear rallies, women's rights demonstrations, and labour protests. She helps students, filmmakers, and researchers with their chronicles of labour and social history. Her typical response to bureaucratic cant is "Piss on them."

Raymond was released from prison in the mid-fifties. He worked in McGill University's Criminology Department, and for five years, he researched and wrote *Les Crimes et Châtiments au Canada Français*. In this systematic study of four centuries of crime and punishment in French Canada—encompassing sorcery, magic, treason; detailing grotesque rituals such as drawing and quartering—Raymond would conclude: "A crime is an act considered prejudicial to society by a group of men whose power gives their opinion the force of law." In his mid-seventies, Raymond is a member of a publishing cooperative named in honour of Albert Saint-Martin, Quebec's early socialist leader. He lives a quiet but politically involved life with his wife Marguerite, with whom he recently collaborated on a collection of interviews and reports on daily life in socialist Chile, before the murder of President Salvadore Allende.

Sydney, almost seventy, is a successful business executive. His desire to change the world has softened, without loss of enthusiasm, to a deep concern for his family and friends. "What is there to regret?" he asks, "I could have devoted myself to my business career. So what? We had dogmatism and sectarianism, but we also had a sense of community, a sense of international concern, friends who are still friends. Brotherhood. The word is almost a joke now." Sydney swims twenty laps a day and greets each new morning with joy.

Norman, sixty-eight, and his wife, live outside a small village on a farm, where they plant, grow, and sell strawberries. Their garden provides their vegetables for the winter, and Norman, the cook, pickles beets and cucumbers, preserves peaches, and bakes a perfect, flaky-crusted meat-pie. Norman says, "We are the architects of our own misfortune," but he and his wife feel that the Communist Party leaders didn't care about people, especially middle-class people. "What we did in giving information to the Soviets was utterly wrong," Norman says. "We were moved by simple anti-fascism. Things were so bad in the Canadian government's attitude that we closed our eyes to dogma and power." When, after six years, Norman was released from prison, he and his wife moved to the country to start a new life.

Gilles and Lilly divorced after their children were grown. Lilly married a millionaire ex-Trotskyite who remembers having been manhandled by communists at a union meeting. Comfortable at last, she sees no point to the years she "wasted" in the Communist Party. Gilles quickly found a good job and he retains a boyish enthusiasm for things physical and spiritual. Although he believes that "the period was romantically idealistic for us but profoundly cynical in the minds of the people who were central to things in the Soviet Union," he is not sorry that he joined the communist movement. "If I had been caught in the ambiance of my family,

I would have remained a cretin. It was worth the negative side to have the *Weltanschauung* that I now have. I have remained curious about social evolution. I am happy that way."

Stanley is a respected professor of political and social history at the University of Quebec in Montreal. He publishes on left-wing political themes and his old, rambling house in the McGill student ghetto is a repository of classic and rare magazines, pamphlets and books. The "categoric, emphatic, rigid frozen dogmatism" of some of the left-wing groups now in Quebec reminds him of the communists in the forties and fifties, and it is odd for him to find himself labelled "an agent of imperialism" because he is a teacher. He hasn't yet written about the 1947 split between the French Canadians and the Central Committee of the Canadian Communist Party, but he has heard that there are books and theses underway. Although Stanley is over seventy and not in perfect health, he is expected to make a pronouncement. Stanley knows this but wishes it would go away.

In the sixties Henri became president of Local 568 of the International Brotherhood of Electrical Workers and vice-president of the Conseil de Travail de Montréal. "I remained a union man," he said. "Tim Buck didn't make me a revolutionary. I did." Much of Henri's recent life has been devoted to writing twelve books of political analysis, which he calls "literature of combat to advance the cause of the workers and the Quebec people." In 1957 he organized seminars so that Emery Samuel could come from British Columbia to meet university students. Emery Samuel and Stanley Ryerson met at his house after last seeing each other decades ago in the acrimonious air of national deviation. "What do you think happened?" Henri asked. "They embraced. It was all forgotten because for twenty years they had fought side by side. It was the twenty years they remembered, not the rest."

David is a jeweller. What he read in 1956, in Khrushchev's report, "boggled the mind." He was one of the Party's toughest and most reliable functionaries and he adamantly maintains that the Communist Party made absolutely no contribution to Canada.

Further, he feels that he and other communists failed to fight Hitlerism as they should have. "Communists all over the world, especially in Poland where the massacre took place, robbed the Jewish people of that sector of their militant youth that should have preserved their generation." Although he denigrates even Communist Party union-organizing, which he says was primarily an attempt at infiltration, David retains his old trade-union friendships, along with the new ones he has made in non-partisan Jewish cultural organizations.

Over seventy, Irene still works to support herself, as she has always done. Recently, friends sent her as part of a Norman Bethune delegation to visit China. Her fine hands cut the air and her voice, as she recapitulates, is matter-of-fact. "The thirties was a remarkable experience: a sense of unity, of comradeship, of trying to bring a new and better world into being. During the war we thought Britain and the Soviet Union would work out a *modus vivendi* and things would improve—the war to save democracy—we were very, very hopeful. Then the Cold War started and the whole McCarthy business and the Rosenbergs—what torture and horror to suddenly realize that you couldn't open your mouth. Nobody wanted to hear about it. Comrades and friends drifted away; they saw we wouldn't have a new society, so they got back up on top of the old one."

Fred Rose died in Poland several weeks after his daughter had been refused a ministerial permit which would have allowed him to end his days with his family in Canada. For him, the past could never be the past. He was politically pinned, an intensely social man who could not give me or anyone else "what was expected" of him. "Believe me," he wrote, "it hurts me to say that to you but my situation forces me to act in that way." During the almost thirty years he lived in Poland, he had only minimal contact with family and friends. In 1980, he met his nineteen-year-old granddaughter for the first time since she was five. The next year, he was introduced to his two teenage grandsons; when they were gone, it seemed a dream. He wrote to a close friend, confiding that "we felt lonelier than ever—our apartment was empty. Actually, the emptiness was within us." Yet, thirty years and seven thousand miles from home, he still sat proudly as we talked: shoulders square under the plaid flannel shirt, chin up. He would die, infuriating many and relieving some, taking his secrets with him, never having explained himself. "Would you do it again, Fred?" I ask, and, eyes twinkling, he shrugs, "Sure. What the hell. There were good years, lean years, but I don't think anybody exactly has a picnic in life."

For better or for worse, all the righteous energy of the Canadian Communist Party ran out with the Khrushchev revelations about Stalin. But Canadian ex-communists, unlike those in societies that achieved communism, suffered, at most, an emotional and intellectual disillusionment: they had never been compelled to imprison each other nor had they ever killed anyone. Their time as communists ended with their dream.

Yet, communists remain an important part of the history of the Canadian Left. They saw the world differently than did most North Americans. They and socialists were keenly aware of existing social and economic injustice, and imbued with a vision of another, better world. They were the impetus for early labour organizing, the popularizers of universal social programs such as family allowance and unemployment insurance, and they were a vocal lobby for fundamental civil rights. Their existence and that of the Soviet Union helped force *laissez-faire* economies to modify themselves.

For most, what remains of their experience in the party is a profound humanism. Many maintain the idea of revolutionary struggle separate from the Soviet Union, which was too much a part of their historical reality. Others question basics such as economic determinism: "It is easy to change economic laws by nationalization," mused Sam Carr, "but the infrastructure— religion, family, language, traditional, national differences—hangs on." Some deeply regret that, having taken the noblest dreams and hopes of mankind as their credo, they "surrendered" themselves in their own Party existence. They are bitter that the whole course of their adherence to the Canadian Communist Party "was cursed" by its subservience to the Soviet Union and angered at the "stupidity" of leaders who would allow their Party to be compromised, setting them all up as "commie spies." They wonder if without the evidence of the post-war trials, connection to an ideology that was central to the intellectual history of the world would have the power to burn so badly. Still, anger as been mollified over the years. Most Canadian communists, looking back, feel the passionate intensity of moments in history of which they were a part, the time of their youth.

When I started researching this book, I had a preconception of what I would find. I knew little about Party politics, but I was close in spirit to the people I was to meet. They, for the most part, were as I remembered them, warm, concerned, energetic, informed. When I was a child, people like these had surrounded me with affection and interest. I was at home in dozens of houses and dozens of people were at home in mine. I learned to have principles, to share, never to give up. I learned respect for people. My songs were of justice, freedom, "love between my brothers and my sisters all over this land." I knew my parents loved peace and when they promised, "We won't have war anymore," I believed them.

It is obviously not how the world is.
It may not even be how the world can be.

Yet, I retain the hope I was given, that people can live together with dignity and decency, a hope I seem to share with others brought up by communist parents. It is my legacy, softer than the fangs of competitive individualism, an echo of the dream.

And the people in the streets below
Were dancing round and round
And swords and guns and uniforms
Were scattered on the ground.

296

Update on Pseudonyms Used In the Book

SYDNEY, called "Danny" in the Vehicule Press 1994 edition of *The Strangest Dream*, was sawing wood with his grandson. When they rested, they talked.

"Do you know who the Weavers are, Grandpa?" the young man asked.

Sydney was pleased his grandson was interested. "Of course. Come."

In the library, he rummaged through his large collection of records and tapes and extracted "Tzena, Tzena" and "A Trip Around the World"—joyful Weavers' songs he thought his grandson would like. The young man tapped his foot and asked for more. Sydney played lyrical songs, political songs, labour songs— "Drill Ye Terriers Drill," "Suliram," "Talking Union Blues," "Joshua Fit the Battle of Jericho," "Michael Row the Boat Ashore"—passing on the culture he knew and loved.

"And do you know who Paul Robeson is?" Sydney asked his grandson when they were packing up.

"No," he admitted, "who is he?"

Sydney decided he would answer the question of who Paul Robeson was and what he meant to him by publishing his real name in the 1994 edition of *The Strangest Dream*, and giving his grandson a copy. When the book was first published, he had worried about his professional reputation and the U.S. border blacklist. These concerns no longer applied, so he could now show his grandson what he had believed in, what he had done, and why he wanted him to know the name, and more than just the name, of Paul Robeson.

Sydney suggested this with such pride, I decided to write an "Update on Pseudonyms" for the 1994 edition.

I began with the people who would not be adversely affected.

Robert is the artist ALLAN HARRISON who painted the Victory and Fred Rose election posters reproduced in this book. He produced posters for the Spanish Civil War ("the kid in the poster is Goodridge Roberts' grandson,") for the *Tribune*, Russian relief, the Drama Playhouse, against nuclear arms. "We broke our asses making banners and posters at night. And Barry Lord does a book on people's art and leaves out posters. That was people's art."

Harrison asked for a pseudonym under duress. "As I get older, I look back and see there was never any mention of my work in the left-wing movement. But I'll tell you, the gang I don't want to know about it, is US immigration." In 1955, living as a permanent resident in New York, he was visited and interrogated by the FBI and in 1960, the RCMP questioned his mother about him. In 1968, the national archives collected his posters and offered to call it the Allan Harrison collection. He said, "Don't call it anything. You have fanatics there who could kill me." Harrison had two major exhibits at the Montreal Museum of Fine Arts (1945, 1968), but neither he nor Fred Taylor were ever invited to exhibit at the National Gallery of Canada, an exclusion Harrison attributed to their left-wing past.

When I interviewed him, he was living in Montreal and wanted a pseudonym so he could continue to go to museums and art galleries in New York.

Allan Harrison died in 1988 and his contribution to left-wing Canadian art can now be acknowledged.

NORMAN remains Norman.

After the "spy" trials in which he was sentenced to five years for offenses under The Official Secrets Act, and an additional year for not testifying against other defendants, Norman lived quietly in the country with his wife. He spent almost fifty years in anonymity "successfully eluding hostile media types in pursuit of where are they now pap" and has recently written his own story. He prefers that I not use his real name in *The Strangest Dream* because "frankly I don't see myself in your characterization." Norman's memoir will be the first look at the Gouzenko Cold War trials written by a defendant. Its working title is, *The Making of a Spy*.

JERRY COHEN, the world-renowned Marxist scholar, G. A. Cohen, grew up in left-wing Montreal and now holds the Chichele Chair of Moral and Political Philosophy at All Souls College, Oxford. He says he asked me to call him "Jerry" (rather than G. A.) but didn't mean to imply I could not use his last name. My reading of his request was a reflex reaction to generalized concern.

In his revealing essay, "The Future of a Disillusion," Jerry describes the culture and values of his family, and their connection to the "prodigiously demanding" socialist ideal to which he is dedicated still:

"Instead of the class exploitation of capitalism, economic equality; instead of the illusory democracy of class-based bourgeois politics, a real and complete democracy; instead of alienation from one another of economic agents driven by greed and fear, an economy characterized by willing mutual service."

Knowing it is hard to maintain dedication to an ideal in a climate where it is regarded as irrelevant, Jerry offers a quote from a letter written by Frederick Engels the day after Marx died, "Well, we must see it through. What else are we here for? And we are not near losing courage yet."

FRED TAYLOR was an independent artist, with an independent income, living in Mexico, and already banned from the United States when I met him.

In our first interview in his apartment in Montreal's Chelsea Hotel, he delivered a three-hour overview of his background, training, politics and war work. The only thing he did not want me to say was that he was E. P. Taylor's brother. He had used his brother's name only once in his life, in 1942, to get permission to paint industrial workers in the war plants. For a year, he wrote letters and went back and forth to Ottawa, aware of the tremendous contribution Canada was making through industrial production, trying to gain access, feeling not a moment should be lost, and yet, "I just couldn't swing it."

Exactly a year after he had written his first letter to C. D. Howe, the Minister of Munitions and Supply, he retyped the same letter word-for-word, except for a single sentence. "For purposes of identification, you should be informed that I am the brother of E. P. Taylor."

He was in Howe's office in Ottawa the next day. "My brother was the head of the buying of everything for Great Britain in the United States and Canada. He couldn't refuse to see the brother of a great lieutenant."

Taylor received permission to paint in the war plants and he sent word across the country to his contacts in the Federation of Canadian Artists saying, "It's possible." His first painting showed five men from the Angus shops of the CPR dragging a tank track into position so it could be locked and welded on. He called that painting, "For Victory." Then he painted a close-up of the men, "For Victory and After" (see photo section), their excruciating physical effort reflected in the face of the man in front. One of his war-time paintings graces the cover of Michael Ondaatje's *In the Skin of a Lion*. The others are stored in the Canadian War Museum.

David is HARRY BINDER. He was the son of a founding member of the Communist Party of Canada and was the Quebec provincial organizer from 1946–56. In the Party hierarchy, it was he who explained, laid down, relayed the Party line to local Party groups such as the Park Extension group to which my parents belonged. He spoke to me unwillingly because he said he had read nothing but garbage about "the movement" and inferred this book would be more of the same. It was he who made me think that the bitterness of people's disillusionment is in direct relation to how deeply they were committed. Except, Lea Roback remembers, "the close ties, the love we felt for one another when we worked together trying to build a new and better world to live in." Perhaps the bitterness is related to the amount of power held and lost.

After I had written about the people I knew could not be hurt by publishing their real names, I began contacting those who were potentially still vulnerable.

Harry, a Canadian Seaman's Union organizer, didn't really see any problem but wanted time to think about it.

"Gilles," a Party Organizer in Quebec in the forties, reread the book and said apologetically, "It isn't that I don't think it's a good book but let's leave it as it is." He was still in business, he explained, and some of his clients were very wealthy but not too broadminded. Once, a sympathizer had actually signed a deal because of his past but others, "Anglo-Saxon and uptight," were very cold. Gilles said "No" because he was concerned about his livelihood. "It's pretty difficult earning a living these days."

I left machine messages for four other people asking if, almost forty years after they had left the Party, they would like to be identified by their real names.

A woman who had cried, age eighteen, at the fall of the Spanish Republic, called to say she did not want her name published because she was financing a research project in conjunction with a university and "it's a Catholic university. It could mess things up. Nowadays, in most circles it's perfectly okay to have been a communist but I don't want them backing off because of it." She felt awkward about her decision, the Cold War was supposed to be history, but it didn't seem to be over.

I called Harry back, He was still not sure. He was assessing if publishing his real name would jeopardize an employment opportunity.

I sent "Danny" the pages I had written about him and left another message on the answering machine of a man who had been in Section 13 (the discreet business and professional group) saying, if I didn't hear from him I'd assume he preferred to leave things as they were. He didn't call back. Neither did the other two I asked.

Finally, Danny called and I heard the hesitation in his voice. He was worried about disappointing me.

"I don't care what you do," I assured him. "Do whatever you want."

"This happened fifty years ago," he said, relieved I wasn't pressuring him, "the thought of anybody bothering me is very, very remote. But I don't want to get a call from anybody raising questions about this. Some smartass kid at a police depot. Some guy whose father was involved with the police. Some big wig who figures I harboured a traitor for two years and shouldn't get away with it. There's still this sneaking fear. I don't want any hassles. I'll give my grandchildren the book, show them my picture and say, "That's me."

"Danny" has died and there is no chance of anyone bothering him now. Over sixty years after he left the Party, I will be able to give his great grandchildren the 2022 revised edition of *The Strangest Dream*, and they can read about their great grandparents, Sydney and Annette.

By the time Sydney called retracting his real name from the 1994 edition of *The Strangest Dream*, I had realized that ex-communists' continuing fear of being identified was as relevant to the 1994 revised edition, as naming names. People wanted to publish their real names, but fifty years after the Cold War spy trials, the mentality which writer David Caute categorized as "the great fear," lived on. Had *The Valour* and *Horror* debacle been less recent, I might have pushed people's desire to claim their place in history, as complex as it is, and been less attentive to their unease. But no one who has felt its power, underestimates the vindictive, self-protective fanaticism of Canada's conservative establishment. Faced with the acid test of publicly declaring they had been communists, people were silenced by the present, not the past.

Response from Readers to the First Edition

A VERY OLD WOMAN

A reader introducing herself as "a very old woman" wrote from British Columbia's Gulf Islands. She had worked for the Wartime Information Board (WIB) and said the Director was Davidson Dunton, not John Grierson: "Grierson was the Commissioner of the National Film Board, certainly a post onerous enough for one man's total responsibility in wartime." She referred me to William A. Reuben's, *The Atom Spy Hoax*, "which examines the mosaic of the whole sordid fraud (the Gouzenko Spy Trials)." What she really wanted was "a private, discreet postal address" so she could contact her old friends through me.

"I, personally, was so embattled by my own hardships that I severed contact with them all and, for fear of questioning, wiped their names from my mind so thoroughly that it is now only with difficulty that I recall them."

Assured the address was safe, she wrote describing her life during and after the witch-hunts, and this letter is included in the Three Letters section that follows.

FRED ROSE

After reading a draft of the manuscript, Rose thought the material quite interesting but containing errors, some he considered very serious:

"The details given by you about RDX are not true. All that was said at my trial in the evidence given by Boyer was that he mentioned the ingredients and saw me writing them down on a piece of paper. No more than that. In fact, Boyer could not have known if I was doodling or actually writing down chemical formulas. The information given to you by Raymond definitely incriminates me, which was not the case at the trial.

"You say, 'Fred Rose did not plead or issue a statement.' I pleaded not guilty but I did not testify because the prosecutor was ready to ask me about dozens of people which would have resulted in serious harm to good and innocent people.

"You say, 'At Yalta Russia got the territories and the Americans got illusive promises of human rights and freedom of movement.' Do you include the other members of the socialist camp as being part of Russian territories? If you do, it's wrong. The Americans got more than illusive promises out of the war. They got the upper hand in western Europe, in the Far East, in South-East Asia, etc.

"Remember: harassment is written with one 'r.'"

STANLEY RYERSON

Ryerson wrote saying the book was "a generous endeavour" then discussed the two major reasons it was flawed: the "glaring inexactitudes" and lack of "substance:"

"My neat classical script written on the train from Montreal to Toronto suffers from the fact that the train was going in the opposite direction. The slip is less a minor one than you might think. There was no CP National Convention, Toronto, Fall, 1947. There was however the provincial party convention in November 1947 (Avakumovic, p256,) 'the Quebec LPP convention of 1947' (*Canada's Party of Socialism*, 1982, p258.)

"Which brings me to my second reason. (Caveat: one's perception of oneself is so loaded with subjectivity that I'm pretty well aware of pitfalls likely to occur in my remembrance of the 1947 split in Montreal. But there are two conflicting versions of what occurred. Neither is treated very satisfactorily in your account, in my opinion.)

"What was involved in 1947 has continued with mutations, into the ML (The Communist Party of Canada, Marxist-Leninist, founded in 1970) and PQ controversies of the 70s and 80s; and the underlying theoretical-political questions of nation and class are far from being resolved. A limited awareness of their depth may be part of the element of validity in the *Gazette* reviewer's argument about lack of "substance" and need to 'dig a little deeper.'

"All the best—for '84 and after!"

RANK AND FILER

L. wrote to say I was amazingly tolerant of Stanley Ryerson. "Some people revered him, I could never talk to him at all. I always had the feeling he was so protected by the Party. There on high, announcing what other people would have to do or think, yet he was never on the street, having to talk to the populace. Then, it took chapters before I translated "David" (Harry Binder). I was on the Rosenberg-Sobell committee with him but he too was someone I felt totally protected and I could never believe his sincerity when he spoke to me. What such people in their nature have to do with the way the Party was shaped, I don't know. What I do believe, is that the book is a history of working-class people's struggles. And so, Party politics and the betrayal, if that's the right word, aside, the book makes those years and that idealism, one of the proudest things our country has to be thankful for, live again.

HARRY

Harry's basic reserve was that the book avoided criticism of Party leaders who "betrayed the people's trust." This, and my "soft" stance on the Soviet Union, was a criticism I was brow-beaten with by another ex-Party leader who read an early draft and invited me to a scrumptious dinner, followed by a chilling criticism session. I left the house of these family friends transferring the outrage the man wanted me to have for the Soviet Union, to him, understanding why writers were always in trouble with the Party (except for inspired periods where absolute visions coincided absolutely.) I felt blessed that this man had never been, nor would anybody else ever be, my leader.

Harry also felt I had not dealt fully with how some Party policies had affected the trade union movement.

"In reference to the assault on the Communist-led unions, there is no mention that I can recall of some of the very real concerns that the government and the leadership of the general trade union movement had, not without justification, of the political consequences of Communist leadership of those unions. I was particularly struck by this in your reference to the scuttling of Canada's deep-sea fleet by the Canadian government. One of the points I was making was that indeed, in terms of national interest, the government could well perceive that under Communist leadership of the CSU the merchant fleet could not be depended on to defend the national interests of this country, at all times.

"Nor is the related question treated of whether the leaders of Communist-led unions, when they advanced political programs as put forward by the Communist Party, i.e. opposition to NATO, etc., rendered their unions vulnerable to attack by government, employers and other unions and, consequently, were unable to best serve the interest of their membership in trade union, bread and butter terms."

Harry made specific points:

"Bethune was not joined by 1239 Canadians in Spain. Canadians were already there when he arrived...

You describe the sharp change in the Soviet and Communist Party line with the rejection of Browderism and a denunciation of collaboration with bourgeois (i.e. Democratic) parties. Would it not have been appropriate to relate this about face with Truman's position and Churchill's subsequent Fulton speech as the beginning of the Cold War, whose origins I am persuaded, can be traced equally to both sides of the Iron Curtain.

Agathe Chapman did not commit suicide in England. It was in Montreal.

The Party meetings you refer to were not held in the Mount Royal Arena (where the Bethune rally took place). They were held in a hall on the north side of Mount Royal near Park Avenue over Dunn's restaurant. The Mount Royal Arena was on the south side of Mount Royal near Clark, about four blocks away.

It seems to me that our major disagreement arises from your supposition that if someone is victimized, somehow they're not guilty. Not so!"

JERRY COHEN

Jerry was grateful to me for writing the book, "having long felt that it was all slipping away and that it would never be recorded." He was impressed by the book's balance, "It is a feat to have been neither idiotically philo-Soviet nor cheaply anti-Soviet in the context of this difficult material."

"Now having said all that, I turn to queries and pinpricks.

How could Gilles have dealt with Sam given that Sam flew the coop on Party orders when subpoenaed in '46 (even though he wanted to turn himself in and have a political trial)?

'No one spoke up for Russian communism' in the meetings after the Revelations. I'm sure plenty did. I heard them. There was a fierce dispute."

Jerry ended by saying, "Congratulations and much love. I shall be grateful to you for the rest of my life."

But for another communist child whose father had been arrested in the spy trials, the book was upsetting. "I cried and cried from the page of the song extracts onward. It is a shame to say this but I hate my father for what he did to his children. The tragedy and blind stupidity of these supposedly brilliant young Turks was absolutely amazing. I am a weak vessel of ill-understood principles that were handed down in a confused fashion by parents who did not have time for their children."

Another child of communists sent me his grade 12 essay describing his version of Utopia: All races of man live together without fear of persecution. Each man is employed at a job for which he is best suited and at which he can best help the community. There is equal opportunity, religious freedom, healthcare, green space, recreation, sound education. The money comes from the people as usual, but no money is needed for defense spending because all the civilized men of Utopia realize that greed, prejudices and war only lead to self-destruction.

Betty read an unfinished draft of the book.

"The role of many other groups trying to improve life in Canada in the '30s should be brought in and the role of the CP not blown out of proportion—the Canadian Co-operative Federation (CCF), the Canadian Civil Liberties Union led by R. L. Calder, Herbert Desaulniers and others, the League for Social Reconstruction with Frank Scott, Leonard Marsh, King Gordon and others, the McGill Committee to help Spain with Francis MacNaughton, Paul Weir, etc.—so that a proper perspective can be obtained. There were many spontaneous self-help movements, too, among the unemployed and poor—to beat the bailiffs or the Electric Light and Gas Company. The Communists have to be seen as part of a mosaic. It is part of my regret that we did not realize it as the time. We felt we were the leaders of the working class and therefore either disdained these movements or thought of them as something to be used, infiltrated (boring from within), distrusted, or taken over. When genuine cooperative efforts were made, we would be called to task for frittering away our time in 'bourgeois occupations.'"

"Also, I get the feeling that you quite rightly blame our idealization of the Soviet Union (S.U.) as the main reason for the breakup of the Communist movement. But you equate that idealization as a motivating power in our becoming communists, with our ideals in working for a better world and for the brotherhood of man and sisterhood of woman. When we joined the movement, it was primarily to prevent war and fascism, and bring socialism to Canada, meaning an end to poverty and ushering in the millennium where all would be free to love one another in a life of comfort and happiness. The S.U., since apparently it had achieved a system that was establishing this kind of society, was looked to as the prime example but I don't recall any feeling of 'allegiance' to them as a country. The problem was, and this is another part of my regrets, we checked in our brains when we did not challenge their policies. It was not only disastrous, it was plain dumb and stupid. But in the day-to-day work here for socialism we weren't thinking of the S.U. What was most powerful in our motivation and gave us the drive and energy was the dream of a better Canada (and lots of religious guilt thrown in).

"Perhaps my most important regret is that the CP members could just possibly have helped change the course of Canadian history if they had used their energy, intelligence and deep feelings for humanity to cooperate with all other sectors of Canadians, pursuing Canadian goals, using our own methods, instead of ending up as a backwater fringe speaking to no one."

GERTRUDE PARTRIDGE said the book made her feel "as if a great load has been lifted in my life—I don't have to keep explaining what we did and why, and how we loved each other."

ARNOLD WESKER made me hope that a book about Canadian communists could be read as a microcosm of a larger, world picture. Communism was an international movement and he and readers from many countries—Dusan Makaveyev, Yugoslavia; Arthur Gavshon, South Africa; Rodney Hall, Australia; Leonard Boudin, United States; Jean Mailland, France—understood and identified with the people and history of *The Strangest Dream*. "Of course you know," Wesker wrote, "you could have changed locations and street names and written the same book in London. The Quest for the millennium is a yearning as old as tears."

The author and Fred Rose, Warsaw, Poland, 1978.

Three Letters

I received many letters after the publication of *The Strangest Dream*. Children of communists thanked me for telling their secret, unexamined story. "It gave me enlightenment and pride," wrote one. Children of American communists, expats in Mexico and Czechoslovakia after their parents fled the witch-hunts, contacted me, and wrote their own books. Readers from England, France, Yugoslavia, said the book echoed their experiences. Many applauded, few castigated.

In this third edition, we include three letters of interest.

Letter from G.A. Cohen, 1984

So, as I just said to you on the phone, you have done it. You have
written a magnificent book, a perfect monument to those wonderful
people and to those wonderful and tortured years. I am _personally_
so grateful to you, having long felt that it was all slipping away
and that it would never be recorded, and having hoped at most for
an historical study by someone, maybe a Ph D student, and now having
received, instead, this beautifully humanly accurate portrayal.

Has a British edition been contemplated? Even before my recent
preposterous elevation I had clout with leading UK publishers.
Now I have super-clout, and I would be delighted to be an unpaid
agent. Let me know. Also: if you want a supersuperlative endorsement
by me on the back of a pb edition then I will break my rule never
to endorse books like that (that is, never, like that, to endorse
books) and gladly oblige.

Among other things what is so impressive is the perfect balance.
Though there is plenty of perfectly appropriate schmaltz, there
is not a sentimental sentence. Nor any cheapness about anti-Sovietism.
It is a feat to have been neither idiotically philoSoviet nor cheaply
anti-Soviet in the context of this difficult material.

Now having said all that, I turn to queries and pinpricks. You can
do what you like with these. _Some_ of them might warrant changes for
the pb edition. There _must_ be a pb edition.

To facilitate reference, imagine each p. as divided into four parts
called a,b,c and d.

   110c "_nothing_ to do"? This is a bit harsh. I think they sincerely
      believed that the end justified the means, and the end was
      certainly, in their minds, to do with all that.

Somewhere you say Robeson ended every concert with OLE MAN RIVER.
I attended two at which he didn't. And I'd bet in at least one of
them he didn't sing it. He did, after all, have an ambivalence ttitude
to the song, which is why he changed those words.

Also, it's a _touch_ misleading to represent him as the son of a slave.
He was the son of a minister who was born into slavery but was never
himself a slave.

Did I not allow you to use my surname? I hope not. I _think_ I wanted
you to call me Jerry Cohen (as opposed to G A Cohen). Perhaps that
generated a misunderstanding. I cd have said "Call me Jerry", taking
for granted you _would_ also use my surname.

My most pedantic point: p.2a Did I say "prastically coincident"?
I hope not. If I said something like that, I said "practically identical".

172c "delayed a year or two". But that would have been no small thing
in the context of an arms race, so this seems to me an unjustified
implicit depreciation of the significance of the transfer of info
(which I think was probably a good thing).

185bc Are you sure most Montreal members were Jews? That wasn't my
impression.

212b How could Gilles (=I presume, Gui) have dealt with Sam when G
was party leader, given that Sam flew the coop when subpoenaed
in '46?

210d Not Feuerbach but Spinoza.

1. It was not called the Mount Royal Arena, but the Beaver Outing Club.
(reference 216c).
2. Names apart, the Mount Royal Arena is said on p. 64 to have had a
15,000 capacity. The B.OC. could have held 200 at most.
3. What, anyway, was the Mount Royal Arena? It certainly isn't there
now.

217a. "No one spoke up..." I'm sure plenty did. I heard them. There
was fierce dispute.

217a You could say there was a Jewish section in the party, meaning
the party members who were Jewish. You could also say there was
a (near-)communist Jewish organization, namely the UJPO, but
that wasn't party of the Party. But there surely wasn't a Jewish
Section of the party, was there, a part of the Party designated
as such?

222d No, the Old did not call themselves the "Old". They called themselves
the "Marxists" and they called those who called themselves the "New"
the "Revisionists".

223,line 10. This is Kashtan to Bella Cohen, I presume, but she wasn't
in fact expelled. She, like the rest of the New, quit,
and not in '57, when the Rialto Hall thing happened, but
in '58. Therefore she was in as long as Fortin, whom you
go on to mention, and contrary to the impression you create
that he stayed longer than most Newies did (of course I
don't know which bits of '58 people left in).

But, once again, congratulations, and much love. I shall be grateful
to you for the rest of my life.

Marxist scholar, G.A. Cohen, or Jerry, was my youth leader when I was
fourteen, the three times I endured a youth study session. One session
was held in a bowling alley where I met Arnie, my husband, who said I
had good form.

Letter from Fred Rose, 1979

Warsaw, January 8th, 1979

Dear Merrily,

I'm sorry I couldn't send my comments sooner. I was busy on some work, then Laura came, then we had a week of very cold weather and snow/drifts and a couple of days of no heat in the apartment.

Your material is quite interesting but I want to point out some errors, some of them very serious ones.

/Léa/

Page 1 - 4th line from bottom: there was no Front Populaire in the late Twenties.

Page 5 - beginning of second paragraph: I ran in St. Louis in 1936. Our election office was on Prince Arthur Street East and not on St. Catherine.

Page 7 - 8th line from top: The name of the leader of Finland was not Mannheim but Mannerheim.

/The Trials/

Page 4 - The details given in the second paragraph dealing with RDX are not true. All was said at my trial in the evidence given by Boyer was that he mentioned the ingredients and he saw me writing them down on a piece of paper. No more than that. Besides, RDX was invented by a German at the end of the 19th century, I believe. In fact, Boyer could not have known if I was doodling or actually writing down chemical formulas. The information given to you by Raymond definitely incriminates me, which was not the case at the trial.

Page 6 - second paragraph: you say "Fred Rose, alleged master-mind in the spy ring, did not plead or issue a statement". I pleaded not guilty but I did not testify because the prosecutor was ready to ask me about dozens of people, which would have resulted in serious harm to good and innocent people.

Third paragraph: You explain the name Debou=z. I don't know who thought up the name but your explanation is wrong. I never asked at parties "where is da booze".

Page 7 - 11th and 12th lines from top: I knew of no formal agreement made between the communists and the government. None existed.

Pages 9 and 10 - Browder's line, which by the way, was not the line of the Soviet Union, was supported by the Canadian Party. But the party did not renounce the "no-strike pledge" and the "liberal-labour coalition". There was no such a thing as a "no-strike pledge". There was never an official "liberal-labour coalition".

Page 10 - 6th line from the top: You say "At Yalta Russia got the territories and the Americans got illusive promises of human rights and freedom of movement". Do you include the other members of the socialist camp as being part of Russian territories? If you do, it's wrong. The Americans got more than illusive promises out of the war. They got the upper hand in western Europe, in the Far East, in South-East Asia, etc.

Page 24 - first paragraph, 5th line: Mike Buhay got 7000 votes not in a provincial election after 1947 but in a by-election in Cartier in 1947 after I was deprived of my seat in the House.

Page 36 - paragraph two: lines 2 and 3: what is the National Congress of Canadian Labour /CCL/. I never heard of such a boy.

314

Page 37 - lines two and three: Was Bob Haddow really a municipal councillor in 1942? Lines 7 and 8: What Garment Workers
were communist-controlled in 1947? In fact no such union existed.
The only union I know of is the International Union of Ladies'
Garment Workers, which was definitely not under communist control.

Paragraph two, line 2: I see that you mentioned the Canadian
Congress of Labour /CCL/. That clears up the mix-up I mentioned in
connection with page 36.

Page 38 - paragraph three, lines 4 and 5: Among the unions
lost by the communists you mentioned the International Association
of Machinists with over a million of members during the war. At no
time did the party control more than a few locals of that union.

Remember: harassment is written with one "r".

Page 47: lines 11 and 12 from bottom: This is a very serious
error. David Lewis visited Poland in 1966. Before leaving he asked
me if he should speak to the Minister about me taking a trip to
Canada. I replied: "If you want, do it". There was no question of
me returning for good. I had in mind a visit. In fact I wasn't sure
that Lewis was really going to speak to the Minister. As you see
Dave gave you a bum steer that could be harmful to me here. There
was no question of discrimination. The Zionist issue that he had in
mind when he told you the story was raised here in 1968.

Appendix, page 3, November 6th - should be: People's Commissar of
Foreign Affairs Vyacheslav Molotov.

Regards to your father and mutual friends. Have a good year

Fred

This letter is from Fred Rose the only elected Canadian communist
Member of Parliament, whose daughter, Laura, was my babysitter. His
comments are based on an early 1979 draft of the book, and as with
Jerry, the factual errors they mention have been corrected.

Letter from "A Very Old woman," 1984

Dear Merrily Weisbord

            I was very happy to receive your letter.
Summer is a busy time here and I am sorry I have delayed an answer.
I have so much to say that several letters will be needed to
express it all. Yes, I remember Harry M. at the Wartime Information
Board and the fine posters he made: one, in particular, the wraith
of a drowned seaman, captioned, "I was a victim of careless talk."

            First I would like to greet those old friends of ours who
remember us and to say how I grieve for their hardships. I,
personally, was so embattled by my own hardships that I severed
contact with them all and, for fear of questioning, wiped their names
from mind so thoroughly that it is now only with difficulty I recall
them.

            I grieve for Fred Rose, our doughty little champion. Eric Adams
and his wife were close friends of our and it is painful to hear they
feel exiled in Poland. And there were others.

            My husband worked under John Grierson and set up Film Societies
all over Canada. He had no connection with any kind of information
they could construe as "top secret" but in due time he got the
treatment anyhow. "Scoundrel time" was beginning, the Film Board
Was purged, he was fired and blacklisted.

            We moved to London, England, where my husband quickly found a
post organizing the film section of the Festival of Britain. I got on
with a government agency, the Central Office of Information, because
of my experience in Ottawa of writing scripts for exhibitions.

            At the King's New Year granting of honours, my husband was
decorated with an M.B.E for his outstanding work in the Festival of
Britain.

            I was not so fortunate. My superior at C.O.I. was an expatriate
Canadian: a confirmed communist hater. The R.C.M.P. had dutifully
informed him of my record (Grierson, who was then employed there, told
me this) and I was fired for an assortment of fabricated reasons.

            My mother wrote there was a crying shortage of teachers in
British Columbia. Since I was a qualified B.C. teacher, I decided to
come home with my young son to my family in Nelson. I got a job

This letter is from a stranger who contacted me after the book was published, hoping to reconnect with Lea Roback. She asked that her name and identifiable parts of the letter be changed because "I am careful not to embarrress my son, nieces and nephews." She introduced herself as, "a very old woman."

immediately in a mining camp in the Selkirk mountains where 14 feet of
snow fell each winter, packed down to seven feet and lay there nine
months of the year collecting all the garbage of the town. It was a
sad, unpleasant, blind alley of a job. I was replacing a young teacher
on the elementary school staff who had fled in disgust and the people
welcomed me as a saviour.

That is, until the second winter when the R.C.M.P. sniffed me
out. Suddenly nobody invited me to gatherings any more and backs were
turned on me in the narrow street. The Vancouver Sun shrieked the
latest scandal. Another dangerous commie was sniffed out red-handed,
corrupting youth as a lecturer at U.B.C. She was my old friend Bea of
the Canadian Labour Defence League, Montreal, and the paper gave the
whole front page to her blown-up portrait and scare-head, "THE FACE OF
COMMUNISM." It was a very pretty face but that served to point the
moral that tigers also are beautiful although wicked.

Sammy, an elderly Italian hardrock miner, knocked on my door one
evening and said, "Wy you not tell me you iss Red Nixon's sister?"
(that was my brother who had once worked in the Sandon mines and was
conspicuous for the colour of his hair and his political opinions).
Until the day I left Sammy toiled up a hod of coal for me every
evening and treated me to a glass of Italian wine.

One weekend the virtuous establishment of the town suffered an
unpleasant set-back. In the small hours of Sunday morning the police
car skidded on the icy road and rolled down a hundred foot embankment.
A passenger in the car was a 14-year-old pupil of mine. She hadn't a
scratch but the R.C.M.P. constable was badly injured. I saw his blood
on the snow. Inspector Harvison quickly replaced him with another
officer warranted immune to schoolgirl temptresses.

The Department of Education, I soon discovered, had also been
alerted and the District Inspector of Schools was instructed to
investigate my competence. He came to my class three times in that
last term. He was a conservative, an austere, exacting man and later
became the Chief Inspector for the whole province. But he recognized
persecution when he saw it. He gave me an excellent report which I
used to get myself a permanent position in Burnaby.

The final victim of the sniffing out and denouncing was a man at
the coast who had done trojan work in a branch library and earned a
promotion to a desirable post in a central library. The difference
this time was that he belonged to the N.D.P. and they had elected
members in the Federal Government who raised an outcry in the House of
Commons. Inspector Harvison had to whistle home his dogs and eat crow.

My former husband continued in the film business in Britain for
many years. A year ago he died. Although I, his poor old first wife in
a succession of three, had not seen him in thirty years, it was a
cruel blow to me and I am still mourning my loss. His old friends
"Norman" and Raymond Boyer may be interested in hearing about him and
maybe Stanley Ryerson and kind, beautiful Libby Park. For myself I
would like to ask dear Leah Roback does she remember me? I could tell
her about our peace movement here.

> Yours in Peace,
> "A Very Old Woman"

Notes

INTRODUCTION

1 From the "Song of the United Nations," music by Dmitri Shostakovich, lyrics by Harold Rome.

2 Vivian Gornick, *The Romance of American Communism*, p. 6.

3 Fred Rose died in Poland, March 17, 1983, while this book was in production. Fanny Rose, age 76, returned to Montreal shortly after her husband's death.

CHAPTER ONE: THE FIRST CONTINGENT

1 After the Russian Revolution, the term "soviet" became associated with a certain kind of parliament elected by members of working-class organizations, for example, the Soviet of Workers', Soldiers' or Peasants' Deputies.

CHAPTER TWO: THE THIRD INTERNATIONAL

1 John Strachey, *What Are We To Do?*, p. 274.

2 The War Measures Act was passed August 21, 1914, as part of the preparation for the First World War. Under the act, the executive of the government has sweeping emergency powers "by reason of the existence of real or apprehended war, invasion or insurrection." Emergency powers extend to arrest, detention and deportation without trial, and censorship and suppression of all means of communication. The War Measures Act is still on the books. It was used in 1946 to detain those suspected of communicating official secrets to a foreign power and it was used again in 1970 in Quebec to detain alleged FLQ sympathizers.

3 Theoretically, the basic unit of the Canadian Communist Party was called the club, group, or cell. When the Party was underground the club was restricted to as few as five people, only one of whom would have contact with a person in another club. When the Party was legal, such as during the Second World War, as many as fifty people from a particular political constituency would hold open club meetings.

Groupings of clubs, called sections or branches, were the next level of Party organization. Some sections were territorial, such as Section

5, the clubs in Fred Rose's district of Montreal-Cartier; others, such as Section 13, the clubs of professionals, as well as the Trade Union Section, were grouped according to similar interests. Section organizers were usually full-time Party functionaries.

The organizational body in each province was the Provincial Committee, made up of about thirteen people elected at the Provincial Convention by club delegates. At the National Convention delegates from the Provincial Committees elected the national organizational body, the National Committee, called the Central Committee in the thirties, a regionally representative group of thirty to forty people.

Over the National Committee was the National Executive, or the Politbureau of the thirties, about twelve national-office people elected by the National Committee. The National Executive was made up almost entirely of people from Toronto, except for a few key representatives from cities outside Ontario. The National Executive and especially its inner circle—Tim Buck, Bill Kashtan, Sam Carr, Stanley Ryerson—directed the Canadian Communist Party.

4 John Strachey, *What Are We To Do?*, p. 275.

5 Jessica Mitford, *A Fine Old Conflict*, p. 67.

6 Written by Joe Hill, troubadour of the Industrial Workers of the World. Joe Hill was executed in a prison yard, in Salt Lake City, Utah, on November 19, 1915.

CHAPTER THREE: SEDITIOUS UTTERANCES, UNLAWFUL ASSOCIATIONS

1 Most of the relief camps were in the Canadian West. Quebec's one relief camp, at Val Cartier, held 1,900 men in 1935.

2 Quoted in Gloria Montero's *We Stood Together*, p. 27.

3 Quoted in Lita-Rose Betcherman's *The Little Band*, p. 172.

CHAPTER FOUR, INROADS

1 Quoted in Gloria Montero's *We Stood Together*, p. 38.

2 Ibid., p. 40.

3 Ibid., p. 43.

CHAPTER FIVE: VORTEX

1 Wendell MacLeod, Libbie Park and Stanley Ryerson, *Bethune, The Montreal Years: An Informal Portrait*, pp. 152–53.

CHAPTER SIX: THE SECOND CONTINGENT

1 "Freedom (The Thaelman Column)," written by Karl Ernst.

2 Ted Allan and Sydney Gordon, *The Scalpel, the Sword: The Story of Dr. Norman Bethune*, p. 160.

CHAPTER SEVEN: PARTY LIFE

1 The twelve sections comprising the Montreal district were coordinated by a Provincial Committee, whose organizer, Fred Rose, sat on the Party's National Executive.

2 Wendell MacLeod, Libbie Park, and Stanley Ryerson, *Bethune, The Montreal Years: An Informal Portrait*, p. 65.

3 G. E. R. Gedye, *Fallen Bastions: The Central European Tragedy*, p. 507.

CHAPTER EIGHT: THE PHONY WAR

1 Walter Duranty, *The Kremlin and the People*, p. 169.

2 Ivan Avakumovic, *The Communist Party in Canada*, p. 142.

CHAPTER NINE: UNDERGROUND

1 "Deutsche Wehr," Supplement to "Die Deutsche Volkskraft," June 13, 1935, in Max Werner's *The Military Strength of the Powers*.

CHAPTER TEN: TOTAL WAR

1 King to Gousev, June 9, 1943, Canada House Files, Public Archives of Canada.

CHAPTER ELEVEN: A COMMUNIST MEMBER OF PARLIAMENT

1 The explosive RDX was known to be militarily superior to nitroglycerin and to Watt Gun Cotton TNT because it was malleable, required only a tiny detonator, acted rapidly, and was extremely powerful. While dynamite would push or shake a piece of steel to blow it up, RDX would cut right through and pulverize it.

2 Leopold Trepper, *The Great Game: Memoirs of the Spy Hitler Couldn't Silence*, p. 180.

CHAPTER TWELVE: THE BOMB

1 *House of Commons Debates*, March 18, 1946, p. 48.

2 In the United States government's *Soviet Atomic Espionage* pamphlet.

3 J. W. Pickersgill, *The Mackenzie King Record*, Vol. 3, 1945–1946, p. 135.

4 Ibid., p. 135.

5 Sir William Stephenson was a close associate of Churchill and was the man who, during the war, built an extraordinary relationship, in the utmost secrecy, between the President of the United States and the Prime Minister of Great Britain. It was Stephenson who convinced Roosevelt to authorize "the closest possible marriage" between the FBI and the British Secret Service—a marriage that originally, for the sake of American neutrality, was kept secret even from the State Department. He established a British Security Coordination headquarters in New York and, in 1942, when the Russians were defending the gates of Stalingrad, arranged with Hoover to further bless the secret marriage by exchanging a careful and exhaustive survey and coordination of domestic communist activities from all sources. He served as midwife to the OSS (later to become the CIA), and was an avid proponent of the protective necessity of security services.

6 John G. Diefenbaker, *One Canada: The Crusading Years, 1895–1956*, p. 225.

7 J. W. Pickersgill, *The Mackenzie King Record*, p. 142.

CHAPTER THIRTEEN: THE SPY SHOW

1 Lester H. Phillips, "Preventative Detention in Canada."

2 M. H. Fyfe, "Some Legal Aspects of the Report of the Royal Commission on Espionage."

3 Quoted in H. Montgomery Hyde's *The Atom Bomb Spies*, p. 95.

4 *The Spectator*, March 7, 1947, p. 236.

5 J. W. Pickersgill, *The Mackenzie King Record*, Vol. 3, 1945–1946, p. 151.

6 Alice Kimball Smith, *A Peril and a Hope: The Scientists' Movement in America, 1945–1947*, pp. 378–9.

7 Ibid., p. 382.

CHAPTER FOURTEEN: THE FRED ROSE CASE

1 The provision in the Official Secrets Act (1939), Sub-section (1) of Section (3), is that communication with a foreign power is an offense if it is "for any purpose prejudicial to the safety or interests of the State...."

2 "The Canadian Spy Case: Admissibility in Evidence of Stolen Embassy Documents," *University of Chicago Law Review* 15: 404–09.

3 *Journal d'un Prisonnier*, p. 115.

4 Although this letter was read and its request decided upon in the justice minister's office, the Justice Department claims still not to have a copy of it in its files.

5 W. L. Mackenzie King Diaries in the Public Archives of Canada September 24, 1945, pp. 1108–9.

CHAPTER FIFTEEN: EVIDENCE

1 Blair Fraser, *The Search for Identity: Canada, 1945–1967*, p. 41.

2 Testimony of Kenneth Howe Cheetham, The King vs. Raymond Boyer, December 3, 1947.

3 David Caute, *The Great Fear: The Anti-Communist Purges Under Truman and Eisenhower*, p. 67.

4 In the United States Government's *Soviet Atomic Espionage* pamphlet.

5 Mackenzie King Diaries, Sept. 24, 1945, Public Archives of Canada.

CHAPTER SEVENTEEN: THE POST-WAR LABOUR PUTSCH

1 J. W. Pickersgill, *The Mackenzie King Record*, Vol. 3, 1945–46, p. 29.

2 President's Speech, Canadian Congress of Labour, *Proceedings*, 1948, p. 23.

3 Irving Martin Abella, *Nationalism, Communism and Canadian Labour: The CIO, the Communist Party and the Canadian Congress of Labour*, p. 163.

4 Quoted in John Stanton's *Life and Death of the Canadian Seamen's Union*, p. 111.

5 J. W. Pickersgill, *My Years with Louis St. Laurent*, p. 147.

6 From Gilles Henault's "Bordeaux-sur-Bagne," *ellipse* 18:21.

CHAPTER EIGHTEEN: THE FINAL YEARS

1 *Maclean's*, September 1, 1949; *Saturday Night*, September 12, 1950; ibid., May 1, 1951.

2 "The Hammer Song," music by Pete Seeger, lyrics by Lee Hays.

3 From the dedication of Howard Fast's *My Glorious Brothers*.

4 From "Lifeitself-manship," an appendix to Jessica Mitford's *A Fine Old Conflict*, p. 326.

Bibliography

BOOKS AND PAMPHLETS

Abella, Irving Martin. *Nationalism, Communism and Canadian Labour: The CIO, the Communist Party and the Canadian Congress of Labour, 1935–1956.* Toronto: University of Toronto Press, 1973.

Allan, Ted, and Gordon, Sydney. *The Scalpel, the Sword: The Story of Dr. Norman Bethune.* Toronto: McClelland and Stewart, 1971.

Avakumovic, Ivan. *The Communist Party in Canada: A History.* Toronto: McClelland and Stewart, 1975.

Betcherman, Lita-Rose. *The Little Band: The Clashes Between the Communists and the Political and Legal Establishments in Canada, 1928–1932.* Ottawa: Deneau Publishers, 1982.

———. *The Swastika and the Maple Leaf: Fascist Movements in Canada in the Thirties.* Toronto: Fitzhenry and Whiteside, 1978.

Blumefeld, Harold. *Sacco and Vanzetti: Their Story in Pictures.* New York: Scholastic Book Services, 1972.

Buck, Tim. *Thirty Years, 1922–1952: The Story of the Communist Movement in Canada.* Toronto: Progress Books, 1952.

———. *War in Europe.* Timely Topics, no. 2. Toronto: New Era Publishers, 1938.

Bukharin, Nikolai. *ABC of Communism.* Translated by P. Lavin. Detroit: Marxian Educational Society, 1920.

Calmer, Alan; Gold, Michael; Hicks, Granville; North, Joseph; Peters, Paul; and Schneider, Isador, eds. *Proletarian Literature in the United States.* New York: International Publishers Co., 1935.

Canadian Chamber of Commerce, Board of Trade. *The Communist Threat to Canada.* Montreal: Canadian Chamber of Commerce, Board of Trade Building, 1947.

Canadian Congress of Labour. *Convention Proceedings.* Toronto: Canadian Congress of Labour, 1948.

Caplan, Usher. *Like One That Dreamed: A Portrait of A. M. Klein.* Toronto: McGraw-Hill Ryerson, 1982.

Carr, Sam. *Communists at Work.* Speech delivered at the Eighth

Dominion Convention of the Communist Party of Canada. Toronto: New Era Publishers, 1937.

Caute, David. *The Fellow-Travellers: A Postscript to the Enlightenment.* New York: Macmillan Co., 1973.

———. *The Great Fear: The Anti-Communist Purges Under Truman and Eisenhower.* New York: Simon and Schuster, 1978.

Claudin, Fernando. *The Communist Movement: From Comintern to Cominform.* 2 vols. New York: Monthly Review Press, 1976–77.

Comeau, Robert, and Dionne, Bernard. *Les communists au Québec, 1936–1956* Montreal: Les Presses de l'unité, 1980.

Communist Part of Canada. *Canada and the 7th World Congress of the Communist International: Outline of Study of the Decisions of the 7th Congress of the Communist International and the 9th Plenum of the Central Committee of the Communist Party of Canada.* Toronto: Communist Party of Canada, 1935.

———. *We Propose.* Resolutions adopted at the Eighth Dominion Convention of the Communist Party of Canada. Toronto: New Era Publishers, 1937.

De Jonge, Alexander. *The Weimar Chronicle: Prelude to Hitler.* New York: Paddington Press, 1978.

de la Mora, Constancia. *In Place of Splendor: The Autobiography of a Spanish Woman.* New York: Harcourt, Brace & Co., 1939.

Deutscher, Isaac. *Stalin: A Political Biography.* 2d ed. London: Oxford University Press, 1967.

Diefenbaker, John G. *One Canada: The Crusading Years, 1895–1956.* Toronto: Macmillan of Canada, 1975.

Dimitroff, Georgi. *The Present Rulers of the Capitalist Countries Are But Temporary: the Real Master of the World is the Proletariat.* Speech delivered at the Seventh Conference of the Communist International, August 1935. n.p.

Doctorow, E. L. *The Book of Daniel.* New York: Random House, 1971.

Dumas, Evelyn. *The Bitter Thirties.* Montreal: Black Rose Books, 1975.

Duranty, Walter. *The Kremlin and the People.* New York: Reynal and Hitchcock, 1941.

Dutt, Rajani Palme. *World Politics, 1918–1936.* London: Victor Gollancz, 1936.

Ellipse 18. Sherbrooke, Quebec: Faculté des Arts, Université de Sherbrooke, 1976.

Fast, Howard. *My Glorious Brothers*. Boston: Little, Brown & Co., 1948.

———. *The Naked Gold: The Writer and the Communist Party*. New York: Frederick A. Praeger, 1957.

Feutchtwanger, Lion. *Moscow*. New York: Viking Press, 1937.

Fournier, Marcel. *Communisme et Anti-communism au Québec, 1920–1950*. Montreal: Éditions cooperàtives Albert Saint-Martin, 1979.

Fraser, Blair. *The Search for Identity: Canada, 1945–1967*. Garden City, N. Y,: Doubleday & Co., 1967.

Gedye, G. E. R. *Fallen Bastions: The Central European Tragedy*. London: Victor Gollancz, 1939.

Gold, Michael. *The Hollow Men*. New York: International Publishers Co., 1941.

Goldberg, Harry, ed. *American Radicals*. New York: Monthly Review Press, 1957.

Gorki, Massimo. *Articles and Pamphlets*. Moscow: Foreign Languages Publishing House, 1950.

Gornick, Vivian. *The Romance of American Communism*. New York: Basic Books, 1977.

Harvison, C. W. *The Horsemen*. Toronto: McClelland and Stewart. 1967.

Heym, Stefan. *Hostages*. New York: Sun Dial Press, 1943.

Howe, Irving. *Politics and the Novel*. New York: Meridian Books, 1957.

Huberman, Leo. *Man's Worldly Goods: The Story of the Wealth of Nations*. New York: Harper & Bros., 1936.

Hutchinson, Bruce. *The Incredible Canadian.* Toronto: Longmans Green and Co., 1952.

Hyde, Montgomery H., *The Atom Bomb Spies*. New York: Ballantine Books, 1980.

Kisch, Richard. *They Shall Not Pass*. London: Wayland Publishers, 1974.

Koestler, Arthur. *Arrow in Blue*. 2 vols. London: Readers Union, 1954.

———. *Darkness at Noon*. Translated by Daphne Hardy. New York: Modern Library, 1941.

Lavallé, Marcel. *Journal d'un Prisonnier.* Montreal: L'Aurore, 1978.

Lenin, Vladimir Ilyich. *Letter to American Workers.* Chicago: Liberator Press, 1975.

Levant, Victor. *Capital and Labour: Partners? Two Classes-Two Views.* Toronto: Steel Rail Educational Publishing, 1977.

Lipton, Charles. *The Trade Union Movement of Canada, 1827–1959.* Montreal: Canadian Social Publications, 1966.

Livesay, Dorothy. *Right Hand, Left Hand.* Erin, Ont.: Press Porcépic, 1977.

Lloyd George [David Lloyd George, 1st Earl]. *The Truth About the Peace Treaties,* Vol. 1. London: Victor Gollancz, 1938.

London, Jack. *War of the Classes.* New York: Regnet Press, 1912.

MacLoed, Wendell; Park, Libbie; and Ryerson, Stanley. *Bethune, The Montreal Years: An Informal Portrait.* Toronto: James Lorimer & Co., 1978.

Marion, George. *The Communist Trial: An American Crossroads.* New York: Fairplay Publishers, 1950.

Marx, Karl. *Wage-Labour and Capital.* Introduction by Frederick Engels. New York: International Publishers Co., 1933.

Meeropol, Michael, and Meeropol, Robert. *We Are Your Sons: The Legacy of Ethel and Julius Rosenberg, Written By Their Children.* Boston: Houghton Mifflin Co., 1975.

Mitford, Jessica. *A Fine Old Conflict.* New York: Vintage Books, 1971.

Molotov, Vyacheslav M., and Stalin, Joseph. *The Soviet Union and World Peace.* New York: New Century Publishers, 1946.

Montero, Gloria. *We Stood Together: First-Hand Accounts of Dramatic Events in Canada's Labour Past.* Toronto: James Lorimer & Co., 1979.

Moorehead, Alan. *The Traitors.* rev. ed. New York: Harper and Row Publishers, 1963.

Pearson, Lester B. *Mike: The Memoirs of the Right Honourable Lester B. Pearson,* Vol. 3. 3 vols. Toronto: University of Toronto Press, 1975.

Penner, Norman. *The Canadian Left: A Critical Analysis.* Scarborough, Ont.: Prentice-Hall Canada, 1977.

Pickersgill, J. W. *The Mackenzie King Record,* Vol. 3, *1945–1946.* 4 vols. Toronto: University of Toronto Press, 1970.

Pope, Arthur Upham. *Maxim Litvinoff*. New York: L. B. Fisher, 1943.

Pritt, D. N. *At the Moscow Trial*. New York: International Publishers Co., 1937.

————. *The State Department and the Cold War*. New York: International Publishers Co., 1948.

Reed, John. *Ten Days That Shook the World*. New York: Modern Library, Bennett A. Cerf, Donald S. Klopfer, 1935.

Rodney, William. *Soldiers of the International*. Toronto: University of Toronto Press, 1968.

Rosenberg, Ethel, and Rosenberg, Julius. *The Rosenberg Letters*, London: Dennis Dobson, 1953.

Ryan, Oscar. *Soon to be Born*. Vancouver: New Star, 1980.

Ryerson, Stanley. *French Canada: A Study in Canadian Democracy*. Toronto: Progress Books, 1943.

Salisbury, Harrison E. *The Unknown War*. New York: Bantam Books, 1978.

Silone, Ignazio. *Bread and Wine*. Translated by Gwenda David and Eric Mosdacher. New York: Harper & Bros., 1937.

Sinclair, Upton. *The Jungle*. New York: Viking Press, 1946.

Skelton, Robin, ed. *Poetry of the Thirties*. Harmondsworth, Middlesex: Penguin Books, 1977.

Smith, A. E. *All My Life: An Autobiography*. Toronto: Progress Books, 1949.

Smith, Alice Kimball. *A Peril and a Hope: The Scientists' Movement in America, 1945–1947*. Chicago: University of Chicago Press, 1965.

Society of Foreign Workers in the USSR. *Resolutions of the Seventeenth Party Conference: Forward to the Second Five-Year Plan of Socialist Construction*. Moscow: Co-operative Publishing Society of Foreign Workers in the USSR, 1932.

Stacey, C. P. *Arms, Men and Government: The War Policies of Canada, 1939–1945*. Ottawa: Queen's Printer, 1970.

Stanton, John. *Life and Death of the Canadian Seamen's Union*. Toronto: Steel Rail Educational Publishing, 1978.

Stevenson, William. *A Man Called Intrepid: The Secret War*. New York: Harcourt Brace Jovanovich, 1976.

Strachey, John. *The Nature of the Capitalist Crisis*. New York: Covici, Friede Publishers, 1935.

————. *What Are We To Do?* London: Victor Gollancz, 1938.

Strong, Anna Louise. *I Change Worlds: The Remaking of an American.* New York: Carden City Publishing Co., 1937.

Sullivan, J. A. [Sullivan, Pat]. *Red Sails on the Great Lakes.* Toronto: Macmillan of Canada, 1955.

Thomas, Hugh. *The Spanish Civil War.* New York: Harper and Row Publishers, 1961.

Trepper, Leopold. *The Great Game: Memoirs of the Spy Hitler Couldn't Silence.* New York: McGraw-Hill Book Co., 1977.

Vance, Catherine. *Not by Gods but by People: The Story of Bella Hall Gauld.* Toronto: Progress Books, 1968.

Weisbord, Vera Busch. *A Radical Life.* Bloomington: Indiana University Press, 1977.

Werner, Max. *The Military Strength of the Powers.* London: Victor Gollancz, 1939.

West, Rebecca. *The New Meaning of Treasons.* New York: Viking Press, 1964.

Wolfe, Morris, ed. *A Saturday Night Scrapbook,* Toronto: New Press, 1973.

Young, Delbert A. *The Mounties.* Toronto: Hodder & Stoughton, 1968.

ARTICLES

Barros, James. "Alger Hiss and Harry Dexter White: The Canadian Connection." *Orbis,* Fall 1977.

Cox, Kirwan. "The Grierson Files." *Cinema Canada,* June–July 1979.

Drobot, Eve. "The Soldiers in $8 Suits." *Weekend Magazine,* October 8, 1977.

Dubuc, Alain, and Jannard, Maurice. "La Grande Dépression des Années Théâtre." *La Presse* (Montreal), October 27, 1979.

Fraser, Blair. "Can McCarthy Happen Here?" *Maclean's,* March 15, 1954.

Friedenberg, Edgar A. "You can have exactly as much freedom as the government allows. That's the Canadian way." *Saturday Night,* April 1979.

Fyfe, M. H. "Some Legal Aspects of the Report of the Royal Commission on Espionage." *Canadian Bar Review* 24 (1946).

Katz, Sydney. "Inside Canada's Secret Police." *Maclean's*, April 20, 1963.

Koulack, Ester. "'It could have been any one of us': An Account of the Atom Spy Hunt and Its Effects in Canada and the USA." *Canadian Dimension* 2, no. 6 (1976).

Langer, Elinor. "If In Fact I Have Found a Heroine." *Mother Jones*, May 1981.

Lévèsque, Andrée. "Le Quebéc et le Monde Communiste: Cowansville 1931." *Revue d'Histoire de L'Amerique Française* 34, no. 2 (1980).

Phillips, Lester H. "Preventative Detention in Canada." *Canadian Forum*, June 1946.

Sobral, Luis De Moura. "Peinture et luttes sociales: 'Talking Union' de Frederick B. Taylor." *Journal of Canadian Art History* 4. no. 2 (1977–78).

Spectator, The. March 7, 1947.

"Statement on Gouzenko Interview." *External Affairs*, December 1953.

"Statement on Harry Dexter White Case." *External Affairs*, December 1953.

Steiner, George. "The Cleric of Treason." *The New Yorker*, December 8, 1980.

"Text of Speech on Stalin by Khrushchev as Released by the State Department." *New York Times*, June 5, 1956.

"The Canadian Spy Case: Admissibility in Evidence of Stolen Embassy Documents." *University of Chicago Law Review* 15 (1948).

"Three-Nation Declaration on Atomic Energy." *New York Times*, November 16, 1945.

PUBLIC DOCUMENTS

Canada. An Act Respecting Official Secrets. Revised Statutes of Canada, 1939, c. 198.

Canada. An Act to Confer Certain Powers upon the Governor in Council in the Event of War, Invasion, or Insurrection. Revised Statutes of Canada, 1970, c. w-2.

Canada. An Act to Protect the Province against Communistic propaganda. Revised Statutes of the Province of Quebec, 1941, c. 52.

Canada. Criminal Code. Revised Statues of Canada. 1927, c. 36, s. 98.

Canada. *House of Commons Debates.* 20th Parl., 1st sess., 1945 (Atomic Energy Declaration), 3: 2632–2652.

Canada. *House of Commons Debates.* 20th Parl., 2d sess., 1946 (Address, Mackenzie King), 1: 44–56.

Canada. *House of Commons Debates.* 20th Parl., 2d sess., 1946 (Official Secrets Act), 1: 4–8.

Canada. Immigration Act. Revised Statutes of Canada, 1927, c. 93, s. 41–42.

Canada. *Report of the Royal Commission on Price Spreads,* "Minutes of the Proceedings and Evidence." Ottawa: Queen's Printer, January 1935.

Canada. *Report of the Royal Commission…to investigate…the communication by public officials and other persons,…of secret and confidential information to agents of a foreign power.* Ottawa: Queen's Printer, June 1946.

Court of King's Bench, District of Montreal, Province of Quebec, Canada. His Majesty the King vs. Fred Rose: Preliminary Hearing, March 22, 1946, and Trial, May 27–June 15, 1946: Appeal Inscription (private collection).

Court of King's Bench, District of Montreal, Province of Quebec, Canada. His Majesty the King vs. Raymond Boyer (Case no. 2155), December 3, 1947 (private collection).

Court of King's Bench, District of Montreal, Province of Quebec, Canada. Raymond Boyer vs. His Majesty the King (Appeal no. 561), November 20, 1948 (private collection).

Court of King's Bench (In Appeal), District of Montreal, Province of Quebec, Canada. Fred Rose vs. His Majesty the King: Appellant's Factum, n.d. (private collection).

Court of King's Bench (In Appeal), District of Montreal, Province of Quebec, Canada. Fred Rose vs. His Majesty the King: Respondent's Factum on Questions of Fact, n.d. (private collection).

Ottawa, Ont. Public Archives of Canada. Canada House Files. A-12. Department of External Affairs to Dominion (on postponement of Fourth Soviet Protocol), March 16, 1945.

Ottawa, Ont. Public Archives of Canada. Canada House Files. Mackenzie King to Feodor Gouzev (re: Third Soviet Protocol, covering a statement of war supplies to be sent to USSR), June 9, 1943.

Ottawa, Ont. Public Archives of Canada. Joseph L. Cohen

Papers, Vol. 1 His Majesty the King vs. Fred Rose (in the Police Court of the City of Toronto on the charge of vagrancy), October 22, 1929.

Ottawa, Ont. Public Archives of Canada, W. L. Mackenzie King Diaries, Lord Addison, the Dominion secretary and Mackenzie King on the question of the "secret" of the atomic bomb, September 24, 1945.

The King vs. Buck et al.: Record of Proceedings. Toronto 1931.

Toronto, Ont. Archives of Ontario. Attorney General's Files. Record Group 4. Series 0-1-1-1. Files 3188, 1931. Communist Party of Canada Archives seized in 1931 police raid on CPC headquarters.

US Congress, House Committee on Un-American Activities. *The Communist Conspiracy. Strategy and Tactics of World Communism: Report 2244.* 84th Cong. 2d sess., May 29, 1956.

US Congress, Joint Committee on Atomic Energy. *Soviet Atomic Espionage.* Joint Committee Prints. 82nd Cong., 1st sess. Washington, D.C.: U.S. Government Printing Office, April 1951.

Index

A World to Win 240
ABC of Communism (Bukharin) 60, 82
Abella, Irving 252
Act to Protect the Province against Communistic Propaganda (Quebec, 1937). *See* Padlock Law
Action Catholique, L' 259-260
Adams, Eric 108, 175, 316
Addison, Lord 206, 229-230
Alger Hiss 195
Allan 105-106
Allan, Ted 21, 28
American Communist League 117
American Federation of Labor AFL) 80, 250, 260
American Federation of Scientific Workers 207-208
Animal Farm 268
Annette and Sydney 97-99, 103-104, 121, 126, 128-132, 142, 145, 147-149, 151, 159-160, 170, 173, 216, 261-270-272, 274, 281-282, 286, 288-289-290, 292, 297-298, 301-302
Anti-semitism 42, 88-89, 95, 246; in Soviet Union 282-283, 286
Arcand, Adrien 89-90
Article 98, Criminal Code of Canada 62-63, 71, 74-75, 82, 86, 91
Asbestos strike 89
Association Humanitaire 43, 47-50, 53, 83
Association of Oak Ridge Scientists 208

Atlantic Security Pact 268
Atlee, Clement 189, 194
Atomic bomb 192, 194, 227, 229, 332
Atomic Energy Commission (US) 194

Ballantyne, Cam 110, 112, 114
Banks, Hal 254-255-256
Barrette, Antonio 258
Bayly, Edward 71
Beirut, Boleslav 279
Bella 64, 67, 80, 180
Bengough, Percy 253
Bennett, R.B. 75, 83-84, 86
Benning, Paulette 151-152, 196
Benning, Scott 151-152, 159, 177-178, 183, 196, 211, 231, 234, 289
Beryl 263, 266, 268, 272-274, 288-289
Bethune, Norman 21, 32, 81, 93, 101, 103, 107-108, 132, 134, 139, 152, 159, 163, 294, 306
Betty 308-309
Bevin, Ernest 196
Biéler, André 164
Binder, Harry 21, 300-301, 305
Bouchard, Paul 88-89
Boutin 82
Boyer, Raymond 21, 88, 93, 110-112, 114, 115, 121, 126-127, 132, 134-135, 137-138, 143, 152, 154, 159, 163, 178, 179, 182-184, 191, 193, 196, 201, 210, 217-218, 228, 230, 289-292, 317

Boyko, John 224
Brais, Philippe, 212, 214, 216, 219
Bread and Wine 116
British North America Act 240
Browder, Earl 187, 314
Buck, Tim 73, 75, 131, 151, 153, 160, 214, 222, 235, 243-244, 277, 279-281, 284-285, 289
Buhay, Mike 239, 314
Bukharin, Nikolai 60
Bury the Dead 134-135)
Byrnes, James 192, 196

Calder, R.L. 308
Caldwell, Christopher 182
Canada Council for the Arts 13
Canada Evidence Act 202
Canadian Association of Scientific Workers 134, 191, 193, 210
Canadian Bar Review 204
Canadian Broadcasting Corporation (CBC) 26-27, 249
Canadian Citizenship Act 24, 226
Canadian Congress of Labour (CCL) 251, 253
Canadian Labour Defence League 64, 75, 317
Canadian Labour Relations Board 256
Canadian League Against Fascism and War 96
Canadian Legion 240
Canadian Merchant Marine 255-256
Canadian Peace Conference 262-263
Canadian Seamen's Union (CSU) 64, 105, 161-162, 176, 249-256, 262, 301, 306
Canadian Security Intelligence Service (CSIS) 23, 25

Canadian Tribune 234, 283
Canadian Youth Congress 96
Caron, Berthe 61
Carr, Sam 101, 138, 151, 176, 179, 219, 277, 295-296
Catholic Church 51, 89, 242
Caute, David 302
Central Intelligence Agency (CIA) 289
Chalmers, David 75
Chamberlain, Neville 112, 115, 143, 152
Chapayev, Vasily Ivanovitch 94-95
Chapman, Agatha 205, 306
Chartier, Monseigneur Émile 88
Cheetham, Kenneth Howe 228
Chrisholm, J. 72
Churchill, Winston 115, 187, 207, 211-212
Civil Liberties Union 96, 109, 112-113, 117, 134, 136, 308·
Claire, Pat 259
Clarion, The 127-128, 145
Clarté 87, 91, 93, 127-128, 145
Cliffside 162
Clutterbuck, Sir Alexander 206
Cohen, G.A. (Jerry) 31, 299, 307, 312
Cohen, Joseph 214, 219-220, 222
Combat 273
Coming Struggle for Power, The 134
Committee to Aid Spanish Democracy 96, 101, 134
Communist International 59-68
Communist Manifesto 82
Confessions of a Red Diaper Baby 22
Congress of Industrial Organizations (CIO) 81, 119
Congress of the American Student Union 117

Conseil de Travail de Montréal, 293
Conseil des Chômeurs de Montréal 70
Cooperative Commonwealth Federation (CCF) 75, 101, 110, 117, 136, 176, 190, 308
Crispo, John 27

Daniels, Dan 262
Dardick, Simon 14-16, 18
David 36, 174, 179, 238, 246-247, 262, 277, 284, 293-294
Davis, Harry 255
Delisle, Paul 47-49, 52, 59-60
Desaulniers, Herbert 308
Diefenbaker, John 197, 226
Dimitroff, Georgi 136
Dinel, Roland 159
Donna 135, 152
Douglas, T.C. 136
Dressmakers' strike 80
Drew, George 257
Drummond, David 14, 18
Dubé, Evariste 157, 246
Dufour, Lucien 70
Dunton, Davidson 303
Duplessis, Maurice 90-91, 119, 152, 160, 216, 257, 261, 263

Eaton's department store 261
Ed 142-143, 157, 190, 239, 247, 262-263, 266, 274, 276, 280, 286-287
Eda 151, 155, 173, 235
Eden, Anthony 143
Éditions Saint-Martin, Les 291
Eight Men Speak 123
Einstein, Albert 263
Eisenhower, Dwight D. 207
Endicott, James G. 262

Fairly, Tom 219
Fallen Bastions 139
Farmers' Union of Quebec 259
Fauteaux, Gaspard 223
Federal Bureau of Investigation (FBI) 192, 236, 238, 269, 298
Federation of Canadian Artists 134, 300
Foreign Investment Act 101
Forsey, Eugene 117, 136
Fortin, Gérard 40, 259-260, 289
Fortin, Willie 83
Fred Rose Defence Leauge 213-214
Friends of the Mackenzie-Papineau Battalion 96, 101, 128
Fur and Leather Workers' Union 250-251

Gagnon, Henri 21, 35, 40, 56-58-59, 61, 81-83, 87, 93-94, 96, 120, 128, 132, 153, 157, 170, 216, 234, 238-240, 245-248, 283, 289, 293
Gauld, Bella 281
Gelbart, Arnie 27
Gélinas, Gratien 88-89
Genreau, L.P. 224
Gershman, Joshua 44, 77-78, 80, 151
Gilles" 117-118, 121, 126, 153, 156, 159, 234, 238, 241, 243-245, 273, 274, 277, 279-280, 283-287, 289-290, 292-293, 301, 307
Godbout, Adelard 160
Gold, Michael 121-122
Gollancz, Victor 144
Gordon, King 110, 308
Gousev, Feodor 167
Gouzenko, Igor 24, 192-193, 197, 200, 204, 216-219, 221, 227, 232-233, 238, 268, 299, 303
Greenwood, Inspector 43

Grierson, John 236, 303, 316
Groulx, Abbé Lionel 88, 99
Guddork, Wilhelm 179

Haddow, Bob 21, 159-161, 170, 250-251, 315
Hands Off China Committee 43
Harrison, Allan 21, 298
Harry 89-90, 135, 249-250, 257-258, 262, 274-275, 278, 285, 287-288, 301, 305-306
Hart, Captain Liddell 149
Harvison, Inspector C.W. 199-200, 216
Hénault, Gilles 260-261
Hepburn, Mitchell 158
Hoover, J. Edgar 238
How the Steel Was Tempered 118
Howe, C.D. 164, 178, 228, 240, 300
Huberman, Leo
Hughes, Langston 25, 122

Industrial Workers of the World (IWW) 50
International Association of Machinists 150, 315
International Brotherhood of Electrical Workers 293
International Ladies Garment Workers' Union 92, 315
International Lenin School 22, 49, 61, 66, 83, 94
International Union of Mine, Mill, and Smelter Workers 250

Janet 277
Jenkins, John Henry 178
Jerry 271-272, 275

Kandai Magyar Munkas 71
Kaufman, Irving 206, 263

Kellock, R.L. 203, 222
King, William Lyon Mackenzie 86, 91, 105, 166-168, 173, 180, 192-197, 199, 206, 218, 231-232, 240, 253
Klein, A.M. 90
Knowles, Major 71
Kon, Irene 32, 107-108, 114, 121, 126, 131-132, 159, 290, 294
Kon, Louis 32, 82, 107-110, 114, 119
Krushchev, Nikita S. 279-281, 286, 288-289, 293, 295

La Voix du Peuple 153, 159
Labor Monthly 25
Labour Progressive Party (LPP) 286
Lahiri, Jhumpa 17
Lapalme, Marcel 246
Laurendeau, André 88
Lavallé. Marcel 222-223
Lazure, Justice Wilfred 219-220
League Against Fascism 136
League for Social Reconstruction 136
League of Nations 100
Legion magazine 23
Leo 51
Leopold, Sergeant 73
Letson, Colonel 184
Lévesque, Georges Henri 128
Lewis, David 117, 172, 226, 315
Lilly 156, 216, 234, 247, 273, 276, 287, 289, 292
Linton, Fred 180
Litvinoff, Maxim 100-101
Livesay, Dorothy 108, 122
Lord, Barry 298
Luxembourg, Rosa 280

MacArthur, General Douglas 182
Mackenzie-Papineau Battalion
96-102, 128
MacLeod, A.A. 174
MacLeod, Wendell 134
MacMahon Bill 207, 209
Marchand, Jean 26
Marsh, Leonard 308
Martin, Paul 198
Masse, Paul 172-173
Masses and Mainstream 25
Masthead, The 163
MacArthur, General Douglas 182
May-Johnson Bill (US) 207-209
McCarran-Walter Act (US, 1952)
37
McCarthy, Senator Joseph 251, 263,
265, 269, 294
McKenna, Brian 26
McNaughton, Francis 308
Mikhoels, Solomon 282
Military Strength of the Powers, The
149
Mitford, Jessica 66, 271
Mohr, Merilyn Simonds 27
Molotov, Vyacheslav 141, 19, 3151
Montagu, Ivor 25
Morris, Leslie 71
Motinov, Lt-Col. 184
Mouvement du Corporatisme 89
Munich Agreement (1938) 115
Myers, Irving 21

National Committee to Save the
Rosenbergs 265
National Council of the Unem
ployed 83
National Film Board of Canada
(NFB) 236, 249
National Unemployed Workers'
Association 71

Needham, Joseph 193
Neilsen, Doris 218-219
New Democratic Party (NDP) 226,
317
New Theatre Group 124-125, 134-
135, 166
Nicolson, Harold 206
Norman 113-114, 181, 183-184, 190,
198-202, 217, 230-231, 289, 292,
298-299
Norris, Justice 255
North Atlantic Treaty Organization
(NATO) 34, 194, 251, 261-262,
306
Nunn May, Alan 193, 206-298, 214,
227

*Official History of the Canadian
Army* 27
Official Secrets Act 201, 204-205,
217, 221, 230
Oppenheimer, Robert J. 208
Ostrovsky, Nikolai 118
Otto 53-54
Our Northern Neighbour 236

Padlock Law 91-92, 103, 109, 115,
117, 119-120, 128, 136-137, 151-
152, 160, 170, 181, 234, 25, 2727
Parent, Madeleine 47
Park, Libby 317
Partridge, Gertrude 269, 309
Partridge, Rev. Glendon 264
Pearson, Drew 195-197
Pearson, Lester B. 157, 207
Pellerin, Gérard 246
Peretz, I.L. 216
Perron, Jean 82
Pfeffer, Itzik 282
Phillips, Lazarus 171-172

Phillips, Paul 277
Pickersgill, Jack 226, 257
Pollitt, Harry 279
Price, Lt.-Col. William 71, 74
Pritt, D.N. 138, 218, 220
Progressive Arts Club 96

Quebec Committee for Allied
  Victory 184
Quebec Labour Relations Board
  257

Relief Camp Workers Union 69, 83
Richer, Philippe 83
Roback, Lea 21, 29, 31, 36, 44-47, 59,
  61, 78-8, 87-92, 103, 115, 119,
  126, 147, 153, 163, 170, 185, 187,
  216, 226, 234-235, 277, 291, 301
Roback, Michael 115
Roberts, Goodridge 298
Robertson, Norman 175, 180, 218
Robeson, Paul 28, 34, 64, 126-127,
  185-186
Rogov, Colonel 200
Roosevelt, Franklin Delano 174, 187
Rose, Chief Justice 73
Rose, Fanny 216, 218-220, 223-224,
  226
Rose, Fred 21, 24-25, 32-34, 36,
  38-39, 41-44, 47, 52, 56, 59-62,
  67, 71, 86, 88-90, 93-94, 102-103,
  132, 137, 141-142, 146-148, 150-
  151, 157-158, 160, 167, 170-173,
  175, 179-181, 183, 188, 194-195,
  200, 204, 211-227, 230, 232-235,
  238, 247, 250, 272, 289-290, 294-
  295, 298, 303-304, 316
Rose, Laura 24-25, 31, 146-147,
  222-223, 226, 235, 270
Rosenberg, Julius and Ethel 25, 36-

39, 206, 263-267, 294
Rosenberg-Sobel Committee 305
Royal Canadian Mounted Police
  (RCMP) 35, 38, 64-65, 71-74,
  84-85, 114, 145, 192, 196, 198-
  199, 201, 203, 232, 234, 239-240,
  253, 255, 262-263, 316-317
Royal Commission on Espionage
  211, 217
Royal Commission on Price
  Spreads (Stevens Report) 94
Royal Northwest Mounted Police
  61
Ryerson, Stanley 53-56, 59, 61, 92-
  93, 103, 113, 119, 128, 135, 150-
  152, 175, 179, 181, 216, 238, 240,
  243-247, 281, 284, 289-290, 293,
  304-305, 317

Sadie 120-121
Saint-Martin, Albert 291
Salsberg, J.B. 141-142, 151, 174,
  282, 284-285
Samuel, Emery 35, 47, 49-53, 59,
  61, 67, 84, 87, 94-96, 126, 132,
  142, 144, 147, 150, 153, 157, 170,
  173, 216, 242, 246-247, 293
Samuel, Nancy 246
Scher, Len 22
Scott, Frank 110, 117, 136, 308
Scott, Marion 110
Seafarers International Union
  (SIU) 254-255
Sedgewick, Joseph 73
Seeger, Pete 270
Seig, John 179
Sise, Hazen 117-118
Skelton, Douglas 175-176
Skelton, Oscar Douglas 175
Slug 157, 159, 170, 173, 216

Smith, Albert E. 132
Smith, Alice Kimball 209
Smith, Stewart 151
Sokolov, Major 151
Spiridonova, Maria 59
St. Jean Baptiste Society 88, 153
St. Laurent, Louis 198, 218, 257
Stacey, Charles 26
Stalin, Joseph 32, 36-37, 119, 137-138, 141-142, 144, 166, 174-175, 185, 187, 189, 244, 247, 259, 268, 274, 279-284, 295
Stephenson, Sir William 195
Stinson, Henry L. 191
Stockholm Peace Appeal 241
Strachey, John 25, 134, 144, 277-278
Strong, Anna Louise 277
Sullivan, J.A. "Pat" 105, 252-253
Sydney see Annette and Sydney

Taschereau, Robert 222
Taylor, E.P. 299-300
Taylor, Fred 21, 93, 112-113, 126, 132, 134-135, 147, 159, 164-166, 270, 291, 299-300
Tedesco, Nick 224
Third International see Communist International
This Magazine 23
Thomas, Gwyn 25
Trades and Labour Congress (TLC) 162, 250-253
Trepper, Leopold 179
Tribune, The 273
Truman, Harry 188, 192, 194, 306

UnCanadians, The 22
Underhill, Frank 136
Unemployed League 57

Union des Bucherons de la Province de Québec Indépendent (UBI) 258-259
Union nationale 160
United Auto Workers Union 250
United Electrical Union 250-251
United Jewish People's Order (UJPO) 98-99, 120, 123, 262, 271, 313
University of Chicago Law Review 221-222
Unlawful Associations Act (1924) 62-63

Valour and the Horror, The 26 28, 302
Varcoe, F.R. 223

Waiting for Lefty 123
Walsh, Red 69-70, 83-84
War Measures Act 136, 152, 181, 193, 196
Wartime Information Board 236, 303
Weavers, The 270
Werner, Max 149
West, Rebecca 229
What Is To Be Done (Lenin) 63
White, Harry Dexter 195
Williams, Major-General V.A.S. 72
Willie 124-126, 154
Wilson, Sir Henry Maitland 207
Wingfield, Harry 161-162, 176
Wingfield, Stan 161-163, 255-256
Winnipeg General Strike (1919) 61-62, 86
Worker, The 70-71
Workers' Educational Association 164
Workers' Theatre 96

Workers' Unity League 81, 83, 92
Workmen's Circle 123

Young Communist League 35, 42,
    56, 93-94, 117, 153, 158, 179

Zabotin, Colonel 179, 213, 217,
    227, 231
Zarkin, Sydney 150
Zynchuk, Nick 41-42